THE DESERT ORCHID YEARS

'The Desert Orchid Years'
first published in Great Britain 1991
by Portway Press Limited
Timeform House, Halifax
West Yorkshire HX1 1XE
Telephone (0422) 330330 Fax (0422) 358645

ISBN 0 900599 58 8

Printed in Great Britain by
Portway Press Limited

CONTENTS

LIST OF ILLUSTRATIONS

by David Elsworth

Desert Orchid is a fantastic horse and everyone at Whitsbury is very proud to have been associated with him. There have been times, however, when it's crossed my mind that if I'd been another trainer I might have become sick of reading about Desert Orchid by now.

However, of all the thousands of articles that have been written about 'Dessie', I think the series of erudite essays that have appeared in Timeform's *Chasers & Hurdlers* annuals take some beating.

'The Desert Orchid Years', based on the Timeform essays, provides a fascinating insight into the story of Desert Orchid, as it unfolded season-by-season and was reported by Timeform at the time. I'm sure you'll enjoy reading it.

November 1991

EDITORIAL NOTES

The essays in this publication were produced for Timeform's *Chasers & Hurdlers* annuals which are published by Portway Press Limited, Halifax, West Yorkshire HX1 1XE, publishers of all Timeform publications including the *'Racehorses of 19—'* annuals, the *Timeform Weekly Black Book* and the daily *Timeform Race Cards*.

With each essay is the Timeform annual rating of Desert Orchid. The Timeform rating represents the number of pounds which a horse's performances would entitle it to receive in a universal handicap embracing all horses in training worth a rating, in which the ratings usually range from around 175 (12st 7lb) for the very best horses down to below 60 for the worst horses.

The form summaries at the start of each essay list Desert Orchid's performances in sequence, and show the race distance in furlongs; an abbreviation for the going; and, in superior figures, what happened to the horse in the race, an asterisk being used to denote a win.

Ratings and form figures preceded by a 'c' relate to steeplechasing, the others to hurdle racing.

DESERT ORCHID 4 gr.c. Grey Mirage – Flower Child (Brother) [1982/3 16g^F Jan 21] useful-looking colt: first foal: dam won over fences: unquoted and just in need of race, ran very well on debut in 18-runner juvenile hurdle won by Boardmans Crown at Kempton in January: took strong hold and was well behind in early stages, but pulled his way up to the leaders on the far side, was full of running turning for home and was just behind leaders when falling heavily at the last: sure to win races over hurdles provided he's none the worse for his fall. *D. Elsworth* —p

The Timeform commentary and rating, reproduced above, appeared on Desert Orchid after his racecourse debut in January 1983. Although he ended up on the deck, there was enough promise in this first race to suggest that he would make his mark as a jumper. But no-one could have foreseen the huge impact that his career was to make.

Desert Orchid has became a public figure and an invaluable standard-bearer for jumping, indeed for the whole sport of horse-racing. He has been the most popular horse on the turf for years.

As a racehorse, he has been exceptional, thoroughly meriting the much-overused description *great.* His highest Timeform rating of 187 has been bettered only by three jumpers—those stars of the 'sixties Arkle, Flyingbolt and Mill House.

The form-book shows that, up to the end of the 1990/91 season, Desert Orchid had won thirty-four races from sixty-eight starts over the jumps, earning a record £542,629 in first-prize money (he has run once on the Flat, tailed off in the two-mile Sagaro Stakes at Ascot as a six-year-old).

Desert Orchid's record over fences, in particular, is outstanding. He has achieved a record-breaking four victories in the King George VI Chase, the mid-season championship for staying chasers, and has also won the Cheltenham Gold Cup, the Whitbread Gold Cup and the Irish Grand National. He has been voted National Hunt Horse of the Year four times.

INTRODUCTION

Trainer David Elsworth and the people who have worked with Desert Orchid at Whitsbury Stables deserve great credit for the way they have handled the horse. No-one knows Desert Orchid better than David Elsworth, who paid this tribute in a *Timeform Interview*:

'There's no one reason for Dessie's greatness. He's got several qualities which, taken with his natural ability, make him so good. He is a particularly athletic horse, a beautiful mover and the best balanced horse I've ever seen; he copes with the ground whatever it is; he jumps better than anything I've ever trained too; and he's a dour, determined sort with tremendous enthusiasm which is the best quality you can have in any athlete, equine or human. Desert Orchid is also blessed with a great constitution and has been a tremendously sound horse who, touch wood, has never had any real injury problems. All these qualities have made him tremendously consistent. It's amazing that he has held his form so well over the years.'

Surprisingly, Desert Orchid's first season ended with him still a novice—he ran four times, coming closest to victory when beaten a neck at Sandown on his penultimate start. *Chasers & Hurdlers 1983/84* takes up the story . . .

THE NOVICE HURDLER

5 YEAR OLD 16f* 16f* 21f² 16f* 16g* 16g* 16g* 16g **RATED 158**

Six wins from eight starts establishes Desert Orchid as the season's leading novice hurdler, though he fails to reproduce his best in the Champion Hurdle, finishing well beaten when second favourite

Horses without a win over hurdles at the start of the season—officially defined as novices—seldom appear in the same season's Champion Hurdle; very few novices are anywhere near good enough or experienced enough for such a demand to be made on them. The five-year-old Brains Trust in 1945 was the last to win the race, the four-year-old Kirriemuir in 1964 the last to be placed. The latest season saw the rapid emergence of a novice markedly superior to his fellows whose form did seem to give him an excellent chance of reaching the frame in the Waterford Crystal Champion Hurdle at Cheltenham in March. That horse, Desert Orchid, had won all six of his races over the championship distance of two miles during the season, most of them in tremendous style, and immediately prior to the Festival had won one of the established trials, the Kingwell Pattern Hurdle at Wincanton. But despite ideal underfoot conditions for him, 7/1 second favourite Desert Orchid finished well beaten—out of the first nine of fourteen—behind the odds-on Dawn Run.

We are certain that Desert Orchid failed to reproduce his best in the Champion Hurdle though we aren't quite so sure of the reasons why. The likeliest explanation is the one in commonest currency that Dawn Run and the rest were too strong for him to dominate. In front from the start in all his previous races during the season, Desert Orchid on this occasion took until the second flight to get on terms with the leader (Dawn Run) and while he showed ahead over the next two he never managed to pull away. Dawn Run went on again descending the hill, and thereafter Desert Orchid gradually dropped back. However, the Champion Hurdle wasn't a particularly fast-run race. The way the others managed to swallow him up, some of them only ordinary horses by Champion Hurdle standards, suggests that all was not well with him; perhaps he was over the top for the season—he didn't race again, at any rate. There's also a possibility, we put it no higher, that some aspect of the track didn't suit Desert Orchid; in considering such a matter one thing which may be overlooked is that Cheltenham is left-handed. The only time the horse had previously appeared in public on a left-handed track, at Newbury on his last outing in 1982/3, he'd run poorly.

Desert Orchid enjoyed a tremendous season up to taking part in the Champion Hurdle, a much more successful one than could have been foreseen after he'd gone four races without a win in 1982/3. His only defeat came on his third outing, when Catch Phrase managed to overtake him near the finish of a race over two miles five furlongs at Sandown in December. That race was confined to novices, as were all the others except the Kingwell Pattern Hurdle. When he'd beaten novices, at Ascot (three times), Kempton and Sandown, he'd won unchallenged, with only I Haventalight and Hill's Pageant of all his opponents able to finish within ten lengths of him in the face of his quick, fluent jumping and his strong running. In the Tolworth Hurdle at Sandown in January I Haventalight, who'd previously been beaten fifteen lengths by Desert Orchid at Kempton, finished an eight-length second with the winners Keelby Kavalier and Dodgy Future soundly defeated; in the Datchet Novices' Hurdle at Ascot in February the newcomer Hill's Pageant also finished an eight-length second with the stayer Brown Trix a thoroughly-outpaced third. On the strength of these performances Desert Orchid started a 2/1 favourite for the Kingwell Pattern Hurdle. Since he was up against the Schweppes Gold Trophy runner-up Stans Pride and the first and second favourite

Foodbrokers-Armour Novices' Hurdle, Kempton—Desert Orchid runs clean away from his field

for that hotly-contested handicap, Very Promising and Admiral's Cup, not to mention Janus and Migrator, this was quite a compliment. He won by four lengths from Stans Pride, giving her 5 lb. He didn't jump so fluently as usual but showed his customary enthusiasm both in containing the very useful front-runner Migrator and in fending off Stans Pride and Janus in the straight, having to meet a strong challenge from the mare. At this stage of his career Desert Orchid was clearly still improving; a little more improvement would surely have put him in the firing line at Cheltenham.

Desert Orchid is young enough to come back for a second crack at the Champion Hurdle. Indeed, he should be a better proposition with another year on his back, but he may not again have the good fortune to find the ground riding fast. He is well suited by good or firm ground; the only time he has run on heavy was in the race at Newbury already mentioned. Other opportunities of winning good races seem sure to present themselves, whatever his fate in the Champion Hurdle. Judging from his defeat by Catch Phrase they will occur at a distance of two miles or thereabouts. We should anticipate Desert Orchid's being a particularly live candidate for the Christmas Hurdle at Kempton, a course where jumping ability and sharpness such as he normally shows are very much at a premium on most occasions.

THE HURDLER

6 YEAR OLD 16g^{3} 16d^{3} 16s^{2} 16g 16d* 16m^{pu} 16s^{pu} 16g^{F}

RATED 159

Only one win from eight starts in Desert Orchid's final season over hurdles

Desert Orchid had nothing like so successful a season as in 1983/4, but he continued to put up some very smart performances, notably when finishing second to Browne's Gazette in the Ladbroke Christmas Hurdle at Kempton. He was no match for the winner in the closing stages and was beaten fifteen lengths, but he easily accounted for the remaining five runners, who included See You Then and Stans Pride, first and third respectively in the Waterford Crystal Champion Hurdle at Cheltenham in March. Desert Orchid, who'd finished well beaten in the 1984 Champion Hurdle, ran an even worse race at Cheltenham in 1985 and was tailed off when pulled up

Oteley Hurdle, Sandown—front runner Desert Orchid is given a tremendous ride by Colin Brown

before two out. Judged on these two runs and on his poor performances in the Irish Sweeps Hurdle at Leopardstown and the Blue Circle Welsh Champion Hurdle at Chepstow there seems no doubt that Desert Orchid is unsuited by a left-handed track, although at Chepstow it did appear that he resented wearing blinkers. Without blinkers and on a right-handed track Desert Orchid can be relied upon to run his race out most genuinely, as he showed in the Oteley Hurdle at Sandown in February. He set a steady pace until quickening and opening up a clear lead early in the back straight, and then kept on well to win unchallenged by ten lengths from Mr Moonraker. Desert Orchid might have added to his success but for falling at the last in a handicap at Ascot in April. Although beginning to tire he still held a clear advantage over the eventual winner Comedy Fair.

Trillium Handicap Hurdle, Ascot—Desert Orchid falls at the last, leaving victory to Comedy Fair

Desert Orchid is to go chasing in 1985/6. If he takes to jumping fences as well as he took to jumping hurdles then he'll be a difficult horse to peg back in two-mile novice events.

THE NOVICE CHASER

7 YEAR OLD 16f^{F} c17g* c16f* c16m* c20g* c16d^{ur} c16s^{2} c16m^{3} c20g^{2} c20g

RATED c135

Desert Orchid makes his mark over fences with four impressive victories; he's also a good third in the Arkle Challenge Trophy at the Cheltenham Festival

In his first season over fences Desert Orchid the chaser proved very similar to Desert Orchid the hurdler: a bold-jumping front runner inclined to make the odd costly mistake, one of the best of his generation though clearly not the best. He made only one appearance over hurdles in the latest season and an eventful appearance it was, for after jumping exceptionally fluently in front at Kempton in October he made a complete hash of the second last when going strongly about fifteen lengths up and paid the penalty. Nothing daunted, he proceeded to reel off four most impressive victories over fences before Christmas by an aggregate of sixty-four lengths. He outjumped Charcoal Wally at Devon & Exeter on his debut. The fences at Ascot and Sandown offer a stiffer test but Desert Orchid handled them well enough for a novice as he picked up valuable prizes in the Hurst Park Novices' Chase, the Henry VIII Novices' Chase and the Killiney Novices' Chase, his most serious mistake being a blunder at the third last in the Killiney which still didn't prevent his coming home unchallenged from Evening Song. A blunder at the fifth, unseating his jockey, cost him his chance of a five-timer at Ascot in January. In fact, Desert Orchid's winning was over for the season, though he had a further four outings and completed each time. His jumping never became consistently fluent: now and again he'd throw himself at a fence, reaching for it. In all probability this chink in his armour will remain for the rest of his career. Formwise Desert Orchid was a model of consistency. His fifth place behind Repington in the Contiboard Novices' Handicap Chase at Ascot in April on his final appearance was a creditable one that might even have been improved on had he been ridden with a little more restraint. On the three other appearances he finished in the frame—close second to Berlin in the Scilly Isles Novices' Chase at Sandown, third to Oregon Trail, beaten just under nine lengths, in the Arkle Challenge Trophy at Cheltenham and close second to Clara Mountain in another novice chase at Sandown.

Desert Orchid the chaser wasn't exactly like the horse we knew, or thought we knew, as a hurdler. Hitherto regarded as a two-miler, pure and simple, he showed in the Killiney and the Scilly Isles that he stays two and a half miles. And after his performance in the Arkle he can no longer be regarded as unsuited by a left-handed track, even though, particularly since he tended to jump right at Cheltenham, there may still be grounds for regarding him as better served by a right-handed one. But other conclusions about his racing character remain unchanged. He acts on any going, except perhaps heavy. He sometimes sweats up, without, apparently, affecting his chance adversely. The experiment of running him in blinkers wasn't repeated in the latest season—not surprisingly in view of the way he'd gone in them the only time they'd been tried before.

Desert Orchid is sure to win more valuable chases. He comes to hand quite quickly and is one to short-list for a successful autumn campaign.

Hurst Park Novices' Chase, Ascot—an easy, all-the-way win for Desert Orchid

HORSE OF THE YEAR

8 YEAR OLD c20d* c20g^4 c16g* c24s* c25m* c25s* c16g^3 c20s* c29f^{pu} **RATED c177**

The first of Desert Orchid's victories in the King George VI Chase is the highlight of a superb season in which Desert Orchid underlines his versatility with top-class performances at two miles, two and a half and three on going ranging from top-of-the-ground to soft

The dictum that horse racing is an unpredictable game is probably repeated rather too often for most tastes. Actually, on occasions, the saying fails to do justice to a sport in which there are few certainties. It sometimes seems that the only thing one can be certain about in racing is that one can be certain about nothing at all. Take, for example, the reasonable assumption that Desert Orchid wouldn't stay three miles in top company, an opinion held almost universally—outside his stable—before his victory in the King George VI Rank Chase. Judged on his pedigree—his sire was a miler

Holsten Export Lager Handicap Chase, Sandown—Desert Orchid shows the way to The Argonaut

and the sire of his dam was effective at sprint distances—and on his zestful, front-running style, Desert Orchid was for long enough regarded as a two-miler, pure and simple. In *Chasers & Hurdlers 1984/85* we went on record as saying that he was 'always likely to be best at around two miles'. In three seasons over hurdles, in which he developed into a good-class performer, Desert Orchid was raced only once at a distance beyond two miles; he was beaten at odds on in a twenty-one-furlong novice hurdle at Sandown, one of only two defeats in eight starts that particular season, the other being in the Champion Hurdle. In his first season over fences Desert Orchid did most of his racing at two miles, but he showed that he stayed two and a half, winning the Killiney Novices' Chase and running creditably in defeat in two other races over the trip. The King George was announced as a target for Desert Orchid after he won the two-mile Frogmore Handicap at Ascot in mid-December with a performance which strengthened our view that he was much more likely to take high rank as a two-mile chaser than as a three-miler; he battled on to

Frogmore Handicap Chase, Ascot—Desert Orchid gives a tremendous display of front running

beat Charcoal Wally most decisively by twelve lengths in a strongly-run race. Desert Orchid started at 16/1 in the King George, four times the odds of his stable-companion Combs Ditch, a close second in the King George in 1984 and 1985 and the choice of stable-jockey Brown.

The King George VI Rank Chase—the event had commercial sponsorship for the first time—drew a huge festive crowd as usual. The field of nine included Wayward Lad, seeking his fourth victory in the race, and Forgive'N Forget, unbeaten in his three races during the current campaign. Recent form pointed strongly to Forgive'N Forget who started 2/1 favourite. Although Desert Orchid hadn't been tested at the King George distance in a race, his rider Sherwood clearly received instructions to ride him on the assumption that he would stay. Sent to the front from the start, Desert Orchid set a good gallop, ensuring a strongly-run race in the prevailing testing conditions. His opponents scarcely saw which way he went! In a sizeable lead for much of the race, he increased the gallop in the back straight on the final circuit and was in a commanding position with four to jump. Only briefly, when Forgive'N Forget took up the chase and moved into second place three out, did Desert Orchid look like being challenged. Stretching out powerfully and with his customary enthusiasm in the final straight, he won in tremendous style, ridden out with hands and heels, by fifteen lengths from the SGB Handicap winner Door Latch, with Bolands Cross six lengths away third, just ahead of the weakening Forgive'N Forget; Wayward Lad was the only other finisher. Combs Ditch was pulled up well beaten before the second last. It goes almost without saying that Desert Orchid's victory in the King George represented a marked improvement on his previous best form—it was a top-notch performance—and another notable feature of his breathtaking display was his fluent and sometimes spectacular jumping. As a novice he wasn't a consistently fluent jumper—now and again he'd throw himself at a fence, reaching for it—and this chink in his armour had again been evident in the

King George VI Rank Chase, Kempton—the second last: Desert Orchid is clear of Forgive'N Forget (right) and Door Latch

very valuable H & T Walker Goddess Handicap at Ascot in November when, starting favourite, he managed only fourth to Church Warden, tending to keep low at his fences and making several mistakes. That said, he had put in a much better round of jumping in the Frogmore and also handled the Sandown fences well enough, though again reaching for the odd fence, when making all in the Holsten Export Lager Handicap on his reappearance.

The King George VI Chase is the most prestigious chase run in Britain before the turn of the year, effectively the mid-season championship for staying chasers, but the Cheltenham Gold Cup in March is more widely regarded as steeplechasing's blue riband event. The Cheltenham Gold Cup is an automatic target for most King George winners but Desert Orchid wasn't even entered in the Gold Cup, connections believing the race unsuitable for him. Desert Orchid had never won on a left-handed track and seemed ideally served by a right-handed one; until the latest season he had never really shone at Cheltenham, his record at the Festival meeting comprising two poor runs in the Champion Hurdle and a third place (to Oregon Trail and Charcoal Wally) in the Arkle Challenge Trophy. In fact, Desert Orchid did put in an appearance at the Cheltenham Festival meeting—in the two-mile Queen Mother Champion Chase—and gave a very good account of himself. Steered slightly wide, he led or disputed the lead most of the way and came home only three lengths behind Pearlyman and Very Promising in a thrilling finish; Desert Orchid finished twenty-five lengths ahead of fourth-

F.U.'s Jeans Gainsborough Handicap Chase, Sandown—Desert Orchid goes from strength to strength; he has Stearsby well beaten at the last

placed Townley Stone and twenty-eight ahead of the fifth Charcoal Wally. The Queen Mother Champion Chase confirmed that Desert Orchid can no longer be regarded as unsuited by a left-handed track and he deserves a crack at the Gold Cup another year. With due respect to The Thinker, Desert Orchid's performance at Kempton, if repeated at Cheltenham, would have seen him a clear-cut winner of the latest Gold Cup. Things are never that simple though. Whether Desert Orchid will stay the extra distance on the much stiffer Cheltenham track in the Gold Cup remains a matter for conjecture, and will probably do so until he faces the test. But he followed up his triumph in the King George with two wide-margin successes over a distance just short of the Gold Cup trip, including a handsome ten-length victory over a leading Gold Cup contender Stearsby in the very valuable F.U.'s Jeans Gainsborough Handicap at Sandown in February. Carrying top weight, Desert Orchid made virtually all and romped home in great style, looking as though he still had a higher gear at his disposal after opening up a winning lead between the third last and second last. Desert Orchid jumped superbly, showing speed and accuracy at the obstacles which neither of his main rivals Stearsby and Bolands Cross could often match. Desert Orchid had a much easier task in the four-runner Jim Ford Challenge Cup at Wincanton later the same month and led throughout to land the odds by twelve lengths from Mr Moonraker.

Jim Ford Challenge Cup Chase, Wincanton—another fine jump from Desert Orchid, leading Mr Moonraker down the back straight

Desert Orchid's victory in the Gainsborough Chase—one of the best performances of recent seasons in a staying chase—took his earnings in first-prize money past the £100,000-mark, one topped by only a select band of jumpers; by the end of the season he had taken his career record to seventeen victories worth £117,303. The gulf in prize money between the jumping game and the highly-commercialised world of the top grade of Flat racing is enormous:

eight horses had *seasonal* earnings of more than £100,000 on the Flat in Britain in 1986 when Dancing Brave and Shahrastani earned more then jumping's top earner Dawn Run in the whole of her career. Yet the top jumpers so often seem to give more pleasure to racing's followers than their Flat counterparts. When did a Flat-racing champion receive a reception to compare with that accorded to Dawn Run after her Champion Hurdle and Gold Cup victories? Perhaps the enjoyment of watching the top jumpers in action gains potency from the antidote it provides to the upper echelons of Flat-racing in which the owners of most of the participants have more on their minds than racecourse achievement. Desert Orchid's popularity was reflected in the applause that greeted him as he was led into the paddock, the star attraction for the last showpiece event of the season the Whitbread Gold Cup at Sandown in April. Desert Orchid was already assured of 'Horse of the Year' honours—in the poll of twenty-six leading racing journalists at the end of the season he received sixteen votes, ten more than See You Then—and it was disappointing to see him run so far below his best. Assessed 5 lb in front of the Gold Cup winner The Thinker—an eleventh-hour withdrawal—in the original handicap, Desert Orchid had to shoulder 12-0; only Charlie Potheen had carried so much to victory in the Whitbread since Arkle's day. Desert Orchid's stable reported afterwards that he had been troubled by a corn, necessitating veterinary treatment, in the days leading up to the race; faith that everything would be all right on the day proved ill-founded as Desert Orchid neither moved nor jumped so well as usual and was eventually pulled up, virtually tailed off, after a bad mistake six from home. Among the qualities which have endeared Desert Orchid to the racing public are his zest and courage, both of which were displayed in abundance in the Peregrine Handicap over two and a half miles at Ascot a little over a fortnight before the Whitbread. Carrying 12-4 and conceding lumps of weight all round to his six opponents, he gave one of the bravest performances seen all

Peregrine Handicap Chase, Ascot—Desert Orchid gamely regains the lead from Gold Bearer before the last to record his seventh win on the course

season, keeping on doggedly to regain the lead approaching the last after losing the initiative to bottom-weighted Gold Bearer through a mistake at the fourth from home. Desert Orchid had jumped splendidly, setting a great gallop, but he looked done for—he had already appeared to be tiring—as Gold Bearer moved into a three- or four-length lead; but Desert Orchid is a grand battler and he got home, almost out on his feet, by two lengths from Gold Bearer with Sign Again three lengths further back in third. It was Desert Orchid's seventh victory at Ascot, and underlined his versatility: he showed top-class form in the latest season at two miles, two and a half and three on going ranging from top-of-the-ground to soft.

It bears repeating that Desert Orchid is as brave and genuine as any horse in training, which coupled with his dashing style—he's a splendid sight out in front throwing down the gauntlet—makes him one of contemporary steeplechasing's greatest assets. He's still young and, with luck, could grace the winter game for several seasons yet. We shouldn't leave him without recording that his career to date reflects great credit on his trainer who, incidentally, said in a *Timeform Interview* when Desert Orchid was only five that he had 'always regarded him as a potential chaser; a three-mile chaser at that'.

CHAMPION AGAIN

9 YEAR OLD c21g* c20d* c16g² c24g² c25v³ c25g² c16s² c25g* c29m*

RATED c177

Desert Orchid suffers a surprising defeat in the King George VI Chase but crowns another remarkable season with victory in the Whitbread Gold Cup

Reams have been written about Desert Orchid's celebrity status. A dashing grey, easy to pick out and in his element bowling along in front, he has become an extremely popular figure, a hero in a time when heroes in jumping are in short supply. His magnificent and almost-universally popular victory in the Whitbread Gold Cup, the season's last major steeplechase, made a formality of a repeat success in the 'National Hunt Champion' award organised by the Racegoers Club; Desert Orchid received twenty-one of the twenty-five votes—Rhyme 'N' Reason got the others—in the end-of-season poll of a selected official panel. No horse has done more for jumping over the past two seasons and provided he keeps his form and steers clear of illness and injury Desert Orchid must have bright prospects of winning a third 'National Hunt Champion' award. Desert Orchid is a symbol of so much that is good about National Hunt racing. He's as tough and courageous as anyone could wish for, and he's a splendid sight in full flow, a supremely quick and accurate jumper. In short, it's a joy to see him racing. He's a durable campaigner into the bargain and runs regularly.

The Whitbread Gold Cup at Sandown in April was Desert Orchid's ninth appearance in a season which saw him facing mostly uphill work, tackling championship or select events and shouldering big weights in handicaps. Desert Orchid (11-11) and Kildimo (11-12) were the only Whitbread runners to carry more than 11-0 and they provided a memorable finish, Desert Orchid having to display all his renowned fighting qualities to beat off Kildimo's persistent challenge. Desert Orchid made virtually all in the Whitbread, being headed only by another confirmed front runner Run And Skip at around halfway and again approaching the third last. Jumping superbly throughout, Desert Orchid warmed the hearts of the big Sandown crowd as he rallied on the run-in after taking the final fence in unison with Kildimo. Kildimo had seemed to be travelling the better from the fourth last but, try as he might, he couldn't get past. Desert Orchid would not be denied and, calling on his last reserves of stamina and courage, he kept on up Sandown's famous hill to win going away by two and a half lengths. Strands of Gold, who had every chance at the second last, came third, four lengths behind Kildimo, with Proud Pilgrim, Run And Skip and Androma next. Desert Orchid met a great reception on his return to the winner's circle, one which can scarcely have been bettered in a Whitbread, an event which has produced more than its share of vintage entertainment and popular winners down the years. The Whitbread provided Desert Orchid with the twenty-first victory of his career and took his earnings in first-prize money to £189,687, which puts him behind only Dawn Run (£259,868), Wayward Lad (£218,732) and Burrough Hill Lad (£195,609) on the list of jumping's prize-money earners.

Terry Biddlecombe Challenge Trophy, Wincanton—Desert Orchid puts in a fine leap

Desert Orchid won three other races during the season, dishing out wide-margin drubbings to small fields in the Terry Biddlecombe Challenge Trophy at Wincanton and the Rank Boxing Day Trial Chase at Kempton on his first two outings, and gaining a comfortable all-the-way victory from Kildimo in the Chivas Regal Cup, a three-mile-one-furlong weight-for-age chase run at the Grand National meeting and designed principally as a consolation event for Cheltenham Gold Cup runners. The Chivas Regal field was reduced to four when the Gold Cup third Beau Ranger was withdrawn after spreading a plate on the way to the start. Desert Orchid was never headed and jumped spectacularly at times as he stretched the field on

Chivas Regal Cup Chase, Liverpool—Desert Orchid records his first success on a left-handed track, at the expense of Kildimo

the final circuit. He came home eight lengths in front of Kildimo who was struggling throughout the finishing straight to make any impression on the winner; Weather The Storm finished twelve lengths further behind in third.

Desert Orchid's two victories over Kildimo in the spring avenged a surprising length-and-a-half defeat at level weights by that horse in the three-runner Jim Ford Challenge Cup at Wincanton in February; Desert Orchid jumped well but couldn't hold Kildimo's finishing effort in a race run at a steady gallop for a long way. Had Desert Orchid won the Jim Ford Challenge Cup in good style it's possible he'd have tackled the Tote Cheltenham Gold Cup at the Festival meeting, rather than the two-mile Queen Mother Champion Chase. Desert Orchid's missing the Cheltenham Gold Cup looked a major misfortune after Charter Party's victory in steeplechasing's blue riband event: carrying more condition than usual, Desert Orchid had fought a tremendous battle, conceding 17 lb, before going down by a little over eight lengths to Charter Party in the Lee Cooper Gainsborough Handicap at Sandown in February (Desert Orchid lost second near the finish to Rhyme 'N' Reason who received 21 lb). In truth, Desert Orchid deserved a crack at the Gold Cup but the rain-softened going finally influenced Desert Orchid's connections to run the horse in the Queen Mother Champion Chase, in which he had finished third to Pearlyman and Very Promising the year before, when he hadn't been entered in the Gold Cup. The return clash of Pearlyman, Very Promising and Desert Orchid again gave the Festival crowd fine entertainment and the race provided Desert Orchid—a very game five-length second to Pearlyman after leading the field a merry dance for a long way—with his highest placing in five successive appearances at the meeting. Desert Orchid's

Cheltenham Festival record comprises two poor runs in the Champion Hurdle and a third place in the Arkle Challenge Trophy in addition to his two placings in the Queen Mother Champion Chase. Some rubbish is still talked and written about Desert Orchid's supposed lack of effectiveness on left-handed tracks, his failure to win a major race at the Festival meeting being cited to support the theory. However, with his two fine efforts in the Queen Mother Champion Chase and his runaway victory in the Chivas Regal Cup at Liverpool, we are surely entitled to hope we have heard the last of this particular subject. Maybe Desert Orchid will get his chance in the Gold Cup another year. He's much better suited by three miles plus nowadays and, though still capable of high-class form at the minimum trip, he's banging his head against a brick wall taking on a top-class two-mile specialist like Pearlyman in top form.

Desert Orchid lost his official ranking as Britain's top chaser to Pearlyman after Christmas (the official handicapper still assessed Pearlyman superior at the end of the season). More specifically, he lost it after a big defeat in the King George VI Rank Chase at Kempton on Boxing Day, shortly after which Pearlyman was an impressive winner under 12-7 of the valuable Castleford Handicap at Wetherby. Desert Orchid's sights had been set on the King George, effectively the mid-season championship for staying chasers, and he started even-money in a field of nine to add to his breathtaking winning performance in the race the previous season. Desert Orchid had completed his preparation for the King George by running over two miles in Sandown's Tingle Creek Handicap, a race named after a horse whose style of running Desert Orchid's recalls. Thought by his stable to need the race, Desert Orchid came a good second in the Tingle Creek, conceding lumps of weight all round, to the much improved Long Engagement; apart from the Queen Mother Champion Chase this was Desert Orchid's only appearance of the season at two miles. All seemed set fair for the King George. But Desert Orchid ran way below his best, beaten fifteen lengths by the comfortable French-trained winner Nupsala; Desert Orchid wouldn't have managed second had Forgive'N Forget not fallen at the last when challenging the winner.

What is to be made of Desert Orchid's failure? Well, perhaps he simply had an off-day, though at least a partial explanation for his performance may lie in the riding tactics adopted on this occasion by his regular jockey Colin Brown. Brown, who announced his retirement from the saddle after partnering Desert Orchid in the Queen Mother Champion Chase, usually rode Desert Orchid very well, but on this occasion he seemed to send him along far too fast for his own good. Desert Orchid used up valuable energy keeping up with Beau Ranger and Cybrandian, two other habitual front-runners who were set alight from the start. Brown would almost certainly have done better to have allowed that pair an early lead, rather than racing with them hell-for-leather well clear of the main body of the field. Desert Orchid lasted the scorching pace better than Beau Ranger and Cybrandian and led from six out until the second last. But the writing was on the wall even before the more conservatively ridden Nupsala and Forgive'N Forget moved effortlessly into challenging positions on the heels of Desert Orchid and Beau Ranger approaching the home straight. The first half of the King George, run much faster than the second, left Desert Orchid with no reserves in hand: he came to the end of his tether after the second last and passed the post very tired. The difference between winning and losing was fifteen lengths, of course, and there is no justification for concluding that Desert Orchid would have beaten Nupsala in the King George ridden differently. Perhaps there will be those who will say, therefore, that criticism of Brown is not warranted. But that's not the way we see it. We can't believe that the riding tactics adopted in the King George were right. Sherwood seems likely to take over as Desert Orchid's regular rider. He rode him in exemplary fashion in

Whitbread Gold Cup, Sandown—Desert Orchid is again too good for Kildimo

the Chivas Regal Cup and the Whitbread Gold Cup, extending his record to three wins from three rides on the horse (he also rode Desert Orchid in the 1986 King George in which stable-jockey Brown chose to partner Combs Ditch).

The sturdy, useful-looking Desert Orchid sometimes sweats up but it's of no significance: he sweated up before his first two victories of the latest season and also before the Chivas Regal Cup. He is very genuine—he seemed to resent wearing blinkers when tried in them once as a six-year-old—and he retains his enthusiasm remarkably well considering the number of hard races he has endured in an honourable career which reflects great credit on those who have handled him at Whitsbury Stables. Desert Orchid is indifferent to the state of the going. His first objective in the next season is sure to be the King George VI Rank Chase in which his prospects of duplicating his 1986 victory appear excellent at this stage.

A PUBLIC HERO

10 YEAR OLD c21g* c16d* c24m* c16d* c25g* c26v* c25s^{F}

RATED c182

Desert Orchid completes the process of turning himself into a sporting legend by winning the Tote Cheltenham Gold Cup after carrying all before him in another brilliant campaign. He becomes the first horse for almost a quarter of a century to win the King George VI Chase and the Cheltenham Gold Cup in the same season

Comparisons between past and present champions are always difficult to make, and claims are so obviously open to challenge as to make the task sometimes seem almost pointless. But when an exceptional and immensely popular horse like Desert Orchid arrives on the scene the desire to make comparisons becomes well-nigh irresistible. Desert Orchid carried all before him in the latest season as he went unbeaten through his first six races including the King George VI Rank Chase and the Tote Cheltenham Gold Cup, the two major championship events for staying chasers. Desert Orchid became the first horse for almost a quarter of a century to win the King George and the Gold Cup in the same season and his election as National Hunt Horse of the Year for the third year in succession—he received all twenty-eight votes from the Press panel—was a formality. Desert Orchid's popularity transcends prejudices within racing—his Gold Cup victory was the result almost all of racing

King George VI Rank Chase, Kempton—a typically fine jump from Desert Orchid, leading from Vodkatini

wanted—and he has made a big name for himself beyond the normal boundaries of the sport. He even has an official fan club!

Television has had much to do with establishing Desert Orchid's enormous popularity. Grey horses have always had a special appeal and Desert Orchid's colour—he is now virtually white—helps to set him apart; out in front, jumping boldly, he creates a spectacular image for the camera—like 'some creature out of legend, a mythological beast', as Hugh McIlvanney described him in *The Observer*. Truth to tell, however, the celebrations of some of Desert Orchid's performances in the latest season were excessive. The public has taken 'Dessie' to its heart like few others before him, but some of the Press and TV commentators, in their frenzy to construct a legend round the horse, showed a marked tendency to exaggerate his feats on the track. Desert Orchid is very much the horse of the moment and unquestionably an outstanding champion in his time. His brave victory in extremely testing conditions in the Gold Cup, the climax of his latest campaign, will long be remembered. But to mention Desert Orchid in the same breath as Arkle, as some did, is something no experienced and rational critic of the game can stomach. When the curtain comes down on Desert Orchid's career, he will leave a memory of brilliant jumping and grinding courage—which was particularly evident in three tight finishes in the latest season—but as things stand you don't have to go back to the halcyon days of Arkle and his brilliant contemporaries Flyingbolt and Mill House to find chasers of at least equal merit. The Gold Cup winners Burrough Hill Lad and Captain Christy, for example, attained ratings of 184 and 182 respectively.

In any argument about 'who was the greatest' the name of Arkle is almost always the first mentioned. He was beaten only four times in twenty-six steeplechases, including on his final appearance when he broke down in the King George VI Chase in 1966. Arkle was in his prime—only nine, a year younger than Desert Orchid—when he ran his last race and before his injury seemed to have excellent prospects of going on to equal, or even surpass, the mighty Golden Miller's record five victories in the Gold Cup. Arkle was a phenomenon, at the height of his powers looking as close to unbeatable as any horse is ever likely to be. For the record, Arkle's achievements included three victories in the Cheltenham Gold Cup, three in the Leopardstown Handicap Chase (once with 12-0 and twice with 12-7), two in the Hennessy Gold Cup (carrying 12-7 each time), and one each in the King George VI Chase, the Whitbread Gold Cup (12-7), the Irish Grand National (12-0), the Gallaher Gold Cup (12-7) and the SGB Handicap Chase (12-7). Arkle's achievements were astonishing and the old black and white television films of his most significant performances certainly convey the impression that he was just about the perfect chaser.

At the end of 1965/6, Arkle's record over the previous four seasons stood at twenty-four wins from twenty-six races (which included two over hurdles and one on the Flat). Arkle had only three more races but in one of them—the 1966 Hennessy—his performance gave a clear indication of the margin of his superiority over his contemporaries. Fighting every inch of the way, Arkle failed by only half a length to hold off Stalbridge Colonist who was receiving 35 lb. The following spring Stalbridge Colonist was beaten only three quarters of a length in the Cheltenham Gold Cup, and in the 1968 Gold Cup he came third, beaten just over a length. What A Myth, receiving 33 lb, was a length and a half behind Arkle in the 1966 Hennessy—and he went on to win the 1969 Gold Cup. Mill House, by the way, came back to win the 1967 Whitbread under top weight. Arkle achieved a rating of 212 in *Timeform* which in his final season described him as 'the greatest chaser ever'; Mill House was rated at 191.

Arkle ended his career with first-prize earnings of £75,107, by some way a record at the time for a British- or Irish-based jumper. Prize money rises steadily over the years as the real value of money falls, yet Arkle's record wasn't surpassed until the mid-'seventies. Between Arkle and Desert Orchid, currently National Hunt racing's leading money earner, eight horses held the record: Comedy of Errors (£94,708), Red Rum (£114,371), Night Nurse (£132,392), Sea

Victor Chandler Handicap Chase, Ascot—Desert Orchid just gets the better of a stirring battle with Panto Prince

Pigeon (£130,395), Silver Buck (£177,184), Burrough Hill Lad (£195,609), Wayward Lad (£218,732) and Dawn Run (£259,868). The figures refer to earnings over jumps only, disregarding place money; Silver Buck had taken over as leading money earner by the time Night Nurse edged ahead of Sea Pigeon again. Desert Orchid passed Dawn Run's mark when winning the Victor Chandler Handicap at Ascot in January; by the end of the season he had hoisted his first-prize earnings to £349,134—his seasonal earnings of £159,447 were easily a record—and taken his record over jumps to twenty-seven wins from fifty-five starts (including twenty from thirty-four over fences). Desert Orchid was 14/1 joint favourite for the latest Cheltenham Gold Cup with Cavvies Clown, Playschool and Kildimo in Hill's pre-season ante-post betting, his odds reflecting considerable uncertainty about whether he would be allowed to take his chance in the race. Much had been made of Desert Orchid's record at the Cheltenham Festival—second to Pearlyman in the most recent Queen Mother Champion Chase was his highest placing in five successive appearances at the meeting—and he had been a notable absentee from the Gold Cup field in 1988 when rain-softened going influenced his connections to run him in the Champion Chase instead. Desert Orchid's Cheltenham target remained in the balance for much of the season though his trainer said in a *Timeform Interview* at Christmas (before the King George): 'We'll make a decision between the two races later, but everyone is dying to see him run in the Gold Cup, myself and the owners included, so I'm sure that will be a very strong consideration. What happens to Pearlyman—presently on the side-lines—would obviously influence

Racecall Gainsborough Handicap Chase, Sandown—another thrilling victory for Desert Orchid, this time at the expense of Pegwell Bay

us a little bit, but even if both races look within Dessie's compass I still think we might go for the Gold Cup because, although it looks as though he's much better than all the two-milers with the exception of Pearlyman, he looks to be a bit better than all the three-milers as well!'

Desert Orchid was regarded as a two-mile specialist for long enough—but victories in the King George VI Rank Chase (before which he was untried at three miles) and the Gainsborough Handicap under top weight in the 1986/7 season underlined his versatility. Few chasers are capable of winning in top company at two miles *and* at three miles—the different trips call for different qualities in a horse—and, remarkably, Desert Orchid extended the variety of his winning distances even further by adding the Whitbread Gold Cup over three miles five furlongs in the 1987/8 season. Desert Orchid's first main target in the latest season was the King George VI Rank Chase in which he had been surprisingly beaten by French-trained Nupsala the previous season. After trotting up in the Terry Biddlecombe Challenge Trophy at Wincanton on his reappearance in October, Desert Orchid completed his preparation for Kempton, as he had the previous season, by running in the two-mile Tingle Creek Handicap at Sandown at the start of December. Desert Orchid's only race over two miles in the interim had been in the Queen Mother Champion Chase. It was almost two years since Desert Orchid's last victory over the trip. His task in the Tingle Creek—in which he conceded between 18 lb and 28 lb to his five rivals—was made easier when the favourite Vodkatini refused to race. Desert Orchid made all, jumping boldly and racing with tremendous zest, for an easy twelve-length win over Jim Thorpe, with Panto Prince half a length away third. Kempton's Boxing Day crowd—the paid attendance was more than 22,500—saw Desert Orchid join Halloween, Mandarin, Pendil, Captain Christy and Silver Buck among the dual winners of the King George VI Chase and leave himself one short of equalling Wayward Lad's three victories. The French hopes Nupsala and Nord Ac, both already temporarily stabled at Lambourn, were ruled out of the King George when their nominations were misdirected and an appeal to the Jockey Club by United Racecourses, who control Kempton, failed to get them reinstated. Desert Orchid, who started at 1/2, faced only four opponents, Vodkatini (7/1), Kildimo and Charter Party (both 8/1) and Cavvies Clown (9/1). Desert Orchid looked in great shape beforehand, bursting with health and moving to the start in fine style, and he won smoothly, confidently ridden throughout, by four lengths and five from Kildimo and Vodkatini. In a strongly-run race, Desert Orchid surrendered the lead to Vodkatini for a while at around halfway but, back in the lead, he put up a spectacular display of jumping over the last six or seven fences and kept on strongly before quickening away from Kildimo and Vodkatini from the last. Immediately after the race, Desert Orchid was offered at 4/1 by Hill's for the Gold Cup with a run.

Ascot's two-mile Victor Chandler Handicap and Sandown's Racecall Gainsborough Handicap over three miles came next on Desert Orchid's programme and he showed great courage in close finishes to keep his unbeaten record for the season intact. Desert Orchid was pushed to the limit at Ascot by Panto Prince, receiving 22 lb, and came out the better in a driving finish by a head after being taken on by his rival from the start; Panto Prince had looked the more likely to win turning for home where the pair were clear of the two remaining runners, their main rival Vodkatini having fallen at the fifth. Three weeks after his close encounter with Panto Prince, Desert Orchid had to ward off another spirited challenge—this time by the Mackeson and A. F. Budge Gold Cup winner Pegwell Bay who received 18 lb in the Gainsborough Handicap. The much improved Pegwell Bay led Desert Orchid on the second circuit and battled on when challenged from the second last; the pair landed in unison over the last and Desert Orchid showed typical gameness to wear down Pegwell Bay up the famous Sandown hill and win by three quarters of a length. The two other runners, Kildimo (received 15 lb) and Charter Party (received 7 lb), did little to enhance their Cheltenham Gold Cup prospects, neither mounting an effective challenge. Desert Orchid's performances in the Victor Chandler and the Gainsborough took his record at Ascot and Sandown to eight wins on each course.

So to Cheltenham. The Gold Cup was announced firmly as Desert Orchid's target a week or so before the Festival meeting and he was withdrawn from the Queen Mother Champion Chase because, in the words of his trainer, 'we don't want to be side-tracked'. Even so, Desert Orchid's participation in the Gold Cup looked to be in the balance for a time after hours of rain turned the going heavy on the day of the race. Snow had also fallen in the morning and the Gold Cup-day programme was given the go-ahead only after passing a stewards' inspection at midday. For those who enjoy their creature comforts, Cheltenham in the open on Gold Cup day was most definitely not the place to be. Conditions were foul and few would have been surprised had Desert Orchid been withdrawn. But Desert Orchid's trainer David Elsworth, to whom the owner reportedly gave the final say, never wavered—'The ground is horrible and conditions are all against him but he is the best horse. Next year, who knows, it might be off or he might have a leg. If the chance is there you have to take it'. The boldness of Desert Orchid's connections was richly rewarded. The crowd of over 50,000 witnessed a Gold Cup which overflowed with emotion and drama and is sure to go down in history as one of the great moments in National Hunt racing. Desert Orchid started 5/2 favourite in a field of thirteen which included two previous winners of the race The Thinker (15/2) and Charter Party (14/1), as well as the previous year's runner-up Cavvies Clown (8/1), the long-time ante-post second favourite Ten Plus (11/2), winner of his last four races, the Coral Welsh National and Racing Post Handicap winner Bonanza Boy (15/2) and the highly-regarded Irish-trained Carvill's Hill, winner of the Vincent O'Brien Irish Gold Cup, who started second favourite at 5/1. The conditions had a shattering effect on some of the runners and only four completed the course without mishap. Desert Orchid made most of the running, jumping with his usual fluency from the start, before being joined by Ten Plus and Cavvies Clown passing the stands for the second time. Ten Plus went on at the fourteenth of the twenty-two fences and was still travelling strongly, two or three lengths ahead of Desert Orchid, with the 25/1-shot Yahoo and Charter Party next, when he fell three from home, fatally injured. Desert Orchid was in the lead again briefly but Yahoo took over approaching the second last, looking all over a winner; Desert Orchid gave every appearance, as he came under pressure between the last two, of having little left. But appearances proved deceptive. Desert Orchid responded gamely and refused to give up. Crossing the last almost upsides Yahoo, Desert Orchid staged a tremendous rally, edging left towards his rival before being straightened and forging ahead halfway up the run-in. With the crowd

Tote Cheltenham Gold Cup Chase, Cheltenham—Yahoo holds a narrow advantage jumping the last .....

..... but it's Simon Sherwood on Desert Orchid who's celebrating at the line

roaring him on, the firmly-ridden Desert Orchid pulled away for a length-and-a-half victory. Charter Party came third, eight lengths behind Yahoo and a distance ahead of fourth-placed Bonanza Boy; 66/1-shot West Tip completed the course some time afterwards. Carvill's Hill was a seventh-fence faller and The Thinker also came down on the first circuit.

Desert Orchid's victory may not have been in the grand manner—it was an around-average Gold Cup winning performance strictly on form—but the Gold Cup will almost certainly be remembered as his finest hour. The reception that met him on his return to the winner's enclosure was reminiscent of Dawn Run's. Desert Orchid had shown all the attributes the jumping public had come to expect from him. His jockey Simon Sherwood, who was unbeaten in nine rides on the horse up to and including the Gold Cup, paid him the following tribute: 'I couldn't believe how well Yahoo was going. On any other horse you would have thought it was all over. But in the end it was all down to guts. I have certainly never ridden a braver horse—and never expect to either'. The stylish Sherwood handled Desert Orchid impeccably after taking over as the horse's regular jockey on the retirement of Colin Brown and his record was spoilt only in the Martell Cup at Liverpool in April when an uncharacteristic lapse by Desert Orchid resulted in a rare fall, the first time he had parted company with his rider since his novice chasing days. Trainer David Elsworth's part in Desert Orchid's emergence as probably the most popular racehorse seen in Britain since Red Rum cannot be praised too highly. Elsworth is a master of his craft and has sent out a host of big-race winners over the jumps and on the Flat as a result of which he is now firmly established as Britain's top all-the-year-round trainer.

If he keeps free from illness and injury Desert Orchid seems likely to dominate the headlines for another season at least. He stands head and shoulders above his contemporaries and looks to have good prospects of adding significantly to his already-splendid record. A record-equalling third King George VI Rank Chase looks very much on the cards and, at the moment, only the up-and-coming Carvill's Hill seems to offer a potentially-serious threat to a second Cheltenham Gold Cup victory. It was announced after Sherwood's retirement from the saddle at the end of the season that Dunwoody would ride Desert Orchid in future.

A TRUE CHAMPION

11 YEAR OLD c25m* c16m² c24g* c21d* c24g* c26f³ c28m*

RATED c187

Desert Orchid proves himself the best National Hunt horse for a long time, the highlights coming in the King George VI Rank Chase (his third win in the race), the Racing Post Chase (the best performance of his career in Timeform's view) and the Jameson Irish Grand National

'Uneasy lies the head that wears a crown.' Desert Orchid added further in the latest season to his glittering list of achievements, winning the King George VI Rank Chase for a record-equalling third time and crowning a fine campaign with a twelve-length victory, conceding lumps of weight all round, in the Jameson Irish Grand National. In between he produced another top-notch display in the Racing Post Chase at Kempton where his breathtaking victory under 12-3 (conceding between 28 lb and 34 lb to his seven rivals) was, by our reckoning, the best performance for many a season in a steeplechase, over any distance. Desert Orchid's tally made his fourth successive National Hunt Horse Of The Year award a foregone conclusion. To win the Horse Of The Year award three times is a rarity—only triple Champion Hurdle winner Persian War achieved the feat before Desert Orchid—and to win four times was without precedent. But the voting for the award—decided by an end-of-season poll of a selected Press panel—was surprising, to say the least, and seemed to indicate that, in the eyes of some, Desert Orchid's magnetism is becoming less powerful. On each of the first three occasions Desert Orchid gained a majority of the votes, receiving sixteen out of twenty-six in 1986/7 (the year See You Then won his third Champion Hurdle), twenty-one out of twenty-five in 1987/8, and all twenty-eight in 1988/9. In the latest season, however, Desert Orchid won with only twelve out of twenty-seven votes. Six of the panel voted for Mr Frisk, four for Kribensis, three for Norton's Coin and two for Barnbrook Again. Notwithstanding the strong claims of these horses, especially Mr Frisk, whose Grand National and Whitbread victories provided some of the most memorable images of the racing season, Desert Orchid's testimonial surely spoke for itself. He is the best National Hunt horse for a long time, in our view the best since the heyday of Arkle and his brilliant contemporaries Flyingbolt and Mill House in the 'sixties: and his exploits have captured the imagination of the general public more than any other since Arkle, with the possible exception of Red Rum. Desert Orchid is racing's most resounding name and, as we have said before, he is a symbol of so much that is good about National Hunt racing and provides a magnificent image for the game. He's tough, versatile, courageous and durable and a joy to watch, his supremely quick and accurate jumping making him a splendid sight out in front in full flow. Could any sport want a more accomplished standard-bearer?

Desert Orchid's defeat in the Tote Cheltenham Gold Cup, a defeat which many considered unthinkable beforehand, almost certainly influenced the voting. No serious challenge to Desert Orchid's supremacy among the staying chasers had emerged by Cheltenham-time, and conditions were considered likely to be more in his favour than the previous year when Desert Orchid had struggled home from Yahoo in conditions of extreme meteorological misery. The fine weather and the prospect of Desert Orchid's becoming only the sixth horse to win the Gold Cup more than once—following Golden Miller (five wins), Arkle and Cottage Rake (three each) and Easter Hero and L'Escargot (dual winners)—drew a crowd of 56,884, thought to be the biggest assembled at Cheltenham. Expectations were high, but, starting at odds on in a field of twelve, Desert Orchid ran about a stone and a half below his best—and, by our reckoning, about 7 lb below his winning performance of the previous year. The 100/1-shot Norton's Coin, an ex-point-to-pointer from a 'one-horse stable', provided the biggest shock in Gold Cup history, holding off Toby Tobias by three quarters of a length to win in record time for the race with Desert Orchid, whose chance had gone before the last, four lengths further back. For whatever reason, Desert Orchid's running was too bad—by his own very high standards—to be true. There's no doubt, however, that his defeat in what is regarded as steeplechasing's blue riband event diminished his worth in the eyes of both the general public and of some in racing. Some days, though, are best forgotten. Why dwell on one particular defeat when there are some splendid victories to recall?

As in previous years, Desert Orchid was trained in the first part of the season for a crack at the King George VI Rank Chase at Kempton on Boxing Day. He won the race in 1986, was surprisingly beaten by the French challenger Nupsala in 1987, and resumed winning ways in 1988, leaving him one short of equalling Wayward

Lad's three victories. Desert Orchid's preparation in the latest season followed a familiar pattern, though he was held up in his work for some time because of the prevailing firm ground. He reappeared in a minor event at Wincanton—cantering over a single opponent in the Silver Buck Chase in November—and then, for the third year in a row, reverted to two miles in the Tingle Creek Handicap ('a good, tough little race, once round Sandown, and an ideal prep-race for the King George', according to his trainer). The Gold Cup and the Tingle Creek Handicap were the only races Desert Orchid lost during the season. Each of Desert Orchid's three opponents at Sandown was officially rated further below him than the 28-lb weight range for the race and Desert Orchid's two-and-a-half-length defeat by Long Engagement (who beat him in the same race on similar terms in 1987) raised doubts in some quarters about whether the horse might be on the decline. However, trainer Elsworth said in a *Timeform Interview* that Desert Orchid (who had had two races before the Tingle Creek the previous year) was 'short of a race' which almost certainly explains why Dunwoody set no more than a moderate gallop

Silver Buck Chase, Wincanton—Desert Orchid makes his reappearance

King George VI Rank Chase, Kempton—a third King George; Barnbrook Again holds on to second place

over a trip that isn't ideal for Desert Orchid nowadays (Long Engagement quickened the better from the last after stalking Desert Orchid all the way). 'We really got stuck into Desert Orchid between the Tingle Creek and the King George', Elsworth told us. 'We had to be more severe with his preparation than one likes to be but he took it well.' Desert Orchid faced five opponents at Kempton and, starting at 6/4 on, led throughout to win virtually unchallenged by eight lengths from his stable-companion Barnbrook Again, who was attempting three miles for the first time; Yahoo came seven lengths further back in third, ahead of Bob Tisdall, the second-favourite Pegwell Bay and Norton's Coin (33/1, beaten thirty-nine lengths by the winner). The early gallop was fairly slow and Desert Orchid's jumping wasn't so fluent as usual but, after making a bad mistake at the ditch after the water second time round, his jumping began to improve and he kept up a tremendous gallop all the way up the straight after his rider had gradually increased the tempo from about a mile out. Desert Orchid took the last three fences in typically dashing style, and came home with tremendous gusto to a rousing reception. His trainer incidentally was the first since Cazalet in 1956 to saddle first and second in the King George in the same season.

Desert Orchid's popularity was as great as ever—he was voted National Hunt 'Horse of the Eighties' by readers of the *Racing Post* at Christmas (polling twice as many votes as his nearest rival Dawn Run)—but his followers had to wait for over six weeks before he was seen out again. Desert Orchid was side-lined by coughing, as were a good number of his stable-mates at around this time, but news in January that Desert Orchid was to be entered for the Seagram Grand National became one of the main topics on the racing pages in the face of a public outcry which must have been unprecedented in advance of a race. A protracted debate ensued about whether the horse should or should not be 'risked' at Aintree. Four of the popular daily papers conducted polls of their readers, all of which were overwhelmingly in the negative. The *Daily Mail* poll, for example, brought in 9,000 votes against and only 48 for. One of Desert Orchid's owners had said at the start of the season that he would never dare to enter Desert Orchid because 'every time the National is mentioned we get a stack of hate-mail'. Desert Orchid was allotted 12-2 in the original handicap, 3 lb less than Burrough Hill Lad had been given in the race in 1985 (these are the only two horses since Mill House—a non-runner with 12-3 in 1965—to be given more than 12-0 in a National). As with Burrough Hill Lad, the handicapper assessed Desert Orchid more favourably—to the tune of 6 lb to be precise—than he would have done at the time for a handicap on a park course, which displeased some of the connections of other leading Grand National candidates. Not to put too fine a point on it, the handicapper leant over backwards to attract Desert Orchid to Aintree. But the strength of the concern of a section of the public—no-one suggested conducting opinion polls when the charismatic Red Rum was appearing year after year in the National—proved too much. Desert Orchid was withdrawn at the first forfeit stage in mid-February. His trainer took the opportunity in his *Timeform Interview* to clear the air:

'As everyone knows, this year's Grand National was a possibility at one time. I discussed it with Richard Burridge and he agreed that we should enter him and see what weight he got. I went on record as saying I thought he'd get 12-2—I said that was as much as we'd want him to get to consider running him. I didn't feel the handicapper could justifiably give him less than 12-2, and lo and behold that's what he got. Now I never said he was going to run because he got 12-2. My interpretation of the conversation with Richard Burridge was that if Desert Orchid got 12-2 we would see how things were after Cheltenham. I certainly thought we ought to consider the National because, for all that it's a marvellous race, a great feature and a great spectacle, it's not always that good a race class-wise, and most years—in theory at least—it's probably not as difficult to win as the Whitbread. And I thought it would be great for the horse if he could win it. I wouldn't run him at Aintree for fun and obviously I thought he had the credentials to win. But I think all the pressure from everybody—should he run or shouldn't he—finally got to Richard and his father. So we withdrew him at the first forfeit. If it was going to cause that much concern and anxiety to the owners, it didn't seem fair to prolong the agony. You can see the point of view of Richard and his father. They are in the game for fun but, of course, owning a good horse brings its pressures and problems. It's a once-in-a-lifetime experience having a horse like Desert Orchid, and it must be very difficult to cope with things logically sometimes. It's difficult enough for me to cope with it—I have never trained a horse like this before—and I can understand any owner reacting to the sort of pressure that was put on Richard. I suppose you might say why the hell didn't we all work that out beforehand and avoid all the controversy. Well, it's like saying you're going to jump off the top diving board at the swimming pool, and when you actually get up there and look down you realise you're not so sure. Obviously with hindsight, if I'd known the way things were going to turn out, I wouldn't even have entered Desert Orchid for Aintree.'

There's reportedly some prospect of Desert Orchid's contesting the Grand National in the next season and, given similarly favourable treatment from the handicapper, he'd surely start a firm favourite. Public opinion might be brought to bear once again but we

Racing In Wessex Chase, Wincanton—Mzima Spring makes a brave attempt to hang on

hope Desert Orchid's owners will take their decision on the merits of the case and not be influenced by a section of the general public's perception of the dangers of Aintree. There probably isn't a tougher race anywhere than the National, and there's no denying that the risks are almost certainly greater than in any other race, but it is only a matter of degree. Risks are inseparable from steeplechasing, at Aintree or anywhere else, and, in our view, the severity of the National isn't a good enough reason in itself to avoid the race. No-one knows Desert Orchid better than his trainer and those who work with him at Whitsbury. We share the view that Desert Orchid has sound credentials for the National and it would be regrettable if the sport was denied what could be one of its greatest sights, because of a fear of exposing such a popular horse to dangers which are, for an experienced and accomplished campaigner like Desert Orchid, in all probability not very much greater than those which he faces every time he sets foot on a racecourse.

An announcement about Desert Orchid's intended defection from the Grand National field was made the day he returned to action with a bloodless victory in a minor race, the Racing In Wessex Chase, at Wincanton in February. It was Desert Orchid's third trip to the races in six days. It had been intended that he would reappear in the Agfa Diamond Chase (formerly the Gainsborough) at Sandown,which was lost to the weather, and he had been withdrawn from the Charterhouse Mercantile Handicap at Ascot the day before Wincanton when the going became heavy after overnight rain. Desert Orchid had little more than an exercise gallop at Wincanton—he won by twenty lengths from Bartres—but he faced a stern test in the Racing Post Chase at Kempton a little over a fortnight later. Only three of the eight runners—Desert Orchid (12-3), Delius (10-3) and Ballyhane (10-1)—were in the handicap proper, but Desert Orchid's

Racing Post Chase (Handicap), Kempton—an exceptional performance even by Desert Orchid's standards

weight included a 3-lb penalty for winning at Wincanton and he had a stiffer task on the form-book than was generally appreciated (he started odds on). Desert Orchid produced a performance to savour, taking command before the home turn after leading or disputing the lead from the start and running on strongly—putting in a blemish-free round of jumping highlighted by a brilliant leap at the second last—to win by eight lengths and the same from Delius and Seagram, with the rest strung out. Desert Orchid was cheered up the home straight and received another thoroughly-deserved ovation after crossing the line. The way we read the form-book, Desert Orchid gave an outstanding performance, his finest to date (represented by his rating of 187); puzzlingly, the official handicapper rated Desert Orchid 182 and Seagram 140 after their performances here, which underestimated Desert Orchid's merit, as it allowed Seagram only 11 lb for the sixteen lengths by which he was beaten (we allowed him the full 16 lb) and raised Desert Orchid only to the mark—including a 3-lb penalty—that he ran off at Kempton. Still more puzzling was the fact that when Seagram went on to run very well for the remainder of the season (earning an official rating of 145) the handicapper chose not to remedy the situation. What price would Desert Orchid have been if he had carried top weight off this mark against the same or similar opposition in his next race?

Desert Orchid's only appearance in a handicap after the Racing Post Chase was under 12-0 in the Jameson Irish Grand National at Fairyhouse on Easter Monday when he gained another

Jameson Irish Grand National, Fairyhouse— that last fence mistake

memorable victory, conceding between 26 lb and 28 lb to thirteen rivals after the late withdrawals of Carvill's Hill (11-4 in the original handicap) and Yahoo (10-6). Desert Orchid showed no ill-effects from his hard battle with Norton's Coin and Toby Tobias at Cheltenham, outclassing the opposition to win going away by a dozen lengths after surviving a bad last-fence blunder. Barney Burnett outstayed Have A Barney, Cloney Grange, Riska's River and The Committee to take second but never looked like posing a threat to Desert Orchid whose fluent jumping allowed his rider Dunwoody—whose partnership with Desert Orchid strengthened as the season went on—to control the race almost throughout; the second favourite Bold Flyer was allowed the lead on sufferance at various stages but once Desert Orchid was sent into a clear lead approaching the second last the race was over, or rather that for first place was, barring accidents. Desert Orchid was only the third British-trained winner of the Irish National, following Don Sancho in 1928 and Rhyme 'N' Reason in 1985 (trained at the time by Murray-Smith, and subsequently transferred to Desert Orchid's trainer for whom he won the Grand National).

The Irish Grand National, which incidentally sets nowhere near so severe a test as its counterpart at Aintree, brought Desert Orchid's record earnings for a British- or Irish-based jumper to £476,739. He has now won thirty-two of his sixty-two races, his victories coming on eight different courses including Ascot and Sandown, on both of which he has won eight times, and Kempton and Wincanton, on both of which he has gained six victories. Desert Orchid's record at Cheltenham isn't so outstanding. His victory in the Gold Cup—on form an around-average Gold Cup winning performance—is the only one he has gained in seven successive appearances at the Festival meeting where his record also includes two poor runs in the Champion Hurdle, a third in the Arkle Challenge Trophy and two placings in the Queen Mother Champion Chase. There's no doubt that Desert Orchid isn't so effective at Cheltenham as he is on some of the other major courses, though it's hard to say for certain why this should be. Cheltenham is left-handed and Desert Orchid's most outstanding performances—judged strictly on the form-book—have been put up going the other way. But it's going too far to say of a horse that has won a Gold Cup (he's also won at left-handed Liverpool) that he is unsuited by a left-handed course. Desert Orchid's superb jumping technique and his excellent stamina are tailor-made for Cheltenham's stiff fences and track; his jumping stood him in good stead when he won his Gold Cup—he outjumped his rivals—and his stamina and gameness were illustrated by his tremendous rally that day at the end of a race which had a shattering effect on some of his opponents (there were only four finishers). Desert Orchid's trainer believes that the firm going may have contributed to the horse's performance in the latest Gold Cup. 'We know Dessie can go on it but his superior jumping wasn't such a great advantage this year, with all his rivals jumping well on the faster ground', said Elsworth. Perhaps there's something in the theory, though such explanations offered for disappointing performances are always a matter for conjecture. It's worth pointing out that ground conditions were similar for the Irish National. Report has it that Desert Orchid may be aimed at the Queen Mother Champion Chase at the next Festival, rather than at the Gold Cup. If so, he'll have to be ridden more enterprisingly than he was in the latest Tingle Creek Chase; he is vulnerable at two miles nowadays unless there's an end-to-end gallop. Desert Orchid stays extremely well and has good prospects of getting the Grand National distance.

Desert Orchid's main target in the first part of the season will again be the King George VI Rank Chase. If Desert Orchid wins the King George he'll set a record of four victories in the race which may never be beaten; if he also goes on to win the Grand National he may well achieve the eminence of an Incitatus, the horse whom the Roman Emperor Caligula made a senator!

A 4TH KING GEORGE

12 YEAR OLD c17g[2] c16m[4] c24d* c16d[4] c25g* c26g[3]

RATED c178

Desert Orchid's ninth season features a vintage display in the King George and confirms his general popularity, a survey showing that he is more widely recognised than a number of public figures, including the Chancellor of the Exchequer who uses the point in his budget speech

'Horses are like strawberries. You must enjoy them while you can because they don't last long. I've been through this a lot of times. You can't look back. Yesterday's sunshine is gone, partner.' The words are those of the American trainer Charlie Whittingham on the retirement of his champion Sunday Silence. Talk of Desert Orchid's being over the hill is almost certainly premature—and Father Time may have even longer to wait if he wins a fifth King George on Boxing Day—but, if indeed, retirement beckons, Whittingham's words are interesting when applied to Desert Orchid. The followers of the jumpers get to know their horses very well. But even though the top horses stay around longer than their counterparts on the Flat it's most unusual to find a horse at the top for so long as Desert Orchid. He began his career over jumps in 1982/3, started second favourite for the Champion Hurdle the following season, and has been a notably durable campaigner. He has now completed nine seasons and has won thirty-four races from sixty-eight starts, earning a record £542,629 in first-prize money. Desert Orchid's record over fences (twenty-seven wins from forty-seven starts) includes the Tote Cheltenham Gold Cup, the Whitbread Gold Cup and the Jameson Irish Grand National as well as his record-breaking four victories in the King George VI Rank Chase. He's been an outstanding stalwart of National Hunt racing and is firmly established as currently Britain's favourite racehorse, his general popularity approaching that of Red Rum. In a survey conducted for Ladbrokes, published in March, 84% said they knew of Desert Orchid, while 94% in the same survey had heard of Red Rum. Desert Orchid was more widely recognised than a number of public figures, including the Chancellor of the Exchequer who used the point in the introduction to his

Budget speech. Desert Orchid's celebrity status actually led to his appearance outside 10 Downing Street in the summer, taking part in the presentation of a petition against allowing the export of live horses for slaughter—not, we hasten to add, fulfilling the prophecy made at the end of the essay in *Chasers & Hurdlers 1989/90*! Few equine heroes have inspired the affection of the general public like Desert Orchid and it was a surprise to see his four-year reign as National Hunt Horse of the Year—decided by a panel of racing journalists at the end of the season—ended so overwhelmingly. Desert Orchid was still the best staying chaser in the country in the latest season—and arguably also put up the best performance over two miles—and yet he received only two of the twenty- eight votes cast in the official end-of-season poll; Garrison Savannah, Seagram and Blazing Walker were less versatile chasers who received more votes in the poll won by Champion Hurdler Morley Street.

If the worst prediction of some sections of the Press had come true, the Desert Orchid era would have been at a close before Christmas. The Jeremiahs wrote him off after defeats in his first two races, the Plymouth Gin Haldon Gold Cup (in which he was beaten six lengths at levels by Sabin du Loir) and the Tingle Creek Chase (in which he came last of four to Young Snugfit, struggling from a long way out). The Tingle Creek over two miles at Sandown has become the traditional stepping-stone for the King George for Desert Orchid—it was his fourth appearance in the race in as many years—and his trainer said afterwards that 'the Tingle Creek was a race I didn't think he would win, the main purpose being to make sure that he had a good, hard race to get him ready for the King George'. Desert Orchid's regular rider Dunwoody, who deserted him at Sandown in favour of Waterloo Boy, was back in the saddle on Boxing Day. 'Running him in the Tingle Creek certainly worked', his trainer said in a *Timeform Interview*. 'He started to give us all the old signals, the vibes were there, and I was very confident even though it looked a very good King George on paper.' The Charlie Hall Chase and Edward Hanmer Handicap winner Celtic Shot was favourite in some of the early betting on the King George, reflecting the doubts about Desert Orchid's form. But Desert Orchid started favourite at 9/4 on the day, in spite of Celtic Shot's keeping his unbeaten record for the season when landing the odds from Garrison Savannah in the Tommy Whittle Chase at Haydock two weeks before the King George. Other notable opponents included: Toby Tobias, who beat Desert Orchid for second place in the 1990 Gold Cup before winning the Martell Cup at Liverpool; Sabin du Loir; French-trained The Fellow, from the same stable that saddled the 1987 King George winner Nupsala; and the

Irish Gold Cup winner Nick The Brief (third in the Tommy Whittle on his reappearance).

Desert Orchid's fourth King George victory—beating the previous record of three wins in the race shared with Wayward Lad—came with a vintage display. When the leader Sabin du Loir fell at the thirteenth of the nineteen fences, The Fellow and Toby Tobias were left as Desert Orchid's closest pursuers. Racing with plenty of zest Desert Orchid galloped on much too strongly for his rivals and, jumping brilliantly, had twelve lengths to spare over Toby Tobias at the post, with The Fellow five lengths further back in third, seven in front of the only other finisher Celtic Shot. Desert Orchid met a great reception on his return to the unsaddling enclosure and it was due in some measure to Desert Orchid's popularity that Channel 4 was able to report its second biggest audience of the year for racing (behind the Derby) with a viewing figure of 2.9m. Incidentally, five of the nine most popular races shown by Channel 4 in 1990 were over the sticks, including the Racing Post Chase and the Irish National, both of which Desert Orchid won.

King George VI Rank Chase, Kempton—an unprecedented fourth win for Desert Orchid who jumps the last clear of Toby Tobias

With the King George safely in the bag Desert Orchid's campaign was mapped out for Cheltenham, his owners—in the light of the controversy the previous year—having had second thoughts about aiming the horse at the Grand National, a plan understood to have been favoured by the trainer. Desert Orchid wasn't entered for Aintree, Elsworth explaining in his *Timeform Interview* that his only serious difference with the owners—'the Burridges have been magnificent and always been very fair to deal with'—had come over the National. 'If it's not fair for a superb jumper like Desert Orchid to run in the National, it's not fair for any horse to contest the race ... but I respect the views of the owners and I can see their point.' Desert Orchid pleased in his preparation for his third appearance in the Tote Cheltenham Gold Cup (his eighth successive appearance at the Festival meeting) and his trainer reported him 'on his very best form, certainly as good as he's been all season, and probably better'. Desert Orchid had put up two highly creditable performances between Kempton and Cheltenham, coming a six-length fourth to Blitzkreig (received 24 lb) in the Victor Chandler Handicap at Ascot in January and making most when winning the Agfa Diamond Handicap at Sandown in February. There were only four finishers in the Victor Chandler—Young Snugfit (received 17 lb) and Katabatic (received 24 lb) came second and third—but Desert Orchid ran his best race over two miles (an inadequate trip for him nowadays) for some time, recording, strictly on the form-book, the best performance seen all season over the distance. Desert Orchid's victory in the Agfa Diamond Handicap was his third in the race—he won it twice when it was known as the Gainsborough Chase—but he had to 'take his coat off and struggle very hard' (in his trainer's words) to regain the lead from Nick The Brief (received 15 lb) on the flat for a three-quarter-length victory. Desert Orchid's performance at Sandown confirmed that he was still the best staying chaser in training and Nick The Brief paid him a compliment when winning the

Agfa Diamond Handicap Chase, Sandown—a fine shot of Desert Orchid jumping ahead of Nick The Brief

Hennessy Cognac Gold Cup at Leopardstown next time. In spite of the fact that Desert Orchid had proved more vulnerable at Cheltenham than on some of the other major courses and that he was the oldest horse in the race, his credentials for the Gold Cup were there for all to see and he started second favourite behind Celtic Shot in a field of fourteen. In what is almost certain to have been his final appearance at the Festival meeting, Desert Orchid finished third behind the outsiders Garrison Savannah and The Fellow, beating all the leading fancies and probably putting up a performance almost on a par with his placing in the race the previous year. For the record, in his six races over fences at Cheltenham, Desert Orchid has never finished out of the first three; he came third in the Arkle Challenge Trophy and was placed twice in the Queen Mother Champion Chase.

A life-sized statue of Desert Orchid is to be unveiled at Kempton on Boxing Day when his legion of followers will be hoping that he goes out in a blaze of glory by winning his fifth King George. Desert Orchid is old to be running in and winning championship races—no twelve-year-old has won the King George since its inception in 1947—and with younger horses coming through into the top flight he's sure to face a stiff task. Blazing Walker and Remittance Man look potentially the biggest obstacles at this stage but Desert Orchid's ability to confound the sceptics seemingly knows no bounds and if he gets to post fit and in top form he's sure to take the world of beating. He's still the champion anywhere except Cheltenham.

THE PEDIGREE

Desert Orchid (gr.g. 1979)	Grey Mirage (gr 1969)	Double-U-Jay (ch 1963)	Major Portion
			Renounce
		Fair Inez (gr 1958)	Prince Chevalier
			Floria Tosca
	Flower Child (br 1967)	Brother (br 1959)	Nearula
			Aunt Agnes
		Grey Orchid (gr 1952)	No Orchids
			Harbour Lights

DESERT ORCHID

Desert Orchid, a sturdy individual in appearance, was for long enough regarded as a two-miler, pure and simple. That he should turn out to stay extremely well couldn't have been predicted in his early days from a study of his pedigree.

Both his sire and dam are now dead. Desert Orchid's sire Grey Mirage, who was exported to Saudi Arabia in 1980, never won beyond seven furlongs and most of the jumpers sired by him showed their best form at up to two and a half miles.

Desert Orchid's dam Flower Child, who gained her only victories as a nine-year-old (finishing alone over two miles at Plumpton and winning a weakly-contested event over two and a half at Fontwell), was by a stallion effective at sprint distances. That stallion, Brother, sired only a handful of winners in a career mostly spent covering non-thoroughbred stock as a National Light Horse Breeding Society (Hunters' Improvement Society) selected stallion. Flower Child's dam Grey Orchid was a winning point-to-pointer sired by a good, game, genuine stayer of the 'forties No Orchids, winner of the Yorkshire Cup and the Ascot Stakes.

Desert Orchid's dam Flower Child has bred only two other winners, the fair hurdler and winning chaser Ragged Robin (by Baragoi) and the modest free-running chaser Peacework (by Workboy), both of whom have been successful at up to two and a half miles.

THE CONNECTIONS

Like most sporting successes, Desert Orchid's magnificent career has been based on teamwork. But the man in the hottest seat whenever a good horse comes along is always the trainer.

David Elsworth, a champion jumping trainer now challenging the big Flat trainers at their own game, has handled Desert Orchid throughout his career. And no-one could have done a better job. He has prepared the horse for his big races with great precision and has coped admirably with the inevitable pressures.

David gave an insight in a *Timeform Interview* into some of those pressures. He was explaining the importance of the smooth relationship between himself and Desert Orchid's owners, Richard Burridge and his father James, who also bred the horse . . .

Desert Orchid (Rodney Boult up) with trainer David Elsworth

'I would like to state in *Timeform* that everything I have done with the horse has been in full consultation and with the agreement of the Burridges who own him. It's one of the most difficult things to cope with the pressure of owning a good horse and the Burridges have been magnificent. I've got a saying that the trainer's worst enemy is the owner's best friend. An owner's friends can sow the seeds of discontent. It's not so bad when a horse is winning but I think every trainer will tell you the same story, that an owner's friends always know better than the trainer! The Burridges, of course, have got millions of friends because of this marvellous horse! They've had plenty of 'advice' over the years, for example about the horse's best distance—in the old days it used to be that he shouldn't be running over three miles, nowadays it's that he shouldn't be racing at two—and the point I'm making is that the Burridges have always

Martell Cup, Liverpool 1989—Desert Orchid is led back (owner Richard Burridge, left) after an uncharacteristic lapse

been very fair to deal with, even when once or twice things haven't gone right. I could think of a lot of people who could have owned this horse and made my job a nightmare! Without the full co-operation of the Burridges, my job would have been a lot more difficult and I'm very lucky to have had them owning the horse. The only serious difference we've had is over running the horse in the National, but I respect their views and I can see their point.'

Others who have played their part in the Desert Orchid story include: the jockeys who have been associated with him, notably Colin Brown, Simon Sherwood and Richard Dunwoody; and the team at Whitsbury, among them one of the head lads Rodney Boult who has ridden Desert Orchid in most of his work, and the horse's devoted stable-lass Janice Coyle who has been with the yard since graduating from apprentice school.

The jockeys most associated with Desert Orchid—left to right, Colin Brown, Simon Sherwood and Richard Dunwoody

RECORD OF WINS

1982/83	**ran 4; 0 wins**	**Winning Prize Money**
1983/84	**ran 8; 6 wins**	
Haig Whisky Novices' Hurdle, *Ascot*		**£1,931.60**
Bingley Novices' Hurdle, *Ascot*		**£2,316.50**
Food-Brokers Armour Novices' Hurdle, *Kempton*		**£3,548**
Tolworth Hurdle, *Sandown*		**£4,482**
Datchet Novices' Hurdle, *Ascot*		**£2,977.20**
Kingwell Pattern Hurdle, *Wincanton*		**£6,059.20**
1984/85	**ran 8; 1 win**	
Oteley Hurdle, *Sandown*		**£4,417.20**
1985/86	**ran 10** *(1 hurdle; 9 chase);* **4 wins**	
Lambskin Products Novices' Chase, *Devon & Exeter*		**£1,607.60**
Hurst Park Novices' Chase, *Ascot*		**£7,987.20**
Henry VIII Novices' Chase, *Sandown*		**£3,759**
Killiney Novices' Chase, *Ascot*		**£5,638.50**
1986/87	**ran 9; 6 wins**	
Holsten Export Lager Chase, *Sandown*		**£4,950.20**
Frogmore Handicap Chase, *Ascot*		**£6,801.30**
King George VI Rank Chase, *Kempton*		**£31,696**
F.U.'s Jeans Gainsborough Handicap Chase, *Sandown*		**£15,666**
Jim Ford Challenge Cup, *Wincanton*		**£6,322.90**
Peregrine Handicap Chase, *Ascot*		**£7,142.10**

1987/88 ran 9; 4 wins

Race	Winning Prize Money
Terry Biddlecombe Challenge Trophy, *Wincanton*	**£3,842**
Rank Boxing Day Trial Chase, *Kempton*	**£7,502.50**
Chivas Regal Cup, *Liverpool*	**£16,040**
Whitbread Gold Cup, *Sandown*	**£45,000**

1988/89 ran 7; 6 wins

Race	Winning Prize Money
Terry Biddlecombe Challenge Trophy, *Wincanton*	**£3,694**
Tingle Creek Handicap Chase, *Sandown*	**£8,812.50**
King George VI Rank Chase, *Kempton*	**£37,280**
Victor Chandler Handicap Chase, *Ascot*	**£21,949.50**
Racecall Gainsborough Handicap Chase, *Sandown*	**£19,340**
Tote Cheltenham Gold Cup, *Cheltenham*	**£68,371.25**

1989/90 ran 7; 5 wins

Race	Winning Prize Money
Silver Buck Chase, *Wincanton*	**£5,076**
King George VI Rank Chase, *Kempton*	**£40,986**
Racing In Wessex Chase, *Wincanton*	**£3,850**
Racing Post Chase, *Kempton*	**£24,100.30**
Jameson Irish Grand National, *Fairyhouse*	**£53,592**

1990/91 ran 6; 2 wins

Race	Winning Prize Money
King George VI Rank Chase, *Kempton*	**£45,190**
Agfa Diamond Handicap Chase, *Sandown*	**£20,700**

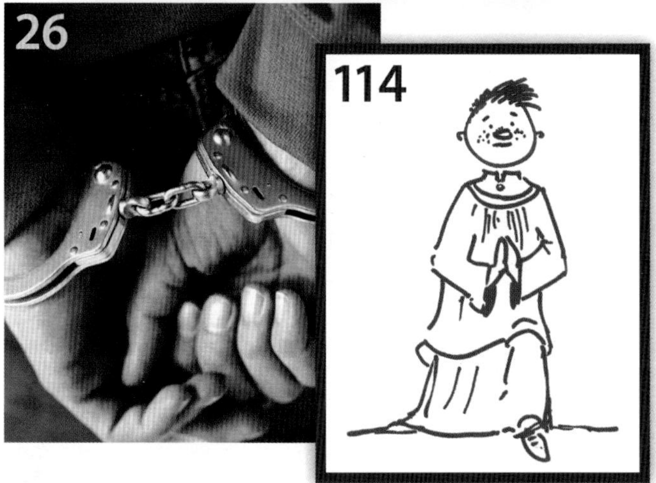

When the Bishop's Conference of England and Wales announced that a National Eucharistic Pilgrimage and Congress would take place in September 2018, they proposed a potential watershed moment.

Big events encourage a feeling of identity and belonging. The Congress, whilst encouraging a deeper understanding and love of the Eucharist, also offers people an experience of strength and solidarity in their willingness to "put God first" in their lives.

Adoremus Extra points towards and beyond the Congress, in some small way accompanying us on our personal pilgrimage, fed and sustained by our Eucharistic Lord. As Pope Francis declared, "a people who adore are a people who walk!" We don't stand still.

The Eucharist is not a one-off event. As Pope Francis said, "The Eucharist communicates the Lord's love for us: a love so great that it nourishes us with himself; a freely given love, always available to every person who hungers and needs to regenerate his or her own strength."

In any living body, the head is an integral part of the whole. In the same way, we cannot cherish the Eucharist, the Body of Christ, in isolation from the parish community in which most of us live and through which we receive and celebrate our faith. Again quoting Pope Francis, "The Body of the Lord makes us a single thing, a single family, the People of God reunited around Jesus, the Bread of life."

In preparing *Adoremus Extra*, a huge variety of both seasoned and first-time writers showed that, in life's ups and downs, Jesus is there for them… and so this magazine kept growing in size and scope during its planning stages. Every contributor wanted to help to renew, rekindle and cherish the parish with the Eucharist as its primary and central focus. We spoke of five "building blocks" of parish life: scripture, understanding the meaning, richness and variety within the Church, mission, formation and music. At the same time, other essential elements such as compassion, liturgy, family, dialogue and social responsibility are qualities which take the "ordinary" parish to the extraordinary.

Adoremus Extra is, therefore, one small pebble helping towards building something exquisitely beautiful: the Church, the Body of Christ, the People of God, on our shared pilgrimage. What more could we want?

God bless,

Fr Denis McBride C.Ss.R. Publishing Director

and *Sr Janet Fearns FMDM* Editor

The Eucharist

Fr Raniero Cantalamessa OFM Cap., Papal Preacher to three popes, describes what happens when bread and wine become the Eucharist, our Bread of Life.

Let's recall a few sentences on the Bread of Life spoken by Jesus in the Eucharistic discourse held in the synagogue of Capernaum:

> "I am the Bread of Life... this is the bread which comes down from heaven, so that a person may eat it and not die. I am the living bread which has come down from heaven. Anyone who eats this bread will live for ever; and the bread that I shall give is my flesh, for the life of the world."
>
> *John 6:48-51*

The sacraments are signs: "they produce what they mean". Hence the importance of understanding what bread means to us. In a sense, the craft of the farmer, the miller, the homemaker and the baker help us to understand the Eucharist better than that of the theologian, because they know much more about bread than the intellectual who sees it only at the moment it comes to the table and eats it, maybe even without thinking.

So let's go to school with these unusual teachers to learn something about bread. If we ask a farmer what the word "bread" brings to mind, he or she will tell us: autumn sowing, waiting, weeding, harrowing, trepidation at the time when the fields are white and a storm could destroy the crop, and lastly, the hard work (harder in the past) of harvesting and threshing.

And this is not all. Many will remember the day when the bread was made as a special time for the family: a feast, almost a religious rite. The last touch was the cross that was traced on every loaf, that the heat of the oven expanded and turned into deep and golden furrows. Then there was the scent of fresh bread that hunger, especially during the war, made even more desirable.

And what about the bread when it comes to the table? The father or mother who breaks it, or just puts it on the table, resembles Jesus. They, too, could tell their children: "Take it and eat it: this is my body offered for you." Daily bread is really in some sense their body, the fruit of their labour and the sign of their love.

So bread is a sign of so many things: work, waiting, nourishment, family happiness, unity and solidarity among those who eat it... Bread is one of the few foods of which we never tire: it is eaten every day and every time its taste is pleasing. It goes with all foods. People who are hungry do not envy the rich their caviar or smoked salmon; they envy, above all, fresh bread.

Well, let's see what happens when this bread comes to the altar and is consecrated by the priest. Catholic doctrine expresses it with one word. I warn you that it is a difficult word, but there are cases (rare though they be) where we cannot avoid using a difficult word if we want to get to the heart of the problem.

One cannot speak of the Eucharist without ever using the word "transubstantiation" with which the Church has expressed its faith in the real presence of Jesus in the Eucharist. What does transubstantiation mean? It means that, at the time of consecration, bread ceases to be bread and becomes Christ's body. The substance of bread – that is, its profound reality that is perceived, not with the eyes but with the mind – gives way to the substance, or rather to the divine person, who is the risen and living Christ, even if the external appearances (in theological language, the "accidents") remain those of bread.

To understand transubstantiation, we get help from a word related to it, but which is more familiar to us, the word "transformation". Transformation means moving from one form to another, transubstantiation moving from one substance to another.

Let's take an example. Seeing someone come out of the hairdresser's with a new hairstyle, we might spontaneously exclaim, "What a transformation!" Nobody dreams of exclaiming: "What a transubstantiation!" Rightly so. In fact the person's form and appearance have changed, "the look" as it is called today, but not their inner being and personality. If they were intelligent before, they are now; if they were not intelligent before, they are not even now (sorry!). Appearances have changed, not the substance.

In the Eucharist, exactly the opposite is true: the substance changes, but not the appearance. Bread is transubstantiated, but not transformed: the appearances in fact (form, taste, colour, weight) remain the same as before, while the deeper reality has changed: it has become Christ's body. The promise of Jesus heard at the beginning is fulfilled: "The bread that I shall give is my flesh, for the life of the world."

Here is how Paul VI, at the time when he was Archbishop of Milan, described what happens at the time of consecration in more modern language: "Christ wanted to choose this sacred symbol of human life to make it an even more sacred symbol of himself. He transubstantiated it, but did not remove its expressive power. Instead, he has raised this expressive power to a new and higher meaning, to a mystical, religious, divine

Fr Raniero Cantalamessa OFM Cap. Image / www.cantalamessa.org

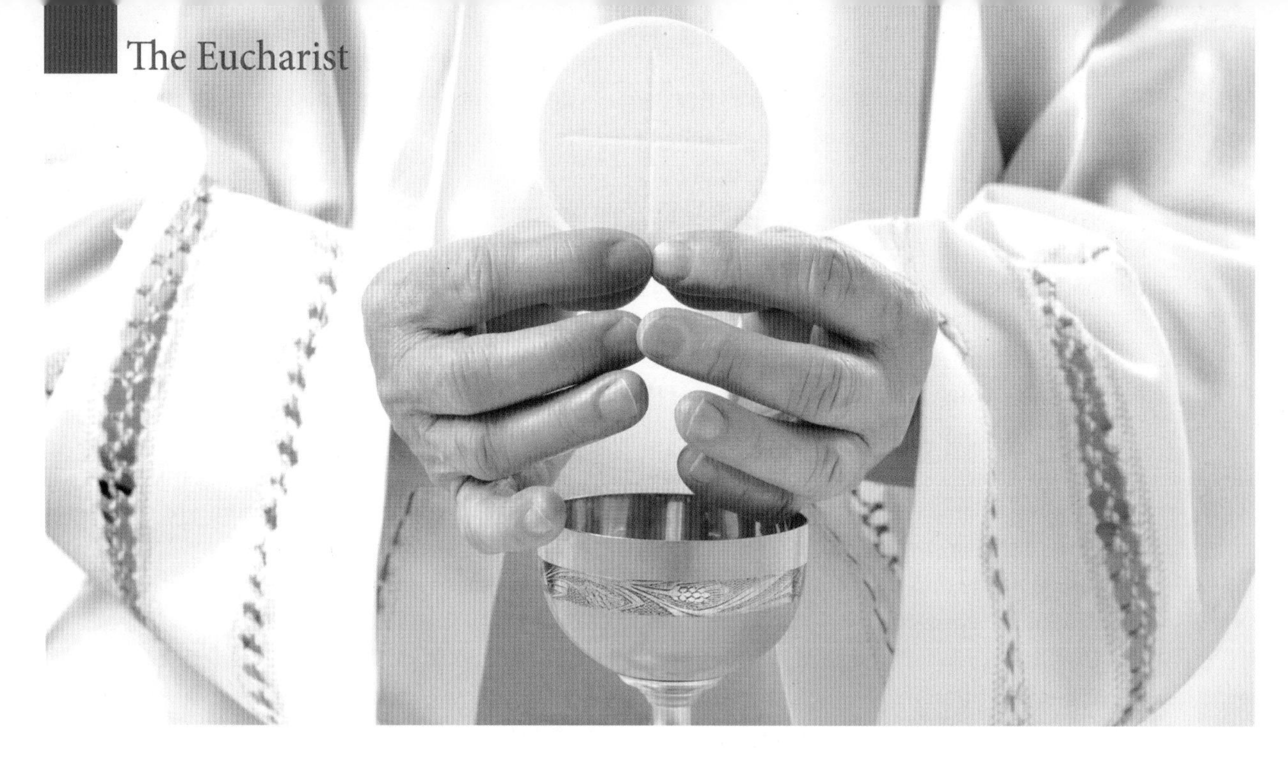

meaning. He has made it a stairway that transcends the natural level. As a sound becomes a voice and as a voice becomes a word, a thought, a truth – so the sign of bread transcends its own humble and pious nature to point to a mystery: it has become a sacrament, has acquired the power to manifest the presence of the body of Christ" (Discourse at the Feast of Corpus Christi, 1959).

That's enough of the difficult things. Let's come down again to the valley, that is, to everyday life. Even if you did not understand much of what I said, do not worry. As it is not necessary to know everything about bread and its chemical components, to eat it with enjoyment and receive its benefit, so it is not necessary to know the theology of the Eucharist to receive its fruits!

In the light of what we have said, the Eucharist illuminates, ennobles, and consecrates the whole reality of the world and of human activity. The new, Eucharistic meaning of bread does not destroy the natural meaning, but rather elevates it. In the Eucharist the same matter – sun, earth, water – is presented to God and reaches its end which is to proclaim the Creator's glory. The Eucharist is the true "Canticle of the Creatures".

"The fruit of earth and of human hands", the Eucharistic bread has something important to say about human labour, and not just about agriculture. In the process leading from the seed to the bread on the table we see the involvement of industry with its machines, trade, transportation and a host of other human activities – all human work.

According to the Marxist vision, work, as it is organised in capitalist societies, alienates people. The worker invests in the product the sweat of their brow, the work of their hands, a part of their life. In selling that product, it's as if the master had sold them. We must rebel...

At a certain level, this analysis can also be true, but the Eucharist gives us the possibility of breaking out of this circle. Let us teach the Christian worker to live well their Eucharist. Let us say that if offered to God for the good of the family and the progress of society, their labour will not end in the product they manufacture, but in that bread which, directly or indirectly, they have contributed to making. It also becomes, in some ways, a Eucharist, secured for eternity, for it is written that "their deeds follow them" (Revelation 14:13).

Deeds are no longer alienating, but sanctifying. The Eucharist, as we see, sums up and unifies everything. It reconciles in itself matter and Spirit, nature and grace, sacred and profane. In the light of the Eucharist, there is no longer any sense in the contrast between the secular world and the Catholic world that so impoverishes our culture, making it "segmented". The Eucharist is the most sacred and, at the same time, the most secular of the sacraments.

On the Sunday on which we hear Jesus' discourse on the bread of life (19th Sunday, Year B), the liturgy gives us an episode taken from the book of the Kings (1 Kings 19:4-8). The prophet Elijah is fleeing from the anger of Queen Jezebel who wants to kill him. He is physically and morally exhausted; he lies under a broom tree asking God to let him die. An angel touches him, shows him a loaf of bread baked on a stone and a jar of water and says, "Get up and eat." He rises, eats, and with the strength given him from that bread, he walks for forty days and forty nights, to Horeb, the mountain of God.

Are we not, at times, that Elijah, tired and disheartened and eager to die? It is also said to us: "Get up and eat." Those who eat this bread that is the body of the Lord will not only walk for "forty days and forty nights", but, as Jesus says, "will live for ever". ■

Fr Raniero Cantalamessa OFM Cap. is a theologian and, since 1980, Preacher to the Papal Household for Pope John Paul II, Pope Benedict XVI and Pope Francis.

We dare to share *with* Jesus

Dom Henry Wansbrough OSB reflects on what happened when Jesus and his disciples shared the Last Supper.

When a Catholic thinks of a Eucharistic Congress a first idea is very often Eucharistic adoration of the exposed Blessed Sacrament. This is indeed a very important aspect of the Eucharist. It is, however, like a still in a video, enabling us to join the dynamic action of the Eucharist at a particular moment and, by that means, to unite ourselves with the Lord and his action at the Last Supper. Gazing in prayer on the consecrated Host has been an important way of revering the Eucharist, particularly at times when frequent reception of communion has not been a common practice. In medieval and Tudor times the elevation of the Host after the consecration was a central moment of prayer. Both Henry VIII and his Chancellor (whom he later beheaded), St Thomas More, would attend several Masses each day, and the ringing of the bell before the consecration was a signal to draw their attention to the elevation.

This is, however, only a still in a video, and can be fully appreciated only if we understand it in the context of the full action. It is an invitation to participate in Jesus' own action at the Last Supper. The earliest account of the Eucharist in the New Testament is not the Gospel account, but is that given by Paul in his first letter to the Corinthians. There Paul is particularly concerned to point out that the selfish behaviour of some members of the Corinthian community is a failure to appreciate the nature of the action. He found them bringing hampers of food to the community supper for themselves and leaving others in a much less favourable position. By their lack of appreciation they are making themselves responsible for the death of Jesus and are eating and drinking, not to their salvation, but to their own loss.

It is in this context that Paul quotes the words of Jesus.

He quotes them as part of the tradition, using the terms of the rabbinic process of passing on central traditional teachings, for already, less than twenty years after the passion and resurrection, they were a set formula, "On the night he was betrayed, he took bread, blessed it and gave it to his disciples, saying, 'This is my body'".

To appreciate the importance of this moment we must see it in its context.

It must have been an electrifying moment, the sort of moment captured in the movie *Of Gods and Men*. The monks, who know that they are at imminent risk of being martyred in Algeria, raise their glasses at their last supper on Easter night and look round at each other as the thoughts of community, death and hope pass through their heads.

At the Last Supper itself the disciples must have known that they too, not only their Master, were at risk. He has already washed their feet as a sign of service, for he was the Servant of the Lord. Now he begins to speak of the shedding of his blood. They were celebrating the Passover, the moment which commemorated the covenant or pact at the Exodus from Egypt which changed the people of Israel into God's special people. That solemn pact between God and the people had been ratified by the sacrificial bloodshed of a lamb. But now Jesus begins to speak of his own blood, of a new covenant in his blood.

In the Gospels the Passover meal itself is not described; the ritual of bitter herbs, certain cups of wine, the lamb and the recital of the story of the Exodus. Concentration is only on particular incidents.

The Gospel of John gives us the story of Jesus washing the disciples' feet. This was a gesture provided by the host, to welcome the guests, honour them and form them into a community. Normally it would be performed by a servant rather than the host himself.

The other Gospels give us two other incidents, both of vital significance. First comes the identification of one of the group

The Last Supper by Leonardo da Vinci. posztos / Shutterstock.com

as a traitor. The name is not given, but we are told only of the depth of his treachery: he is one who not only shares the meal but also puts his hand in the same dish as Jesus. This should be the ultimate expression of sharing in loyal friendship: in fact it is the work of a traitor about to betray his master. Then comes the moment of sharing the bread and wine, the basic supports and means of life: this forms a community of life. Jesus tells them that they are to do this in memory of him.

The whole scene must have been full of a mysterious dread for them. Threatened as they were, the meal was a sort of prequel for what was to happen, the arrest, torture, humiliation and death of Jesus. Jesus was explaining to them the significance of what was to come. In the context of the Passover-covenant he was announcing to them a new covenant, which he was making with them, which was to be sealed by his own blood and which they were to repeat.

So there were three moments involved: the covenant at the Exodus, the new covenant at the Last Supper and the future when they were to transact its repetition.

It is in this context that we must see our Eucharist of today, the Eucharist which is being celebrated in the Eucharistic Congress. We are being brought into the action of Jesus and his disciples at the Last Supper. They were being authorised to repeat this moment in all its dread and vital significance of the final meal before Jesus' death, when he showed the meaning of his death. Familiar as they must have been with the prophecies of the Old Testament, they would have known that this "new covenant" was the fulfilment of God's plan for the world, the eschatological moment, when God was to bring to a conclusion the purpose of creation. It was to be brought to completion in the death of Jesus and in the acceptance of this act of loving obedience, marked by his resurrection.

So today we are also invited to enter into the same community, the same covenant, the same death and resurrection. The action of the Eucharist is a memorial, not in the sense of a mere commemoration or reminder of what happened, but as an effective re-presentation. It brings into the present the offering of Jesus in the past, enabling us to enter into the same moment. So we can and must reflect on whether we are traitors, masquerading as faithful friends. We must unite ourselves with Jesus' offering, just as his disciples did (and some of the Corinthians to whom Paul wrote were failing to do). By sharing the meal of Jesus' body and blood we are united to his offering and accept his invitation to become part of his fellowship in the great act of obedience.

It is not without its dangers that we dare to share with Jesus, for each time we receive Communion we are putting ourselves in the frame of that still of a video which carries on to the crucifixion and to the resurrection. ■

Dom Henry Wansbrough OSB is a renowned biblical scholar and a monk of Ampleforth Abbey.

I am the *Bread of Life* and food for the *journey*

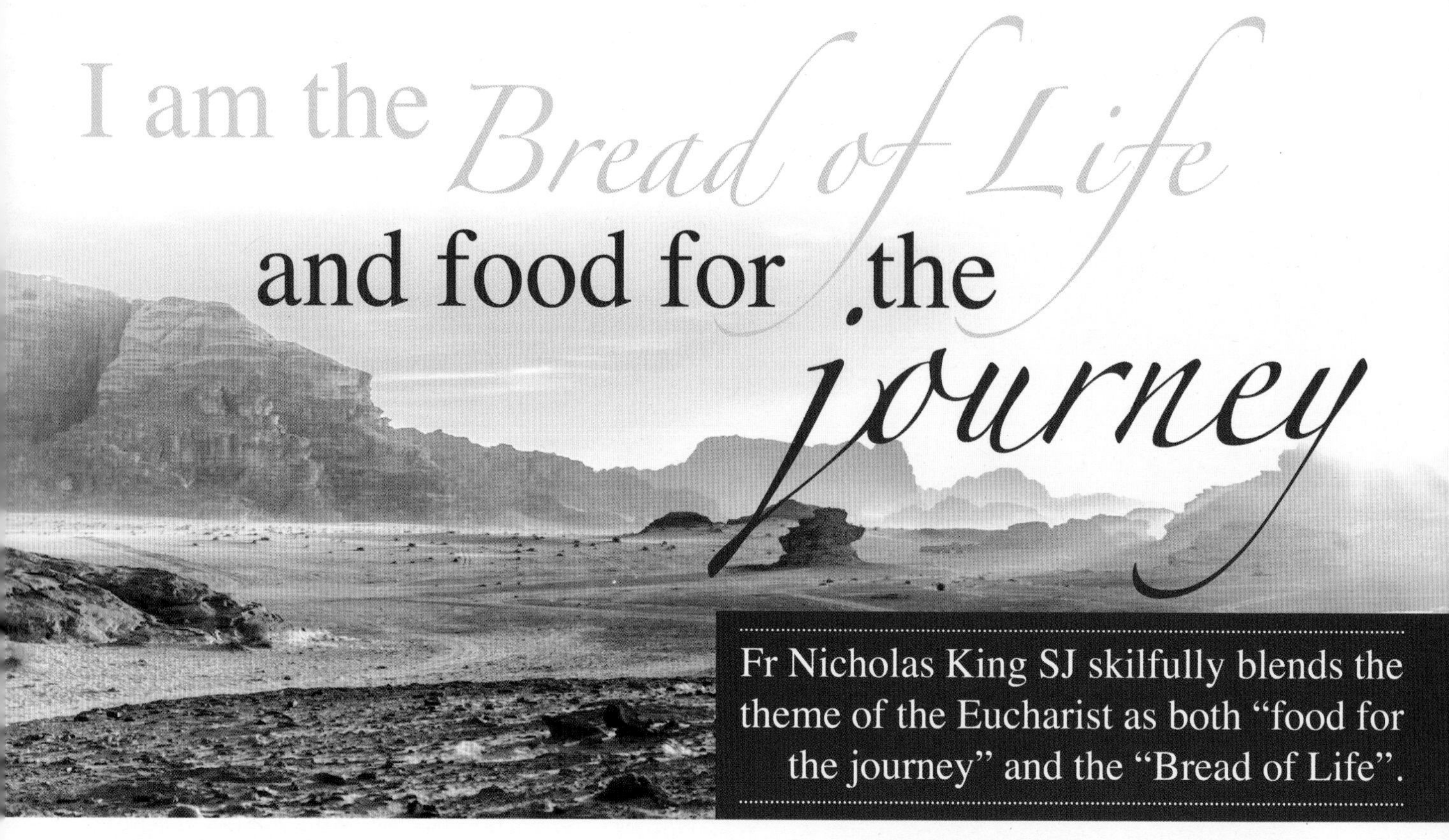

Fr Nicholas King SJ skilfully blends the theme of the Eucharist as both "food for the journey" and the "Bread of Life".

At a time when Christians, and indeed Catholics, are not showing much enthusiasm for the Eucharist, it is appropriate to be asked to reflect on the overall theme "I am the Bread of Life", under the sub-heading of "food for the journey". For these two phrases capture a good deal of the richness of our theology of the Mass.

Food for the journey

This last idea, "food for the journey", takes its starting-point, I think, from 1 Kings 19 (and I'd ask you now to blow the dust off your Bible and read the first seventeen verses of that chapter). The story so far is that Elijah has won a spectacular victory over the prophets of Baal on Mount Carmel. If you have forgotten the details of that lively event, then go back to the previous chapter and see the competition that Elijah had set up, about whether Baal or the real God could produce fire from heaven.

There is more than a touch of comedy in this story, as the prophets of Baal spend the entire day calling on their god. Elijah helpfully suggests that they should shout a bit louder, in case Baal is asleep, or attending to his bodily functions. Naturally they fail and, equally naturally, Elijah succeeds, having first insisted on dousing the wood with water no less than three times, and the people decide that, after all, "The Lord is God! The Lord is God!" This is followed by a mass slaughter of the prophets of Baal. The blood-letting creates something of a complication, because the king's wife. Jezebel, was rather an admirer of Baal and his prophets and so she announces that she is going to have the prophet killed – and she is a very determined women.

Not unreasonably, Elijah flees into the desert, sits down under a broom tree and falls asleep, after asking God to kill him. However he is not permitted to sleep for long, for "the angel of the Lord" wakes him up and orders him to "get up and eat"; at his head is a cake and a jug of water. Elijah does not quite put two and two together, but goes back to sleep. So the angel wakes him again: "up you get and eat – otherwise the journey will be too long for you". Now, finally, he has got the message: "he got up, ate and drank. Then, strengthened by the food, he walked forty days and forty nights to Horeb, the mountain of God".

That is "food for the journey". Does it speak to your life today? One element in this story that may speak to you now is that Elijah is one example of God's personal care for each individual, no matter how ghastly things may feel, or how frail we are. That is one important element of the doctrine of the Eucharist.

Prophet Elijah receiving Bread and Water from an Angel by Alessandro Bonvicino – Moretto (1498-1554). Renata Sedmakova / Shutterstock.com

I am the Bread of Life

Another such element (though still with that strong sense of personal care on the part of God) appears in the well-known discourse on the Bread of Life that you find in chapter 6 of John's Gospel. The evangelist repeats the story of the feeding of the five thousand and then invites us to reflect on what has just happened, taking us (as always in this Gospel) deeper into the mystery of who Jesus is.

After the feeding, Jesus goes up alone into the mountain (to avoid being made king) and comes to them, walking on the water. Not unreasonably, they panic as he draws near to the boat, but his response (once again notice the strong sense of personal care here) is "I AM – don't be afraid". That "I AM" could be translated as "it's me", but it is also the ancient name of God, rumbling down the ages: we go deeper into the mystery of who Jesus is. This leads to a prolonged meditation on what has really happened in the multiplication of the loaves, taking us deeper into the idea of "food for the journey".

As always, Jesus starts where we are (as God had done with Elijah in the desert). The crowds want signs (you might think that the feeding was already quite enough to be going on with!) and Jesus gently educates them into understanding about Moses feeding the Israelites in the wilderness. We understand, and so we feel ourselves superior to the crowds, who do not understand when Jesus says, "the bread of God is the one who comes down from heaven and is giving life to the world". Not unreasonably they ask for more of the same, and are not the wiser when he responds with another "I AM": "I AM the Bread of Life: the one who comes to me will not go hungry, and the one who believes in me will never be thirsty again".

Like Elijah in the desert, Jesus' hearers are in thoroughly complaining mood and simply don't understand how Jesus can be both "Jesus the son of Joseph, whose parents we know" and "the Bread of Life that came down from heaven". Twice more he utters this great "I AM", and adds, "if anyone eats of this bread they will live for ever". Then it gets really uncomfortable: "the bread that I am going to give is my flesh for the life of the world". We shiver and they resist: but he is talking of "food for the journey", of course, and all they can say is "How can this one give us his flesh to eat?". And Jesus does not give an inch: "Amen, amen I'm telling you" [this very strong assertion is found only in John's Gospel] "unless you eat the flesh of the Son of Man and drink his blood, you do not have life in you".

Now uncomfortable as this is, it gets worse. At this point Jesus starts to use a different word for "eating", one that means to eat as animals do, "munch" or "crunch", perhaps: "the one who crunches my flesh and drinks my blood has eternal life; and I am going to raise that person up on the last day". It is, you see, food for the journey; and Jesus does not retreat by an inch from the profound and difficult reality that is our Eucharist: "my flesh is genuine food and my blood is genuine drink. The one who munches my flesh and drinks my blood remains in me, and I in that person."

It is important not to run away from the costly reality of the Bread of Life that is on offer; we have to take it seriously and then we may start to glimpse why it matters that we receive this extraordinary food whenever we can.

Just to make sure that we have got the message, Jesus repeats himself: "the one who munches my flesh and drinks my blood remains in me and I remain in that person. As the Living Father sent me, and I live because of the Father, so the one who munches me, that person too will live because of me."

So it is indeed food for the journey; but it is not comfortable, this Bread of Life. So (if we have been paying attention to the text) we are not really surprised to hear Jesus' audience, including some of his disciples, muttering, "This is hard talk. Who can listen to him?" If you find yourself nodding in agreement with this restiveness, then listen as Jesus turns to you and asks, "You don't want to go away too, do you?" That is quite a challenge and I hope that you applaud as Simon Peter simply responds, on your behalf, "Lord – who are we going to go away to? You have the words of eternal life".

That is the real Bread of Life, and it is food for our journey. So, with Simon, we can say, today, "We have come to believe and know that you are the Holy One of God". It is not easy and it is not comfortable, but this certainty of God's personal care for us will keep us going ever deeper into the mystery. May it be food for your journey. ■

Fr Nicholas King SJ is a biblical scholar and Fellow in New Testament Studies, Campion Hall, Oxford.

The road to Emmaus

– a journey to Eucharist and beyond

The disciples at Emmaus met Jesus and their lives changed. Fr Denis McBride C.Ss.R. reminds us that knowing Jesus compels us to spread his Good News.

Santiago de compostela memorial

A pilgrimage of the heart

When pilgrims walk the Camino de Santiago, they deliberately head for a religious destination, whatever personal reason they might have for making the journey. It is an official road of pilgrimage, no matter what motivates the travellers.

Most roads we take in ordinary time, however, are functional: to get us to where we need to be or to head back home. Other roads are taken, with family or friends, to head for a pleasant destination or a longed-for holiday. There is another road we might take in life, to escape the sorrow and disappointment we want to leave behind us: we take that road in the fond hope that we can leave both the place and the sadness securely over our shoulder. We soon learn that however easy it is to leave a place behind us, it is more difficult to leave the hurt.

Hurt, it has to be said, travels easily.

You see this writ large in the journey to Emmaus. Luke is the only evangelist to tell this story: how two disciples leave Jerusalem, the great place of pilgrimage, to get away from this sacred place; how a stranger joins them on their escape route; how he listens to them tell of the death of Jesus of Nazareth as the death of their own hopes; how he responds to their story by opening the scriptures; how he accepts their offer of hospitality to stay with them; how he reveals himself as the risen Lord in the breaking of the bread. The story of the mysterious wayfarer, whose revealing word and presence give hope to his disappointed followers, has appealed to many Christians as a moving summary of the Gospel. It takes account of how Jesus finds people and how he leaves them; how he addresses their pain and confusion with his own story of God's purpose in life.

As the geographical journey moves from Jerusalem back to Jerusalem, there is an inward journey, an actual pilgrimage, which moves from desolation to hope, from bewilderment to understanding, from the real absence of Jesus to the presence of the risen Lord. In the Emmaus account, the real destination of the disciples is in meeting the Lord in the breaking of the bread. Unknown to them, they are on a pilgrimage to a person, not a place: their flight from Jerusalem turns out to be a pilgrimage of the heart to meet the Lord.

Les pèlerins d'Emmaüs © ADAGP, Paris and DACS, London 2018

On the road

We meet two disciples heading away from Jerusalem, the place that is identified as the graveyard of their hopes. Although we cannot identify the village of Emmaus, it is the road that is important, one of the famous lost roads of history. The narrative focuses on the condition of two disciples who are overcome by their own loss, frankly bewildered by the violent turn of events that have recently happened. We listen to Cleopas as he puts together both the disciples' experience of Jesus and their expectation of him.

Cleopas shares the sad news that he and his companion's expectation about Jesus have been brutally ended: "But we had hoped that he was the one to redeem Israel" (Luke 24:21). Their hopes are in the past perfect tense: it is not only the body of Jesus that has been buried, but their hope in Jesus has been entombed as well. Who they were was tied to who they believed he was: they were disciples because he was their master and teacher. Their governing self-identity as disciples of Jesus has been shattered; they are identified by what they used to be. Their situation is reflected in the lines of Lord Byron:

And all that memory loves the most
Was once our only hope to be.
And all that hope adored and lost
Has melted into memory.

Everything they cherished is now memory. The disciples look on the death of Jesus, as many probably did, as the end of a promising calling, not the fulfilment of a promised one. Their hope that Jesus would prove to be the awaited Messiah is now cancelled by their experience of what has happened to him. Their hope has been reluctantly laid down in the tomb, beside the dead body of Jesus.

There is a sense in which we can see the two disciples on the road to Emmaus as our contemporaries, fellow travellers journeying through a grey landscape of ambiguity and disappointment, where, in the uncertain light of what is sometimes seen and sensed, so many cherished hopes, now withered, have been relegated to lost causes. Yet the story of their loss is what we call "Gospel", what we name as scripture. When their story is proclaimed in the assembly, the priest or deacon adds the words, "The Gospel of the Lord." What the disciples saw as hopeless, we interpret as good news, not least because we interpret their story in the larger frame of scripture. And that is what the risen Jesus does in his response to his two disciples.

The risen Jesus, still a stranger, re-interprets his disciples' experience of recent events in the light of the past story contained in scripture. He offers a different interpretation of the same events the disciples have described, one that tries to make sense of pain and rejection and brokenness. The dynamic, used in therapeutic counselling, is to stop staring at the present moment, the place of pain, and travel backwards into the old story in the hope that, seeing the new event in this larger context, one can understand not only what has happened but also what is going on now. In using the scriptures to reinterpret recent events, Jesus is illuminating the disciples' recent experience.

The risen Jesus' reinterpretation leads to burning hearts and an invitation to the stranger to stay with the two disciples: "they pressed him to stay with them. 'It is almost evening and the day is now nearly over.' So he went in to stay with them." (24:29)

The breaking of the bread

The drama now moves from the road to the table: the house-guest now takes bread, blesses it, breaks it and hands it to the two disciples. In that action the disciples' eyes are opened to the revelation that their guest is the risen Lord. The stranger reveals himself by giving himself away in the breaking of the bread, something that continues to happen today in the Eucharist. This meal stands at the point where the whole movement of Jesus' life, death and resurrection is first revealed in its full significance and as a pointer to how the Christian community will meet the risen Lord in the Christological interpretation of scripture and in the breaking of the bread.

Thus a journey that began in confusion ends with revelation; it moves from hiddenness to openness. The scriptures were opened because of what Jesus said; the disciples' eyes are opened because of what Jesus shares with them. In the light of their new experience, the disciples are enabled to see their past experience as a source of significance rather than a memory of disappointment, as a word of life rather than a word about death. The word that Jesus spoke registered in hearts burning with joy.

In the light of their new experience, their recognition of the risen Jesus, the disciples again reassess their past: a recent past of injured hope is now healed in this fresh revelation. They are now able to understand why their hearts were burning within them. Their new experience enables them to make sense, not only of the last few days, but also of why they felt the way they did on the road when the stranger was unfolding scripture to them. New insight can change our reading of the past. The recent and the immediate past are reappraised in the light of the new awareness and insight; they are liberated from their own tragic interpretation of the last days of Jesus and their own self-image as leftover disciples of a dead prophet.

The Supper at Emmaus by Caravaggio. The painting depicts the moment when the resurrected but incognito Jesus reveals himself to two of his disciples (presumed to be Luke and Cleopas) in the town of Emmaus. Image/ Wikimedia commons.

Experience and mission

The disciples' new experience gives them a new sense of purpose and a new authority, so they go back to the place they longed to leave over their shoulder. Jerusalem is now their chosen destination, the same city they discarded earlier in the day. Even though the day is far spent, they go back. Their return is not only to a place but, more importantly, to a community, one which they presumably believe to be as wretched and desolate as they were at the beginning of their journey.

Their engagement with the Lord sends them out of doors, on mission. They do not stay in Emmaus to build a monument to the place where they met the Lord: instead they feel compelled to share what happened with others as good news.

The structure of the Emmaus story gives us, the Christian community, a perfect reminder of coming to know Jesus as Lord in the Eucharist:

the coming together
the personal acknowledgment of defeat
the hearing of the old story anew
the gathering around the table
the breaking of the bread
the recognition of Jesus as Lord
the renewal of personal discipleship
the departure to share the new experience as good new

When we gather to celebrate the Eucharist we too listen to the word of God and break bread together. Jesus comes among us, not as the stranger; rather, he comes to us in word and sacrament to give us new hope to face the future with faith in him. Our own stories may not sound very different from the two forlorn disciples on the road to Emmaus: we may also be covered in disappointment; may have a past that bewilders and hurts us. But we are invited to tell our stories to the Lord, to listen to him as he speaks his word, to recognise him in the breaking of the bread and become one with him in communion. Only with him can we look with understanding at the past, and with hope look to the future. Only in his name can we share the good news with others. ■

Fr Denis McBride C.Ss.R. is a biblical scholar, author and the Publishing Director of Redemptorist Publications.

Many books, CDs and DVDs by Fr Denis McBride are available from Redemptorist Publications, www.rpbooks.co.uk. These include The Road to Emmaus and Beyond: a journey from Easter to Pentecost.

Pilgrimage

The Eucharist *and the sea*

Greg Watts describes the important role of the Apostleship of the Sea.

Father Colum Kelly remembers celebrating Mass on a ship in Immingham in Lincolnshire when the temperature was -6˚C. "Yet the men, all from the Philippines, still took off their hats and balaclavas. Two of the crew had to keep watch on deck, but they opened the portholes in order to receive Holy Communion."

During his time as an Apostleship of the Sea (AoS) port chaplain, Father Colum has celebrated Mass on many ships. And it's something that always gives him great joy, he said. "Because seafarers are often at sea for such long periods they don't get many opportunities to receive the sacraments or talk to a priest."

Most of us probably never give much thought to seafarers. They can seem remote from our daily life. Yet they play a vital role.

Without the world's 1.5 million seafarers we wouldn't have many of the things we take for granted. Cars, computers, clothes, fruit, vegetables… these are just some of the items that are transported to Britain by ships.

In 2017, when the captain of a container ship sailing from New York to Tilbury in Essex was found dead, the crew were distraught. Father Colum went on board the ship when it docked in Tilbury to say Mass for the crew and to bless them.

"I spent time listening to the crew and hearing of the stress that they had been feeling during the voyage. It emerged the death took place one week into the voyage. It was the first time the crew had sailed with that captain so they knew very little about him," he said.

"The captain's body was laid in his sealed cabin for the remainder of the voyage. Particularly distressed was the young seafarer who had discovered the body. It was the first time he had seen a corpse."

The crew requested Mass to be said and for specific areas of the ship to be blessed, including some cabins and the spot where the body was found. Fr Colum said the atmosphere seemed to change after Mass and there was a sense of relief among the crew. "I did what I was able to do for the crew; talking to them and trying to bring some consolation. It was a terrible time for the seafarers, but at the end of the day there was a sense of joy in the midst of the grief, stress and bewilderment," he said.

"This tragic incident is a powerful example of AoS' ministry of going to where the hurt is… the Church in outreach to those on the margins, where the Holy Father encourages us to go."

Many seafarers have a deep faith and are keen to nourish it, explained Rev Roger Stone, AoS port chaplain in Southampton and a permanent deacon in the diocese of Arundel and Brighton. "I offer them Christ in the form of Holy Communion, leading services on board whenever I'm asked. For seafarers who are strong in their faith, being unable to receive Holy Communion is a real problem."

Catholic parishes can play a vital role in supporting seafarers, he added. "Seafarers derive comfort from knowing that someone cares. They leave their homes and families and risk their lives so we can enjoy the goods we use every day.

"Our Christian vocation is to be Christ to seafarers when they visit our ports. Without the support and generosity of people in parishes we wouldn't be able to function and seafarers would be completely abandoned." ■

Images © Apostleship of the Sea
Top: Fr Coluum Kelly gives communion
Middle: Rev Roger Stone at Port
Bottom: Rev Roger Stone on board

Greg Watts writes for the Apostleship of the Sea (www.apostleshipofthesea.org.uk) and is also Editor of the Southwark archdiocesan magazine, The Pilgrim.

APOSTOLATUS MARIS

Apostleship of the sea
Supporting Seafareres Worldwide

Feeling warm beside Our Lord

Jesus met Dr Adrian Treloar when Adrian was a small child accompanying his parents to Mass. The encounter was an unforgettable milestone on his journey.

As a small child, one Friday evening, Mum and Dad took me to Mass. It was dark, quiet and late autumn. I was, I think, about six years old. I remember after Mass going up to the statue of St Joseph. He had some magnificent tools in a basket and looked kindly and gentle. He, I thought, would have loved my Dad's shed.

That night, with my parents and before the Blessed Sacrament, I remember feeling a deep sense of warmth, safety and calm gentleness. To the right of St Joseph was the Blessed Sacrament. Friday evening Mass had ended and in the peace and still of the evening all was well.

Throughout my life the Blessed Sacrament has been there, beside the little red light, gently burning as a sign of God's presence to us. It was the same Blessed Sacrament when I was in an African mission hospital; the same Blessed Sacrament at midnight Mass in the Nigerian bush; the same Blessed Sacrament on my journeys across Europe and even in those tiny chapels made of reeds that I visited on the high lakes of Peru. The Blessed Sacrament truly is Our Blessed Lord physically present and so close to us all.

Some who have doubted that truth have been surprised. In the eighth century, a priest in Lanciano (a little town in Italy), doubting the real presence while saying Mass, was shocked to see the sacred Host bleeding.[1]

There are many more Eucharistic miracles which show us the way towards Jesus, true God, true Man and truly present in the Blessed Sacrament.

But for me, the Blessed Sacrament has become the central cornerstone of my faith and life. The Blessed Sacrament is, after all, Jesus physically present among us.

Alongside him, we find Our Lady. Mary bore Jesus and cared for him. She shows us the way to him. Indeed she holds our hands on the journey and helps us on the way. She draws us towards the warmth and love the Eucharist.

But it is in the Blessed Sacrament that we truly find Jesus. And through the Blessed Sacrament, he strengthens us and feeds us. We eat his body and drink his blood and are given eternal life.

Benediction and Blessed Sacrament processions

As a parent, I have found Benediction and Blessed Sacrament processions to be very helpful. We go to Mass every Sunday (and more often if we can) but it is really good to be able to adore Jesus in the Blessed Sacrament at other times and in other ways.

First among these is Benediction. We kneel before and specifically gaze at our loving Lord. The devotions of Benediction are quiet, holy and draw us towards the recognition of our infinitely great Creator, who is so humble that he sits upon the altar in front of us.

I think that when children begin

[1] *You can read more about Lanciano at http://www.therealpresence.org/eucharst/mir/lanciano.html*

The Last Supper (1325–1330) by Ugolino da Siena Metropolitan Museum of Art Image /Wikicommons.

to be able to see Jesus' true and real presence in the Blessed Sacrament they are really getting to know him. Blessed Sacrament processions, exposition and pilgrimages to Marian shrines build and strengthen that faith further – as does faithfulness to Mass when away travelling on holiday or on business. It is very important to show yourself and your children that the Holy Mass is so important that you will always go to Mass, even on holiday, even on Holy Days of Obligation.

And every time we are in church, we should show how much we respect him by genuflecting (bending our knee in worship) as we cross in front of the tabernacle. It is very helpful to encourage children to make these little devotions. And very beautiful to see two- and three-year-old children doing so.

My Eucharistic journey

My Eucharistic journey started, of course with baptism, but took a great leap with my Mum and Dad at my side one Friday evening at Mass. And that journey has carried on with my family and children, hugely aided by my wife and children.

Jesus wants us to be with him in church every Sunday and also, if possible, during the week. If we do not journey to be with Our Lord, we lose our sense of his warmth, his love and his friendship. He wants us there. He wants us to make him central to our lives. Visiting him in the Eucharist is an absolutely central part of that journey.

I still go regularly to Friday evening Mass in my church. Mass is as still, calm and warm as it was all those years ago. Just recently I went to a Friday evening Mass in South London. There were about a hundred people there, gently and quietly surrounded by the love of Jesus in his Blessed Sacrament. Such a gift! ■

Dr Adrian Treloar is a consultant psychiatrist. His books Dementia: hope on a difficult journey *and* Depression: caring for yourself and others *are available from Redemptorist Publications, www.rpbooks.co.uk*

The inner journey

As Dr Lucy Russell has discovered, chronic illness does not stop someone from taking an active part in the Congress nor from making a pilgrimage within the limitations imposed by illness.

Last summer, my friend Isaac walked the Camino: eight hundred kilometres to Santiago de Compostela in five weeks. Listening to him talk about his experience, I wished it were something I might one day be able to do. This kind of pilgrimage is one which is perhaps largely for the young or the old. I couldn't imagine many families taking part in such a pilgrimage, or indeed taking my children along to walk between twenty and thirty kilometres a day for five or six weeks. There is a chance I might walk the Camino one day, but it is a slim chance. I have been very lucky with my MS, but I get tired and the tiredness triggers shooting pains and such like. My friend's Dad has similar issues, which meant that he didn't feel he could accompany his son on his Camino walk. Isaac's Dad, Alan, has ME and fibromyalgia. There would have been days he could have walked with his son, but Alan couldn't foresee whether his health would allow him to walk with Isaac every day for over a month.

We aren't all able to make physical pilgrimages, for all sorts of reasons – which is, of course, why we have the stations of the cross in our churches. For those who can't get to Jerusalem, we are able to meditate on these holy places in our homes.

The stations of the cross, as we know them in our churches and our homes today, developed from an early tradition in the Holy Land, following the way of the cross, stopping and contemplating the events of Christ's passion at sites where tradition held they took place.

The desire to reproduce this devotion to the holy places in or near our homes was developed for pilgrims who could not actually travel to the Holy Land. We are all able to reflect on the stations in a devotional, spiritual way in our own hearts: we don't have to be physically present in a particular place.

This is something which Pope Francis himself has talked about: "The Christian journey is simply about changing hearts. One's own heart first [of] all, and then helping to transform the hearts of others." This is what real pilgrimage is all about: transforming our own hearts so that we can become closer to God, and in turn help to bring others closer to God.

It is perfectly possible to have a spiritual journey anywhere, without even needing to leave home. In his book *Eternal Echoes*, John O'Donohue wrote that, "Ideally, a human life should be a constant pilgrimage of discovery. The most exciting discoveries happen at the frontiers. When you come to know something new, you come closer to yourself and the world. Discovery enlarges and refines your sensibility. When you discover something, you transfigure some of the forsakenness of the world."

These frontiers don't have to be physical land borders. Take for example the character of Mary Lennox in Frances Hodgson Burnett's *The Secret Garden*. Mary's pilgrimage and the transformation of her heart happen in a single place. It is because Mary has nowhere else to go and nothing else to do, that she begins to wonder about a locked-up garden in the grounds of Misselthwaite Manor. It is her wondering that starts to change her. Mary starts talking to the gardener. She makes friends with a robin who helps her to find the key to unlock the garden door. Now Mary starts to interact with nature and notice the changing seasons. Her relationships start to change and grow as she begins to tend the garden and grow plants and flowers. The secret garden itself is a catalyst for healing the characters who see it. They don't have to travel to take part in a pilgrimage: they embark on a spiritual journey of transformation in their own home.

At the beginning of his journey, my friend Isaac was disappointed his Dad couldn't join him on his pilgrimage. This is perhaps something that he reflected upon while he was completing his gruelling walk across Spain. Alan, like all of us, is on his own pilgrimage, one that he doesn't need to leave his home in order to take part in.

My latest book, *Who Do You Say You Are?* had just been published when Isaac left for Spain. I had invited his family to lunch the day before his flight. Noticing a couple of copies of my book in the kitchen, Alan picked one up. I saw his interest and told him he could have it. He asked me to sign it and also to write something meaningful and personal for him.

My book reflects on issues of identity and how chronic illness impacts on that. Does a diagnosis of chronic illness change who you are? The book is a reflective and spiritual one. It is a book which would be of interest to those who have not got a diagnosis of chronic illness, but it is also a companion to those who have, or who have friends or family members who have.

When Isaac told me he was going to complete the Camino de Santiago de Compostela, I did some reading about it. Writer Malcolm McKay's *Daily Mail* article about his experience of the Camino struck me: "...walking the Camino was one of the greatest experiences of my life. And that's because of the people I met. In my opinion, if you seek the spiritual, it's right there in the man or woman walking beside you. And did I find the answer to the question I asked?... No I didn't. But I can tell you this: the person asking it was different by the time he arrived in Santiago and perhaps that was the answer he was seeking." There you have it.

I signed my book for Isaac's Dad: "For Alan. A guide book to your own 'Camino walk'..." Living with a chronic condition is its own pilgrimage. Without physically travelling anywhere, we are all able to discover new frontiers within ourselves, and allow our hearts to be transformed. ■

Dr Lucy Russell is an author, teacher, mother and regular contributor to The Pilgrim, *the Southwark archdiocesan magazine. Her book* Who Do You Say You Are? *about coming to terms with chronic illness, is available from Redemptorist Publications: www.rpbooks.co.uk*

The pilgrims' tale

Church historian Fr Norman Tanner SJ tells the tale of pilgrimages through the ages.

Jesus provides the model on which our pilgrimages of life are based. For his example, we give unbounded thanks. There are differences, of course: Jesus came down from above, as we say in the Creed on Sundays: "Son of God… he came down from heaven… and became man" – whereas we start here on earth. But thereafter, our pilgrimages have much in common. From his birth in Bethlehem and exile in Egypt, through his early life in Nazareth, then two or three years of public ministry, culminating in his passion and death in Jerusalem, followed by his glorious resurrection and ascension into heaven, Jesus gives us both encouragement and example in our pilgrimages of this life into – we hope – the unending joys of heaven.

Early Church

During the first three centuries of the Church, when persecution was frequent, martyrdom provided the crown and model for pilgrimage – following the example of Jesus.

Some martyrs hardly travelled at all. Many of the early Christians, however, undertook extensive travels – linked to their work of evangelisation – either before martyrdom – Peter and Paul are obvious examples – or without ending in martyrdom. Thereby the relationship between martyrdom and pilgrimage began to be stretched.

This connection was further stretched by the Emperor Constantine's conversion to Christianity in the early fourth century. His conversion, alongside the establishment of Christianity as the official religion of the Roman Empire, brought an end to the chronic persecution of Christians. Pilgrimages began to be undertaken without the likelihood of death.

Two women were archetypes during this period of transition. Helena, mother of the Emperor Constantine, made a pilgrimage in 326 to the Holy Land, where she founded churches on the Mount of Olives and at Bethlehem and, according to later tradition, discovered the cross on which Jesus had been crucified.

Then, towards the end of the fourth century, a devout woman, who probably came from Spain or France and is usually identified as Egeria, went on pilgrimage for three years to Egypt, the Holy Land, Edessa and Constantinople. Her copious observations during these journeys were written up into a fascinating book, *The Pilgrimage of Egeria*.

Irish monks were notable pilgrims during the sixth and seventh centuries. Columbanus, according to his biographer Adomnan, sailed from Ireland "as a pilgrim of Christ" and founded a monastery on the Scottish island of Iona, later founding other monasteries and churches in both Scotland and Ireland. Pilgrimages thus benefited other people as well as the pilgrim. Columba travelled much further, cultivating the idea of life as a perpetual pilgrimage. First he was a monk at Bangor in Wales. Then he founded monasteries in France and finally settled with his companions at Bobbio in northern Italy.

Middle Ages

The rise of Islam quickly brought the Holy Land under Muslim control. As a result, pilgrimages to Jerusalem – the archetypal focus for Christian pilgrimage – became much more difficult. Crusades to recapture the lost territories, which began with the first crusade in 1098/9, continued throughout the Middle Ages and, later, were regarded as pilgrimages. Peaceful pilgrimages, however, were usually possible even though difficult.

Margery Kempe, who journeyed from her home

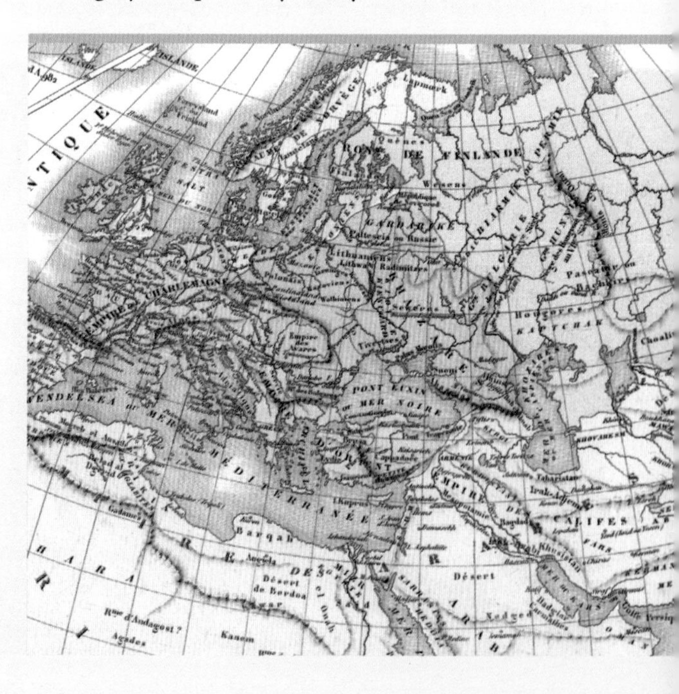

in (King's) Lynn in England in the early fifteenth century, provided a graphic account of her feelings, as well as the good treatment she received from Muslim inhabitants, in these words:

> "And so we proceeded into the Holy Land until we could see Jerusalem. When I saw it – riding, as I was, on the back of an ass – I thanked God with all my heart; and I prayed that just as he had brought me to this earthly city of Jerusalem so, of his mercy, he would give me the grace to see the city of Jerusalem on high, the city of heaven... Great was the grace our Lord showed me during my three weeks in Jerusalem... Afterwards I rode to Bethlehem on an ass... The Saracens also fêted me. They escorted me and guided me to all the places I wanted to visit throughout the country and I found everyone good and kind to me except my own countrymen.
>
> *Book of Margery Kempe, chapters 28-30*

After Jerusalem, Rome enjoyed pre-eminence. Peter and Paul had been martyred there; Peter's body was believed to have been entombed in the crypt of St Peter's Church and the city had a wide range of religious and other attractions for pilgrims. Access, too, was relatively easy, unlike Jerusalem. Popes, who were bishops of Rome, promoted their own city. Boniface IX proclaimed a "Holy Year" in 1300 when special indulgences were granted to pilgrims to the holy city and popes have repeated this initiative at regular intervals ever since.

There were many other places for pilgrimages. Besides her visit to the Holy Land, Margery Kempe managed to combine life with her husband and bringing up a family of fourteen children with journeys to Santiago de Compostela in Spain, where the body of the apostle James, brother of John, was believed to be buried. She also visited shrines in Norway and Danzig (Gdansk) and the two most famous shrines in England: Walsingham, associated with Mary and the Holy Family, and Canterbury Cathedral, the place of Thomas Becket's martyrdom. Pilgrimages to Becket's shrine were immortalised by Geoffrey Chaucer's *Canterbury Tales*.

There were, however, critics of pilgrimages: John Wycliffe in England and Jan Hus in Bohemia; also Thomas à Kempis, who lamented that "they that go much on pilgrimage seldom grow in sanctity" (*Imitation of Christ*, Book 4, chapter 1).

Reformation onwards

Criticism reached a crescendo with the Reformations. Martin Luther began his protest in 1517 by condemning the granting of indulgences for those who contributed towards the rebuilding of St Peter's Church in Rome, the central focus of pilgrimages to this city.

In England, pilgrimages to the Shrine of Our Lady in Walsingham ended with the desecration of the shrine at the instigation of King Henry VIII. The Catholic response at the Council of Trent (1545-1562) was to approve pilgrimages but in a somewhat restrained manner.

As a result, pilgrimages have remained part of Catholic devotion, to Jerusalem and Rome as well as to many shrines dating from the Middle Ages and earlier, but also to more recent shrines around the world: Lourdes, Fatima and Medjugorge in Europe, Our Lady of Guadalupe in Mexico, the shrine of St Thomas the Apostle at Chennai (Madras) in India, the Martyrs shrine at Guelph in Canada, to name only a handful. There has also been some revival among churches of the Reformation: the Anglican shrine of Our Lady of Walsingham, for example, as well as Protestants frequenting Catholic shrines.

Pilgrimages, moreover, have always been considered opportunities for interceding for one's family and friends, and others in need, as well as benefiting the pilgrim.

There is, too, the inter-religious dimension: Christian respect for Muslim pilgrimages to Mecca, for Hindu pilgrimages to Benares (Varanasi) on the river Ganges, and for Buddha's way of life as a pilgrim. In recent times, indeed, this aspect of pilgrimage as a way of life has flourished among Christians, alongside the earlier focus on pilgrimage as a journey.

Fr Norman Tanner SJ taught Church History for many years at the Pontifical Gregorian University, the Pontifical Beda College and the Venerable English College in Rome. He now lives with the Jesuit community in Bournemouth.

Pilgrims from Canterbury / Wikimedia commons

To know a *heart-shaped, heart-sized* God

A pilgrimage is about finding God, but a few memorabilia collected on the way play their own part on the journey, as Sr Janet Fearns realised when the relics of St Thérèse came to Britain in 2009.

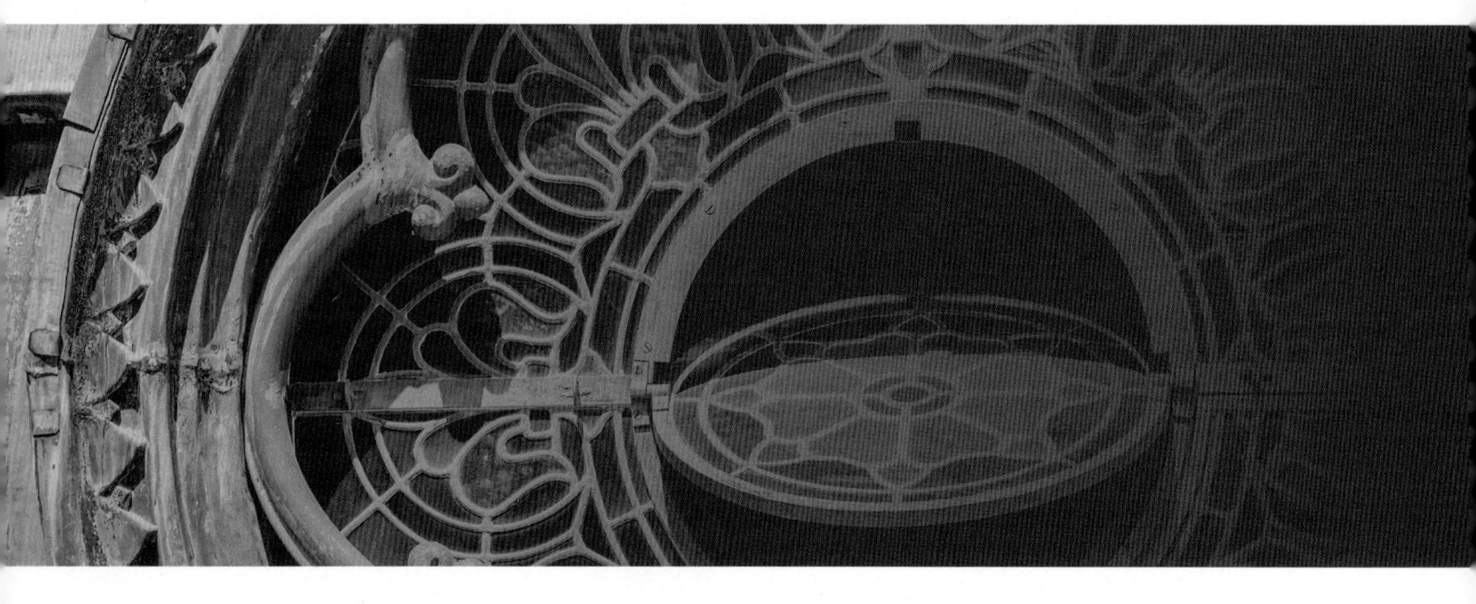

In 2009, when the relics of St Thérèse of Lisieux came to Britain, I found myself standing outside Westminster Cathedral for several hours, distributing prayer cards at a rate of eight hundred per hour as the crowds filed through the cathedral door. The cards' popularity was for a reason we had not foreseen: as people processed past the beautifully ornate casket inside its thick glass canopy, they used it to touch the glass, by which small gesture the card became a memento to be treasured.

In our days of (comparatively) cheap travel, we bring back souvenirs of places we have visited in order to recreate the sights and sounds of unforgettable moments which we want to keep for ever. How many of us have returned from Lourdes with several plastic statues of Our Lady containing water from the Grotto, or from Rome with assorted rosaries, medals and pictures, blessed by the Pope during the Wednesday General Audience or at Sunday's Angelus message?

In the early Church, the Eucharist was originally celebrated at the tomb of a martyr and then, subsequently, at the graveside of an outstandingly holy person. There was a slight problem as Christianity spread beyond Israel and Rome to new areas where nobody local had yet been martyred or canonised. Did this mean that people in new mission territories should be denied the Eucharist?

The ever-growing need for direct, tangible contact with the sacred led to the transporting of relics in portable altars and other frequently valuable and extraordinarily beautiful reliquaries.

Several hundred years ago, holy memorabilia accompanied journeys which were truly once-in-a lifetime affairs. The one-way walking distance between the tomb of St Thomas of Canterbury and that of St James the Apostle in Compostela is, according to Google Maps, a distance of 1,092 miles. Canterbury and Jerusalem – again, one way – are 2,818 miles apart. A pilgrim who had walked that distance in both directions wanted proof of a trip which lasted for several years, involved considerable hardship and, frequently, danger from illness, bandits or warring armies. He or she needed to feel an unbroken connection with the sacred even across huge distances and perhaps many centuries. The distinctive pilgrim's badge mentally transported someone back to a life-changing time and place.

As time progressed, the greater the saint, the more important (and valuable) the relic became. Naturally, the most highly prized would have some direct link to the apostles, St John the Baptist, St Joseph, Mary – or even Jesus, the most precious memento that anybody could possibly dream to possess.

Inevitably, this offered an ideal opportunity to fraudsters. (Yes, I do know of someone who was offered – and bought – a feather which apparently fell from the wing of the Archangel Gabriel at the annunciation!) The number of fragments of the True Cross, for instance, would probably recreate a forest. How many relics in the collection of King Louis IX of France in La Sainte Chapelle are actually genuine? Probably only God knows the answer!

Perhaps the link between a pilgrimage and its memorabilia is best summarised in a quote from William Blake's poem, "Auguries of Innocence:"

To see a world in a grain of sand
And a heaven in a wild flower,
Hold infinity in the palm of your hand
And eternity in an hour.

That's all we really want: to know a heart-shaped, heart-sized God. That's what pilgrimage memorabilia are all about. ■

Sr Janet Fearns is a Franciscan Missionary of the Divine Motherhood.

The pilgrimage behind bars

A serving Catholic prison chaplain constantly sees that prison often brings people to God.

By pilgrimage we usually think of a long journey, a kind of quest to reach a holy place, usually to worship, pay homage or give thanks. Behind bars many similar journeys are embarked upon. The withdrawal of one's liberty and freedom is an unorthodox start to a pilgrimage, but then the Lord does indeed move in strange ways. The quest is indeed to reach a holy place and that place is a better self, a rehabilitated self. On the way there can be many opportunities to worship and give thanks; in fact the ultimate success of the pilgrimage relies upon the seizing of such opportunities. Like any pilgrimage there are highs and lows, challenges and successes. Inside a prison environment the extremity of these can be somewhat magnified. Perhaps the end result therefore is all the more worthy of celebration.

Pope Francis, speaking to prison chaplains in Rome, said, "Thinking about this is good for me: when we have the same weaknesses, why did they fall and I didn't? This is a mystery that makes me pray and draws me to prisoners."

Our catechism teaches us that it is a Corporal Work of Mercy to pray for the prisoner. By doing so, we play our small part in the pilgrimages that go on each day behind the walls of our prisons. We should never be in doubt about the power of such prayer.

There is no one reaction to being sentenced to a period in custody. Sadly, and all too often it is a familiar experience, an occupational hazard. Sometimes it is the expected outcome of a grave mistake or a terrible decision. It can be a great shock or even the knock on the door that was always expected. Yet however a custodial sentence starts, it can be the beginning of a quite remarkable journey of faith.

Within twenty-four hours of arriving in prison a chaplain will have visited to gather general information, provide some reassurance and establish whether or not any specific faith needs can be met. It is at this very early moment that a faith that may have been greatly lapsed, indeed all but forgotten, stirs itself. The pride with which "I'm a Roman Catholic" is sometimes uttered can be extremely moving. It can very quickly be followed by stories of Grandma's insistence on Mass attendance, of Catholic school or about the art of altar serving. Moments long forgotten and ignored can take on a new and powerful resonance.

The great privilege of being a chaplain lies in being a fellow pilgrim. Over time these footsteps of faith become uncovered, shared and explored in ever greater depth. Conversations in a cell, on the wing, on a corridor, at work, in Bible class or before and after Mass allow the exploration of the heart to develop. In the hubbub of daily prison life the words of St Alphonsus ring true, "Your God is ever beside you – indeed he is even within you." Great reassurance for a chaplain, I can assure you, but a stark reminder to a searching soul that the pilgrimage has already begun.

Like any pilgrimage there is the need for preparation. The real preparation however is in acceptance of the need to start. This is often as simple as the realisation that the messages given by family, catechists, clergy and teachers do indeed ring true. A point has been reached, the lowest point perhaps, where a new direction is being sought. After all this time, the direction had always been there, from baptism.

Sometimes the pilgrimage begins with a jolt, a shock, or the death of a loved one, for example. At such news we gather around each other and offer prayer and support. Behind bars this brings home the loss of liberty. The prison service does all in its power to enable direct family members to attend the funeral of a loved one. Cuffed to officers, this can be challenging for the prisoner and the family. Yet it can work. A prisoner saw me at Mass a few days after his father's funeral. He was full of praise for the staff who made sure that his attendance was as normal as possible. It meant a great deal to him and his family. It spoke highly of the decency and humanity of the prison staff and reinforced his pilgrimage of faith.

Accompanying a man to the chapel in times of real crisis are among the most blessed moments of prison ministry. These can be very tearful times. As a chaplain one can only be present to the grief, offering comfort and prayer. Many times I have experienced real moments of soul searching and sincere sorrow among the sobs of grief. To leave a candle, lit in the memory of a love one, before the Blessed Sacrament, provides enormous consolation. Rarely have the "Eternal Rest" and the "Our Father" failed to pour out a tangible balm, to return the grief stricken to the care of the Saviour. These moments of true pain can be powerful prayer stations on the pilgrimage.

Throughout any pilgrimage behind bars the chapel is a source of comfort and solace. It is a sacred space of welcome, where bars are usually unseen and a rare quiet is found. Here men and women are reminded that they are children of God, pilgrims, not a number. Familiar symbols, the crucifix, the stations of the cross, statues… all play a supportive role. It is here that the strength of the Eucharist can be sought and found. People of all ages rediscover and rekindle the embers of faith, slowly but surely allowing the power of the Body and Blood of Christ to recreate them in his image. It is both a painful and a joyous experience.

In the Eucharist, the weekly progress of the pilgrimage can be measured and celebrated. The Gospel message can be seen to dovetail seamlessly with the daily rehabilitative agenda. Another week of the journey goes by and the strength to reach its end is replenished by the word and the Bread of Life. ■

Faith Inside: a guide for Catholics in prison *is available from Redemptorist Publications, www.rpbooks.co.uk*

Wisdom and faith behind bars

The writers of the following articles have travelled a million miles within the confines of their cells. All are serving prison sentences, but, in finding God, have discovered freedom and hope. We congratulate them for their courage in writing for *Adoremus Extra* and pray that they will be blessed in all that they do.

The new, old me

"I am the new, old me because you live in me. The truth will always haunt me, but it set me free."

My name is Janet and I am an addict. I have been off methadone for thirteen months. Last year I chose to break the chains of addiction.

I was released for three months and stayed clean.

Thirteen months ago in here, I worked with a prisoner in the gardens. Her name is V. She was my spiritual mentor, guide and teacher. She told me the hand of God was on me.

I used drugs for many years. I was a thief, a liar and a fraudster. I hurt the people closest to me. I have asked God for forgiveness, my family for forgiveness and I have forgiven myself. I believe God has forgiven me.

This process of asking for forgiveness took me six months, every night writing down my sins, repenting them – and forgiveness followed.

I am blessed now. My Father and best friend gives me his strength to live a new life.

My job here is Recovery Mentor, helping ladies who are detoxing from drink and drugs. I love this job. I help others and they help me.

Praise be to God.

*"Every day is a winding road.
Every day is a faded sign.
Every day I get a little bit closer
to feeling fine."*

Cheryl Crow, songwriter

"Change the gears of your life out of reverse and into fourth gear."

The way, the truth and the life

"I am the way, and the truth, and the life. No one comes to the Father except through me."

John 14:6

During the past two years of my life, I was touched by some life events (those that people normally never think to live) that addressed me as immense in a very profound, personal spiritual journey, seeking for answers to questions, solutions to issues and clarifications to doubts in regards to the meaning and purpose of my life, my beliefs and my faith.

This journey included long hours of reflection and meditation on readings, debates and conversations with other people, but, as well, with the Lord. People could be thinking that it is not very humble to state that I have conversations with the Lord, but the reality is that I have those moments and I have got important answers as well, which provide me with a peace that I never had got before, a peace that gives an incredible joy to my heart and soul.

I have grown up in a Catholic family. Despite that background, when people used to ask me about my faith, I normally answered that "I am a Catholic by tradition but not by conviction." I described myself as a "social Catholic", which is like saying that "I am a social smoker or a social drinker."

Thanks to the love and mercy of God, this self-perception has changed dramatically. Now I clearly tell people that, "I am a Catholic by conviction."

This journey has allowed me to find my God, my Lord and my new vocation in life. This spiritual journey is a work in progress. Every day I discover new things. I am blessed by the Lord with new graces and I learn more and more about him, his attitudes, his thoughts, his works and his will.

People are constantly asking how you can find the Lord. It is a very simple answer:

"Open your heart to him. Surrender yourself to him and his will and you will find that 'the Lord is merciful and gracious, slow to anger and abounding in steadfast love'. ”

The best way that I found to open my heart was to begin to read the Bible, pray, involve myself in studies of the scriptures, confession etc. Basically, I have begun to get knowledge about my faith and my Lord. There is not a formula. This is a very personal journey, but what I can assure you is that, step by step, day by day, you will find him when you were not expecting to do so. You will realise that your heart is full of love, patient understanding, generosity and self-control.

That day, you will realise that you have been filled with the fruits of the Holy Spirit as God promised through Jesus Christ.

Be patient. You will get there. Trust in Jesus. Whatever will be God's will, it will be good for us. He is our Father and he will always be caring for us. If you look for him, he will be waiting for you to open that door, to give you light and show you the road to everlasting life. ■

"Teach me your way, O Lord, that I may walk in your truth; give me an undivided heart to revere your name."

Psalm 86:11

Walking in the life

I would like to get to a place in the South,
and never came back.

I left my life, my love, I left my beach... I forgot God.
How many lost things!!!! How many tears spilled,
and there is just one question. Why? Why oh Lord?

The life and years are happening and with them the change.
I returned to God, my mysteries and above all I returned to myself. I believe in myself. I will return to my life, with my love, to my beach and I will never forget God, my faithful companion.

I would like to get to a place in the South and never come back,
My life
My God
My beach
My Love
They wait for me!
Forever! ■ ”

Translated from the original Spanish by Jeackson SJ.

A poet for the *pilgrimage*

Images © John Bradburne Memorial Society. Used with permission.

John Bradburne was killed in 1973 because he cared for people with leprosy. Professor David Crystal shows how Bradburne's poetry reveals his inner journey towards God.

The missionary poet John Bradburne was killed in Zimbabwe in 1979, having refused to leave the lepers he cared for in Mutemwa, a village one hundred miles north of Harare. Mutemwa is now an African Fatima. Every 5 September, on the anniversary of his death, thousands come to celebrate his life, climb Chigona hill where he walked and prayed, and hear Mass. His cause for beatification is progressing, slowly, but as far as the pilgrims are concerned, he is already a saint.

What makes him unique is the combination of a caring, selfless character (shared by many saints) with an ability to express his mission and vision in high-quality poetry (which has little precedent). The word "unique" is not too strong, for the poetic oeuvre he created makes him the most prolific poet ever to have written in the English language – over five thousand poems and one hundred and seventy thousand lines – an output that is roughly three times as much as Wordsworth.

His poems, as the John Bradburne poetry website puts it, "display a single-minded enthusiasm and clarity of vision that is compelling in its intensity and endearing in its humanity". He writes compassionately and vividly about the people with leprosy in his care, but his main themes are universal and hugely significant for Catholicism: the nature of the Trinity, the importance of the Eucharist, the centrality of Mary, the place of the Bible, the necessity of Christian unity, the critical role of prayer. And it is a vision which becomes a reality only through a life of service to others.

His story is especially appropriate for a Eucharistic pilgrimage, for those two words echo throughout his poetry. For him, Catholic Christianity is seen as special because of the special role of the Blessed Sacrament, which adds an extra dimension to everything else we do:

"A thankful heart, a contrite heart,
A heart aflame for love of Christ
Is far above all human art
Without the Holy Eucharist.

But in the furnace of His Love
The Host can lift our hearts above
And make them melt for love of Him
Who sits above the Cherubim."

It is a vision that for him becomes a reality only through a life of service to others. Why is John Bradburne important? The people of Mutemwa would tell you: because he provided them with their daily needs in the form of food, medicine, and loving care. It is this continual relating of the realities of this world to those of the next which is the unwavering focus of his writing, and which gives his Mutemwa experience a universal significance. In A "Ballade of Non-Despondency" he writes:

"I'll stay to watch and pray and try
To bring about undoubted ill's decrease
By standing sentinel in Christ and by
Issuing rations where the rations cease."

He sees an intimate connection between the two worlds of daily survival and eternal life. As he puts it in a poem about the leprosy settlement:

"Mootamewa is God's darling; those who come
And go or stay may thus work out salvation."

It was many years before he found his vocation among people with leprosy. His journey took him from his home in

Cumbria and later Norfolk, the son of an Anglican vicar, to the war zones of the Far East (leaving from Liverpool in 1941, a day gloomily remembered in one poem for its "clogging fog and filthy haze"!). Then, after the War, he stayed in several religious houses – Buckfast, Parkminster, Louvain, and Prinknash – exploring each monastic rule until deciding it wasn't for him. He was sacristan at Westminster Cathedral for a while, describing the place as "a temple that had done much towards my conversion" (he became a Catholic in 1947).

Journeys to the Middle East and North Africa reinforced a strong desire for Christian unity, as seen throughout his longest poem, *Ut Unum Sint* – "that they may be one". It reflects the diversity of his spiritual background. Raised as an Anglican, after his conversion he frequently signed his letters as "Jew", and in his travels had close encounters with Islam and Buddhism. He concludes:

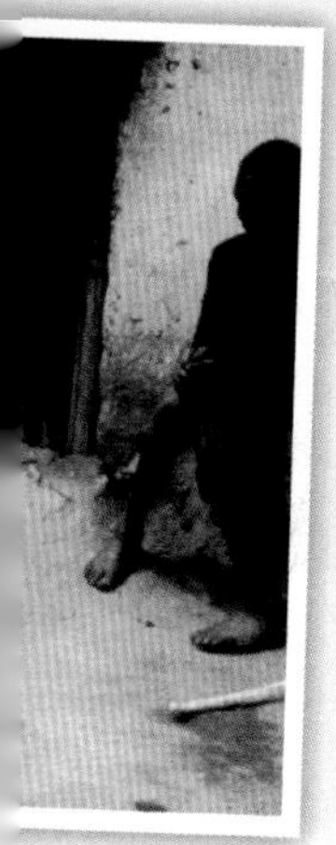

"Hindoos and Buddhists, Anglicans,
And many quaint Americans
And legion others, if they seek
Sincerely, are the Saviour's sheep.

'Tis men of Faith whom God doth choose -
And pray remember that the Jews
Of old were His own faithful race:
We are adopted by His grace."

The theme of the Pilgrimage and Congress is a recurrent motif in his writing. The Eucharist is the subject of over a hundred poems; pilgrimage another hundred. The "Bread of Life" is vividly described in one poem as our "primal ration". In another he uses a metaphor from music:

"The Bread of Life, our Madrigal,
Is sacrificed in One for all:
Discern The Body of our Lord
The King as ye surround His Board."

For more on John Bradburne visit: www.johnbradburne.com. His poems can be read at: www.johnbradburnepoems.com. His biography, The Vagabond of God *is by Didier Rance (Darton Longman Todd, 2017). Also: David Crystal,* My Life in Words: the poetry and thought of John Bradburne *(2017, available through www.davidcrystal.com)*

In another, the analogy is with clothing:

"Wear The Son who is The Word made flesh,
At the Eucharist receive Mine Host;
Put Him on as often and afresh
As may move thee to The Holy Ghost:
Being moved to Him who is thy moving
Soon thou shalt be proved to be improving."

As always in his writing, the Blessed Virgin is never far away:

"Holy Eucharist, the Bread
At sight of which the angels dance,
Is Jesus risen from the dead;
It seems but bread that greets our glance
But, if we meet Him with our gaze
Of Faith, it is no wraith who sways
Such sweet dominion that we
Grow conscious also of a She
Who means 'The Seas': Maria, hail,
The Lord is with you without fail!"

And, as if in an anticipatory nod to this magazine, he writes in "Rosario":

"To be a light, to lighten us
Adopted Gentiles, Christ
Has remained where ADOREMUS
Is owed at Eucharist."

With his anniversary occurring just two days before the event begins, John Bradburne surely has to be thought of as the poet in spiritual residence at the 2018 Eucharistic Pilgrimage and Congress. ■

Professor David Crystal is described as "the foremost writer and lecturer on the English language". An academic, broadcaster and author, he is also at the forefront of promoting the cause and writings of John Bradburne.

Reflections

To help you on your journey, the following six weeks of daily reflections can be started anywhere and continued in any sequence. They might also be useful for discussion groups.

Compassion Week One

David Wells reminds us that showing compassion to others is the quickest way of finding God.

> "What does love look like? It has the hands to help others. It has the feet to hasten to the poor and needy. It has eyes to see misery and want. It has the ears to hear the sighs and sorrows of men. That is what love looks like.
>
> *Saint Augustine*

Monday

Give them something to eat

Matthew 14:13-21

Sitting eating my lunch in a poor neighbourhood, I congratulated myself after sharing half my sandwich with a small impoverished little boy. He possessed nothing but the glimmer of hope that I might give him something to eat. Feeling rather pleased with myself and my good deed, I was challenged to see him run across the street and tear his half into smaller pieces to distribute amongst his friends. In that small boy I saw Christ, multiplying the little compassion I had demonstrated. Acts of compassion can always be multiplied. Jesus never asks us to give what we don't have. What he asks is that we allow compassion to grip our hearts and so to be generous with what we have.

Lord, help me to see generosity as multiplying what I have rather than depleting it. Amen.

Tuesday

No celebrity status

Matthew 15:29-31

Pope Francis teaches us that the greatest of truths can be taught by the smallest of gestures. Jesus didn't defeat huge armies with lightning bolts from the sky; he didn't miraculously swoop and cavort above the crowds to attract their admiration. Jesus is not living as a celebrity. His miracles are always gestures of compassion. In our Gospel reading for today, Jesus encounters the pain and loneliness of the bruised, hurting and dirty people who place themselves at his feet. His response is compassion and love. What is happening in these encounters is that Jesus is proclaiming his kingdom, not by edict or earthly power, but by divine gesture. The crowds are amazed. For those who really "get it", their amazement will slowly mature into conversion. For those who don't, he remains just a celebrity.

Lord, help my amazement at "things" to mature into gestures of compassion. Amen.

Wednesday

How often must I forgive?

Matthew 18:21-35

Have you grown up with the ideal that "To forgive is to forget?" Sometimes I can forgive but I can't always forget. Does this make my forgiveness fake? At night and again the next morning, I must forgive those who have offended me. This happens repeatedly until the hurt is slowly released, the debt cancelled and I let go of the grip the damage has done. I have to dig deep into compassion and repeatedly forgive if I am to be released from my resentment or else I will remain enslaved like the unforgiving servant in today's story, consumed by bitterness. Compassion frees us from ourselves.

Lord, grant me the depth of compassion I need to cancel the debt I hold on others. Amen.

Thursday

Moved with compassion

Matthew 20:29-34

We frequently read in the Gospels that Jesus is moved with "compassion" or "pity." Here Jesus is moved by the plight of two blind men. Often the root of Jesus' compassion is translated from the Greek word *eleos* partly meaning "gutted." When we feel gutted we are close to the word *eleos*. We gaze upon the plight of others and our stomach knots up inside us. To be "moved with compassion" in this way is the love Jesus calls for. Jesus does not ask us to be sympathetic. Sympathy can be passive. Jesus calls upon us to be moved by compassion; to see where love is needed and to respond accordingly. Love like this both hurts and heals, it feels and prompts movement. There is no looking away.

Lord, help me to see with my heart where love is needed and to act accordingly. Amen.

Friday

Catch Jesus' attention

Mark 2:1-12

Sitting in the cinema I notice a small boy in front of me. Before the film begins he takes himself to the toilet. When he returns to the auditorium the lights have dimmed and he can't find his family in the darkness. He walks up and down the aisle repeatedly trying to find them. Finally, standing in front of the screen he declares, "Does anyone here know me?" His effort to be recognised is to be applauded. When we know we need help we must have the humility to ask for it. In this remarkable story it is the tenacity and inventiveness of the stretcher bearers who draw upon Jesus' compassion. How generously Jesus responds! It is essential to accept our need of Jesus and to be resolute in catching his attention.

Lord, help me to accept my need of you and to call upon your compassion and mercy. Amen.

Saturday

Jesus tears down the gates

Luke 7:11-17

Death comes frequently to first-century Israel. Life is hard. It is at the gate of the town where Jesus encounters the widow and her dead son. It is hot. His body is being removed from the town. With no husband and no children, the woman's fate is sealed; she is consigned to a life of isolation. One of the many fruits of compassion is that people are reunited. Compassion brings people home, into the town and into the bosom of family love. The compassion of Jesus tears down the gates we build, nothing can withstand it, even death. It is perfect compassion which reunites this son to his mother and them both to a shared life. Jesus will repeat this moment on the cross, ensuring that his mother, also a widow, will have a son in the disciple John.

Lord, help me to have the compassion to bring others together, to unite rather than divide. Amen.

Sunday

Hold open the door

Luke 15:11-32

When children become adults their parents have to adjust. Children must take control and parents have to let go. A child's vulnerability now becomes the parent's.

Parents have to trust that their children will be responsible. At home we have a rule. When our sons and daughter come home at night (long after we have gone to bed) they have to turn the hall light off. This tells me and my wife that they are home safely.

Jesus understood that love waits in hope of a return. In today's story, the father waits, longing for his boy to come home. This is the compassionate disposition we must all adopt. As a Church we look with the eyes of a loving Father, holding open the door, ready to greet and welcome everyone as they appear on the horizon.

Lord, help me to keep open the door of my heart and the light on ready for when someone needs me. Amen.

Discussion points

On a bad day, my life is all about me. My world shrinks until I'm bubble-wrapped inside concern for myself. Compassion draws me out. There are two consequences.

Firstly I have room for others.

Secondly I notice I am having a better day.

In this week's readings Jesus shows us his compassion, thereby revealing, not only how to love, but also how to be happy.

Are you bubble-wrapped inside your own worries? How might more compassion make you a happier person?

David Wells' books The Reluctant Disciple *and* The Grateful Disciple *and DVDs are available from Redemptorist Publications, www.rpbooks.co.uk*

Community

Week Two

Sr Thérèse Garman SMP describes some of the ways in which we can be community builders.

> You may be poor yourselves in material ways, but you have an abundance of gifts to offer when you offer Christ and the community of his Church.
>
> *Pope Francis*

Monday

You must love

Matthew 22:34-40

Relationships are at the core of Christian living. Love of neighbour, however, is necessarily self-sacrificing. Let's reflect on how much we ourselves have been enriched by the self-sacrificing love of many people. We show our love of God in how we relate to those around us. Do I really love my neighbour as myself? This means unconditional acceptance of others just as they are, forgiving them and asking for forgiveness.

In receiving the Eucharist, each one in our Christian community is to become "bread that is broken" for others, working actively to build a more just and loving world, because, "A Eucharist which does not pass over into concrete practice of love is intrinsically fragmented" (Benedict XVI).

Lord, may the Eucharistic mission of our community help us transform our neighbourhood and world. Amen.

Tuesday

I have come to call sinners

Luke 5:29-32

This is Jesus' mission statement. He goes out to the despised and marginalised; to re-integrate the excluded. To follow Jesus, therefore, requires me constantly to reach out to those who need him most, showing them his love and compassion. Do I visibly reach out to them?

The party at Levi's house is Eucharistic. For Jesus it's about eating and drinking with all the "wrong" people, thus welcoming everyone into God's reconciled and loving community. Do we see continuity between the Eucharistic celebration in our parish community and the liturgy of our daily life? When we receive the bread broken and shared out, we are missioned to live a life of compassionate understanding and forgiveness.

Lord, forgive our self-righteous attitudes, so that our parish community may welcome those who need you most. Amen.

Wednesday

Intimate connections

Acts 2:42-47

This passage is a powerful description of community, connecting to God, each other and the wider community. These three intimate connections are vital. Our Eucharistic mission is first to "be" community, then "do": make disciples, together creating a church community in which everyone feels at home.

These first believers are doing their best to incarnate what the kingdom of God should look like. They break the bread of their own life and live the Eucharist in order to give others "something to eat". Living the Eucharist involves us being available, selfless, building up – it involves sacrifice. Can I truly say and demonstrate to those with whom I find it difficult to relate: "This is my body given for you"?

Lord, in your love, may we courageously become "bread, broken" for others. Amen.

Thursday

They continued to testify to the resurrection

Acts 4:32-35

For the early Christians, the powerful sign of the resurrection was not an empty tomb but a loving, vibrant and unified community whose lives had been transformed, in which sharing was a way of life; sharing rather than giving. Giving can remain impersonal, whereas sharing begs for relationships. Can we challenge ourselves to move beyond giving towards truly sharing, taking time to build relationships?

We who gather at the Lord's table, and enter into a real personal encounter with God in the Eucharist, will identify ourselves as witnesses of the resurrection by practising the sharing love, compassion and mercy of God, in ways which are powerful and life-changing. Is this my witness?

Lord, may our loving and compassionate sharing be life-changing for others. Amen.

Friday

Gifts differing

Romans 12:3-13

The combination of the body of Christ that we share in the Eucharist and the body of Christ that we form as a community reminds us that the Eucharist is profoundly social. This passage calls us to celebrate unity in diversity and to appreciate our differences. The way we appreciate differences is to acknowledge and rejoice that God has given each of us different abilities and gifts and also the responsibility to use them. God graciously uses us to bless others and others to bless us. Paul's communities are his audiovisual aids, giving credibility to his statements about new life. Let us look for concrete ways in which we can be a blessing to others.

Lord, thank you for my gifts: may I recognise and use them to the full for others. Amen.

Saturday

Do all you can to live at peace

Romans 12:14-21

On the cross, totally broken and stripped of everything, Jesus prays for his executioners. This same love is offered to us in the Eucharist. How do we take it to others? Whom do we have difficulty in loving? To love means having true care, concern, understanding and forgiveness towards them. We offer them to God in prayer. Praying for them is the key to letting God foster a real love and concern in our hearts. This leads to reforming our emotions and feelings. We open up, with God's help, the possibility of changed relationships and building a peaceful community.

Benedict XVI reminds us that, "All who partake in the Eucharist must commit themselves to peacemaking in our world."

Lord, let there be peace on earth and let it begin with me. Amen.

Sunday

Clothed in the beauty of holiness

Colossians 3:5-17

We are spoiled masterpieces needing restoration to rediscover God's image in us. Holiness is about being a Christ-transformed community. It is relational. We are to put on something new, make choices in the light of who we are. Our new life depends, not on "dos" and "don'ts", but on being united with Christ in treating others as he has treated us.

We all struggle to discard old habits, but let's challenge ourselves to be examples of humble service towards everyone, not simply those we like. In John's Gospel, the washing of the disciples' feet during the Last Supper, where Judas was present, is a powerful example of Eucharistic behaviour, truly humble and caring.

Lord, help us to rediscover your image in each other and so become a transformed community. Amen.

Discussion points

This week's readings focus on community and how the Eucharist transforms the relationship between individual and community.

- How do I see the continuity between the Eucharistic celebration in our parish community and the liturgy of my daily life?
- Can I honestly say to those with whom I find it difficult to relate: "This is my body given for you"?

Sr Thérèse Garman SMP is a Sister of Our Lady of Providence.

Comfort Week Three

Raymond Friel reminds us that if we want to experience comfort, we must be prepared to give comfort.

"We should ask ourselves: 'how is my heart? Is it open and steadfast in faith; does it let itself be led by the Lord's love?' With these questions, let us ask the Lord for the grace that each one of us needs.

Pope Francis

Monday

Blessed and comforted

Matthew 5:1-12

Pope Francis called the beatitudes the "identity card" of the Christian. The Catechism calls them the "countenance of Jesus Christ", the very self-portrait of God. They challenge each generation to reflect on what persons and actions they consider to be important or blessed. The exemplars Jesus provides of those in proximity to God, or "blessed" – the poor, the meek, the mourners, the peacemakers – are all in some ways vulnerable, dependent, precarious. They do not follow the way of the world, which esteems the rich, the confident, the emotionally tough, the warriors. This was a new way of being human and for those who lived this way, like Jesus, there would be persecution because they were a threat to the established order: but there was comfort; they were blessed.

Loving Father, grant me the grace to grow in the humility of the beatitudes. Amen.

Tuesday

Take refuge in Jesus

Matthew 11:25-30

At around the age of thirteen, a Jewish boy becomes *bar mitzvah*, literally a "son of the commandment". He takes on the "yoke" of the Law and is from then on obliged to keep the commandments and to study Torah. This is not seen as a burden, this is after all the revelation of God, albeit incomplete, to begin to bring about the kingdom. Jesus uses the same language but puts himself in place of the Law – "come to me" – and makes it clear that what awaits those who come to him is not an impossible burden but rest for our souls, which are so often agitated. So many people today are burdened by anxiety, guilt, depression... The gentle Jesus offers them a refuge in himself.

God of peace, calm my tired and troubled soul. Amen.

Wednesday

Christ the victim

Matthew 25:31-40

On what will we be judged at the end of our life? How many times we went to Mass? What we believed? What group we belonged to? Important as these surely are, Matthew's Last Judgement does not refer to them. In this scene, we have another set of beatitudes and this time Christ says that "those whom my Father has blessed" are those who reached out to help the hungry, thirsty, naked, sick, the prisoners and strangers; in other words, the victims, in one way or another, of society's indifference and violence. And why should we reach out to help them? Because whatever we do to them, we do to Christ the victim: lying asleep in a shop doorway, clinging to an overcrowded dinghy, scraping at the dry earth for food.

God of those who are poor, help me to see your presence in those who are most vulnerable. Amen.

Thursday

Room even for doubters

John 14:1-3

This is a moment of high anxiety in John's Gospel. Jesus has celebrated his Last Supper with his disciples and astounded them by washing their feet, an act which would take years for them to understand. Judas has gone into the night to betray Jesus. Simon, despite his dramatic declarations of loyalty, was about to deny him three times. And what does Jesus say in the middle of this emotional turmoil? "Do not let your hearts be troubled." He tells his anxious disciples that he is going to prepare a place for them in his Father's house, where there are "many places", even for doubters and deniers, for people like us.

Forgiving Father, bring me safely to your heavenly home. Amen.

Friday

Guided towards the light

John 14:27

Jesus is preparing to leave his disciples, but he will not leave them alone. In the Christian tradition, there is a strong memory of a transition from the presence of Jesus to the presence of the Holy Spirit. This is the "peace" which Jesus is leaving us: his risen presence. The Spirit of Christ brings peace because it teaches us and leads us further into the depths of the revelation that was the life, death and resurrection of Jesus. Like the disciples, it takes us quite a while to get the point and we often forget what is most important. The Spirit, said Jesus, "will teach you everything". This is what brings peace. We are not left in the dark. We have a teacher who guides us towards the light.

Come, Holy Spirit, fill our hearts with wisdom and peace. Amen.

Saturday

From the depth of my heart

Romans 8:26. 27

Prayer is not always easy. We are often distracted and our best resolutions fall away. It's reassuring to know that the first person to write about the Christian life, St Paul, knew that too. He said that "we do not know how to pray as we ought". Paul's great insight is that all is not lost: the Spirit of God prays within us, with a depth that is beyond our imagination. *YOUCAT*, the *Youth Catechism of the Catholic Church*, puts it this way: "Basically prayer means that from the depth of my heart, God speaks to God." So what is our role in this divine conversation? By some kind of regular simple silent prayer, we just have to get out of the way and let it happen.

Holy Spirit, pray in us with sighs too deep for words. Amen.

Sunday

Life's great love

Romans 8:28-39

When St Paul was "seized" by Christ on the road to Damascus, he clung on and did not let go for the rest of his life. He had an unshakeable faith that Christ would not let him down or leave him. No hardship – and he suffered many – not even death itself, would separate him from his life's great love. He knew he was loved, he was "justified", to use his word which has caused so much argument. And how did he come to be justified, to be right with God? Through faith. Jesus often told people that their "faith" had saved them. Faith in what. In a complex system of doctrine? It was much simpler than that. It was faith as a childlike trust and openness to the overwhelming grace of God.

Loving God, grant me faith in your everlasting love. Amen.

Discussion points

The readings highlight some of the key characteristics of the Christian life: humility, simplicity, purity of heart, faith, and a call to reach out to help the victims in society, since Christ is for ever identified with them.

- To what extent can I describe the beatitudes as a self-portrait?
- What is my encounter with those who are poor?
- Am I committed to a daily discipline of prayer which seeks to diminish my ego and allow the Holy Spirit to pray in me?

Raymond Friel's books, CDs and DVDs are available from Redemptorist Publications, www.rpbooks.co.uk

Commitment

Week Four

Catherine Pepinster encourages us to follow Jesus in all that we say, think and do.

> Are we ready to be Christians full-time, showing our commitment by word and deed?
>
> *Pope Francis*

Monday

Not a second thought

Matthew 4:18-22

We have all been asked life-changing questions: "Will you accept this job?", "Will you marry me?", "Shall we move house?" And so often, the response is: "I'll have to think about it; I can't make a decision like that straight away!"

But when Jesus called the fishermen Simon Peter and his brother Andrew to follow him, they didn't hesitate, even though he warned them metaphorically of what lay ahead.

As "fishers of men", they would be casting into the deep, sometimes facing terrible storms. But they left behind their jobs and their families and placed all their trust in him.

Give me the courage, Lord, to answer your call, just as the fishermen did, and let me, like them, place my trust in you. Amen.

Tuesday

Be utterly focused

Mark 6:7-13

Christ's instructions to his apostles encourage all of us to be utterly focused on our mission. Jesus wants his disciples to strip away everything that doesn't matter and instead direct all their energies towards his service. Mark records a sense of urgency about what Jesus calls them to do: if people show little interest in what the disciples have to say, he tells them to leave immediately. Today, we might find talk of urging others to drive out demons and impure spirits unusual, but there is a sense of Christ commissioning his followers to do all the work of the Lord.

Following you, Lord, requires my unerring dedication and commitment; help me live this calling day by day. Amen.

Wednesday

Commitment is not easy

Luke 9:57-62

Nothing can come before our commitment to God. Answering this call has to be everything and nothing must get in its way. There is no place for "Yes, buts", or for any kind of hesitation. Luke records that Jesus told one man that even burying one's family cannot come before God. And for all of us, these are difficult words to hear. Human beings are encouraged to think first and act later; we are constantly told that being cautious can be a wise option. But following Christ is a demanding vocation and Jesus leaves us in no doubt how total our response must me.

Lord, you are everything to me. Never let be parted from you. Never let anything come between me and your love. Amen.

Thursday

Beyond our understanding

John 3:16. 17

For any parent, their child is the most precious thing in life. Imagine then, the gift given freely that God gave the world: his Son who would redeem it, who would be the sacrificial lamb. God asks that we give our all, but it is no more than he has given us: his all, his Son. But another gift awaits those who make that all-encompassing commitment that God seeks. He promises eternal life. In other words, to be with him and his Son for evermore. It is hard to imagine, with our limited human understanding, what this means, but we have been offered a divine promise.

Lord, you gave me the gift of your most precious Son. Help me to follow him and freely give my commitment to you. Amen.

Friday

The bride is only for the bridegroom and yet…

John 3:29. 30

Marriage is of great significance in the Bible, not only literally but also metaphorically. It symbolizes an unshakeable bond. God is often depicted as a groom and his people, or the church, as his bride. John the Baptist is like a best man, supporting Jesus, but making way for him too. There can only be one groom, one Lord with whom we have our bond and to whom we make our lifelong promise. It is Christ alone who is come to redeem the world. We are called to play our part in the history of salvation.

Just as spouses do on their wedding day, I make my pledge of commitment to you, Lord, my lifelong promise to follow your path. Amen.

Saturday

No wishy-washy sentimentality

Philippians 3:7-16

When Paul writes to the Philippians about knowing Christ, this is not a need for facts; it is about a desire for a relationship, for a connection. Paul warns that this is not about some wishy-washy sentimentality: there is a price to pay. This commitment surpasses everything else in life and the cost to followers of Jesus may be giving everything up that was once held dear. But there is so much to be gained: what Jesus himself describes as the peace that the world cannot give - and a share in his resurrection.

Teach me to be generous, Lord: to give my everything and not count the cost; to have the courage for true discipleship and to discover the true joy of this commitment. Amen.

Sunday

Live in God

1 John 4:7-16

To love God is not a narrow love. The Holy Trinity of Father, Son and Holy Spirit is an eternal sign of love as relationship - and the love of God embraces the whole of humanity. This love is a continual relationship. John tells us that those who love one another love God and similarly, those who love God must in turn love one another. Therefore our commitment to God is to humanity and indeed to this world in which we live. As John writes, if we love one another, God lives in us.

As Christ stretched out his arms on the Cross to embrace the world, so Lord, may I reach out in love to humanity and to your creation and serve you each and every day. Amen.

Discussion points

- Can you think of a time when you unhesitatingly answered a life-changing request? If so, what inspired to you to do so?
- Could you commit to Jesus in the way the apostles did, if it means giving up everything? If not, what is holding you back from such a life of discipleship?

Catherine Pepinster is a former editor of The Tablet *and the author of* The Keys and the Kingdom: the British and the papacy from John Paul II to Francis, *published by T&T Clark.*

Commemoration
Week Five

Jo Siedlecka suggests that actively remembering the past can have a positive influence in our present.

> This is why the Eucharistic commemoration does us so much good: it is not an abstract, cold and superficial memory, but a living remembrance that comforts us with God's love.
>
> *Pope Francis*

Monday

Taking for granted?

Luke 22:14-20

There must have been a holiday atmosphere in Jerusalem at this time. Jesus knows he must shortly endure great suffering – but he spends this day of celebration with his friends and, during their special meal together, he tells them about how eagerly he has desired to eat the Passover with them. Then he gives them the great gift of the Eucharist.

Can I imagine the disciples happily gathered around the table for this festive meal? When I hear the words of the consecration, do they really sink in with me? When I go up to receive Communion do I feel that sense of eagerness – or have I got too used to this precious gift?

I pray that I may never again take the sacrament of the Eucharist for granted. Amen.

Tuesday

Too busy to see?

Luke 24:13-35

When the disciples walked along the road that day – did they notice the passing scenery, the stones under their feet? Did they hear the birds in the trees? In this account, they seem so preoccupied with the events of the last few days, so busy chatting away together, that they don't realise the man walking alongside them is Our Lord.

How often do we miss something under our nose? How often are we so busy thinking about a past event or planning a future one that we just miss that turning in the road or just not notice something very important?

Let us pray for the gift of being really present in a situation and to be thankful when we do "get" it. Amen.

Wednesday

Actions speak louder than words

Luke 24:36-53

How difficult it must have been for the apostles to accept that Jesus was really with them once again after all they had been through. Yet he had told them many times all this was going to happen. And now he tells them again. But it seems that it wasn't until Jesus asks for food and they see him eat the fish that they begin to trust that this is really true.

We all need reassurance. It's often practical acts like sitting down with someone for a shared meal or a cup of tea that build trust, more than complicated words. Hearts speak to hearts without words.

Lord, help us to show our love for others through practical actions. Amen.

Thursday

Spread the Good News

Matthew 28:16-20

Here Jesus commands the eleven disciples to go out and spread the Good News to all peoples around the world – to baptise and make disciples of all nations. That means us too. Through our own baptisms we have also become disciples – and we have been commissioned to continue this work.

In my own life am I following this commandment? It's hard to take on board. Do I talk about my faith or demonstrate to others through my behaviour and the choices I make, that I am a follower of Jesus?

Lord, help me to be faithful to the task you have set for me and not to fear because you are with me every step of the way. Amen.

Friday

Bemused and bewildered

John 12:12-19

What a bewildering day this was! The crowds were so enthusiastic to greet Jesus at this time – but the high priests were angry and later we know the crowds would curse Jesus.

Who of us could say that we have never run with the crowd, even against our better instincts? This is the world, our world, into which the love of God incarnate has come to establish the kingdom.

The crowds greeting Jesus were right. This was a new and definitive moment in history. Only this time it is a kingdom of the heart that Jesus is creating; a movement of followers who will seek to bring into everyday life the love of God and neighbour that Jesus himself taught and lived.

Lord, help me to hear the truth and remain faithful when those around me fall away. Amen.

Saturday

Humanity needs hope

John 14:23-26

This reading is so comforting. Pope Francis once tweeted: "Humanity needs hope in order to live and needs the Holy Spirit in order to hope." Here Jesus promises us the gift of the Holy Spirit to teach us all things and to remind us of all the teachings he gave to the disciples.

Do I call on the Holy Spirit as I go through my life's daily challenges? Do I invoke the light of the Spirit when I prepare myself to read and meditate on the scriptures?

I pray that in the future I will be quieter and more aware of my need of the Holy Spirit in my life. Amen.

Sunday

Not so different

Acts 10:34-43

This reading has been described as an early Christian creed. Here St Peter, in the house of Cornelius the Roman soldier, affirms that God's love is for everyone: not just the people of Israel, but all who fear him and do what is right. In Peter's day, the inclusion of Gentiles in God's mission was very controversial. Many of the original followers of Jesus could not imagine a messiah meant for non-Jews – even though God's promises to Israel always had a universal meaning.

We are not so different. We tend to build our own "private" Church, objecting to others whose style of worship may differ from our own.

Lord, I pray for a pure heart that loves others equally and does not judge them. Amen.

Discussion points

Commemoration, honour, celebration, remembrance, veneration… These are all words associated with the Eucharist.

What words describe what happens for me when I go to Mass and receive Holy Communion?

Jo Siedlecka runs the Independent Catholic News website: www.indcatholicnews.org

Communion
Week Six

Mary Bell encourages us to look more deeply into our appreciation of the Eucharist.

In the Bread of Life, the Lord comes to us, making himself a humble meal that lovingly heals our memory, wounded by life's frantic pace of life.

Pope Francis

Monday

How far would you travel?

John 6:1-15

How far would I travel to encounter Jesus? Would I walk all day, like those people by the Sea of Galilee, desperate to be with him in spite of rocky, stony paths? Jesus loved them and pitied them in their physical need, providing an abundance of food to nourish their bodies.

Their persistence was overwhelming. Is our reception of him in Holy Communion as enthusiastic? In some countries people walk for miles to attend Mass. Do we eagerly bring our whole selves, opening up our lives to him?

Lord, may we seek you with the determination and fervour of those crowds who followed you and benefited from your direct nourishment. Strengthen my faith I beg you with your generous gift of yourself. Amen.

Tuesday

Not all food lasts

John 6:12-27

Imagine the buzz that must have gone round: Jesus had fed thousands of people with just a few loaves and fish. Our social media would have had a field day.

But not even the disciples actually understood what he had shown them in his miracle. The real needs of human beings are not just bodily but spiritual. There is no lasting value in ordinary food. The bread that is Jesus is for ever, a heavenly food because it comes from God. Food is necessary for life; without it we die. Jesus himself is our spiritual food necessary for our spiritual lives.

Dear Jesus, help me to understand: feed my soul with your divine presence and bring me to our heavenly home. Amen.

Wednesday

The Bread of God

John: 6:28-33

We all live in the physical world where we need to see things with our own eyes. Jesus knew this. The people asked for signs and his basic symbol of bread was simple and obvious but they did not recognise its true significance.

He told them they must believe that he was sent from God and have faith in him, as we also must believe that the bread and wine we receive in Holy Communion is his gift that can bring us to perfection and everlasting life.

However, too often we fall short; we fail in faith and understanding.

Lord, forgive my lack of belief, my doubts when I look for physical signs and further proof of your presence and love. Amen.

Thursday

What a promise!

John 6:34-40

What a promise! What can this mean for us? Although at Holy Communion we take the bread and wine into our bodies, our souls take in the spiritual substance of Christ's flesh and blood, thereby strengthening the spirit so we can face up to our troubles, meet the demands of ordinary life and commitments and be strong in faith, hope and love.

Furthermore, no one who believes and who seeks Jesus will be rejected. This is his promise because it is God's will. All who seek him will gain eternal life.

Dear Lord, we have to listen to your words and believe in your promise: may our reception of the Eucharist strengthen our hope of life with God in the future. Amen.

Friday

The Bread that lives

John 6:46-51

This must have seemed such an outrageous claim to his hearers. We are accustomed to the idea that if we go to Holy Communion, taking the bread and wine, believing that it has changed into the substance of Jesus' body and blood we shall not die spiritually, only physically. Jesus is himself the "living" bread. It is his flesh sent by God. No wonder they were shocked.

We have Jesus' words from the Gospel. However difficult the concept, which is a mystery, it is stated quite plainly. We weren't fed with manna or loaves and fishes but we can receive the bread and wine of Holy Communion at any time. We can receive Jesus himself. He has said so.

Lord, please help me to believe your promises. Amen.

Saturday

My flesh is real food

John 6:52-58

If anything could shock those who heard him, this would. No wonder the Jews were beside themselves. For us the concept is also hard to grasp. It is no surprise that controversy has accompanied its interpretation.

Really it is simple if we have faith. We can be united with the Lord in a special way: Jesus is giving the whole of himself to us for our nourishment of body and soul. If we identify with this, let go of the apparent irrationality, then we accept an enormous strength to see us through our lives. If only we could let go and ACCEPT.

Jesus, be our help always in life as in death in the hope of our resurrection. Amen.

Sunday

It all began here

1 Corinthians 11:23-27

It all began here at a Jewish supper where Jesus linked the Passover bread and wine with his body and blood and commanded all his followers, including us, to continue to eat and drink in his memory, uniting us with his suffering and death forever.

We hear these words at Mass so often that we don't tend to think about them in their original context. Saint Paul's account is the oldest; written within living memory of the original event so the more likely to be accurate. That is a profoundly moving thought: my reception of Holy Communion links me directly with Jesus in a tangible, unbroken line.

Lord Jesus, please come to me, a humble sinner, trusting in your promise of eternal salvation. Amen.

Discussion points

- Have we allowed our reception of Holy Communion to become too casual?
- Do we receive it with sufficient reverence as is suitable to receiving the body and blood of Jesus himself?
- In modern times has our faith in Jesus' promise become diluted; do we make enough effort to get to Mass?

Mary Bell is a grandmother and a retired teacher who continues to use her skills in the University of the Third Age.

Pilgrims Past and Present

We become *what we adore*

Fr Jim McManus C.Ss.R. explains that we ourselves are transformed by sharing in Jesus' gift of himself in the Eucharist.

Adoration monstrance with the Blessed Sacrament. Thoom/ Shutterstock.com

For the past thousand years, Catholics have loved to gather around the Blessed Sacrament exposed on the altar in a great community act of adoration. Our faith in the real presence of Jesus Christ in the Blessed Sacrament, the sacrament of love, evokes in our hearts a deep yearning to respond in love. When we act on this yearning we find ourselves kneeling in profound adoration of our Lord and Saviour in the Blessed Sacrament.

We become what we adore

Our act of adoration is our response in love to the great love that Jesus has for us in the Blessed Sacrament. St Alphonsus expressed our Catholic faith at the beginning of his famous little book *Visits to the Blessed Sacrament* with these words:

"My Lord Jesus Christ, I believe that you are really here in this sacrament. Night and day you remain compassionate and loving. You call, you wait for, you welcome everyone one who comes to visit you".

Once we hear the Lord's call and respond with faith and gratitude we begin to experience more personally the great mystery of God's love for us. As we worship Jesus in the Blessed Sacrament we are spiritually transformed into his image. St Paul describes this grace well when he writes: "All of us, with our unveiled faces like mirrors reflecting the glory of the Lord, are being transformed into the image that we reflect in brighter and brighter glory; this is the working of the Lord who is the Spirit" (2 Corinthians 3:18). That spiritual transformation takes place in us as we lay our whole lives before Jesus in the Blessed Sacrament. We enter into a deep, personal friendship with Jesus. In our act of adoration we become like him. We become what we adore.

Our relationship with Jesus

Our loving, personal relationship with Jesus is the essence of our Christian faith. As Pope Benedict XVl wrote,

"Being a Christian is not the result of an ethical choice or a lofty idea, but the encounter with an event, a person, which gives life a new horizon and a decisive direction." *(God is Love, 1)*

Our time of adoration is our "heart to heart" time with Christ. We gaze in faith on Christ truly present on the altar. More significantly, we allow Jesus Christ our Redeemer to gaze into our hearts with his eyes full of love.

We open our hearts to Jesus and we speak to him about everything that is going on in our lives. We converse in the language of love. We find ourselves saying words like, "Jesus I love you with my whole heart", "Jesus, I place all my trust in you", "Jesus I want to belong completely to you." This is the language of the lover, speaking to the God who is love. And, as you listen for a response, you will hear in your spirit the Lord saying "I love you too with my whole heart", "I love you so much that I died for love of you."

Starting again

If you haven't knelt in adoration of the Blessed Sacrament for some time, or perhaps you never had that prayer experience, this welcome initiative of our bishops to hold a National Eucharistic Congress is a good opportunity for you to experience afresh the love, joy and peace that will fill your heart as you spend time in adoration before the Blessed Sacrament. He is waiting.

Cardinal Nichols, in his pastoral letter announcing the Eucharistic Congress, said that its aim is to "rejuvenate Eucharistic adoration in our parishes as the source of strength for our lives and for our mission, that of making present the love and compassion of Jesus in our society".

Love alone can bring about this great renewal of Eucharistic devotion in our parishes. Adoration, not theology or philosophy, transforms the heart, opens the heart to the love of our Blessed Lord and fills our heart with joyful hope.

Living hope

Pope St John Paul II wrote, "The Eucharist plants a seed of living hope in our daily commitment to the work before us" (*Encyclical on Eucharist, 20*). As we kneel in adoration of the Blessed Sacrament that seed of living hope germinates and grows within our hearts, filling us with a strong, Eucharistic confidence in our daily life, a confidence that touches the hearts of our families, our parishes, our friends and everyone we meet. That living hope, nourished through our time of adoration, gives new meaning and direction to our lives.

Evangelisation

Since we become what we adore, we now have the very person of Jesus within us. Whoever meets us meets the Lord in us. We are now able to love our neighbour as we love ourselves. As people consistently experience our love they are evangelised. Pope Francis always emphasises that, "It is not by proselytising that the Church grows, but by attraction." Our love reveals God's love.

Coping with distractions

We pray with our hearts, not with our thoughts and, in spite of distractions, our hearts remain with Jesus in the Blessed Sacrament. There is no need to be discouraged. Becoming aware of our distractions is the grace of the Holy Spirit, a contemplative grace and an invitation to continue our adoration.

St John gives us great encouragement for our time of adoration. He writes, "When he [Jesus] is revealed we shall be like him, because we shall see him as he really is" (1 John 3:2).

As we kneel in adoration of Jesus in the Blessed Sacrament our spiritual transformation into the very likeness of Christ is taking place within us.
Let us be patient with our weaknesses as we wait in joyful hope for the coming of Our Saviour, Jesus Christ. ■

Fr Jim McManus C.Ss.R. is a well-known retreat giver, spiritual writer and the author of many books, available from Redemptorist Publications, www.rpbooks.co.uk

Taste and see

Patti Gallagher Mansfield discovered that consciously inviting God into her life transformed it for herself and others.

As a "cradle Catholic," my faith always meant a great deal to me. Our family couldn't afford a Catholic school education but we were faithful Catholics and never missed a Sunday Mass. I decided to attend a Catholic university so that I might deepen my knowledge of the Catholic faith. In 1964 I entered Duquesne University in Pittsburgh, Pennsylvania.

After taking a few theology courses, I realised something very important. Simply learning "about" God wasn't enough. I was hungry and thirsty to actually "know" God… to experience God personally.

I began to attend daily Mass on campus and, on occasion, I became aware of that "peace that surpasses understanding" during the Eucharist. The Lord was drawing me closer through the Eucharist and I joined a scripture study group that met weekly to pray and discuss the word of God. But I sat quietly within this group, sure that everyone else understood more about God and the word than I did. I was even afraid to offer a spontaneous prayer out loud.

Then everything changed!

In February 1967, this scripture study group made a retreat based on the Acts of the Apostles. To prepare for the retreat we were told to read Acts 1-4, the story of Pentecost, and a book entitled *The Cross and the Switchblade*, the story of a Pentecostal minister who was led by the Holy Spirit to leave his small town and minister to gangs in the heart of New York City. This was the first time I had even thought about the Holy Spirit since I was confirmed at the age of twelve!

I began to ask myself the question, "Why isn't the Holy Spirit active in my life the way he was in the lives of the apostles and in the life of this minister?" There was a longing growing in my heart. I thought, "Wouldn't it be wonderful if an ordinary person like me could actually have an intimate relationship with God?" But I concluded that this kind of intimacy was only for "special people" – priests and religious. Yet in the depth of my heart was a little mustard seed of faith that caused me to kneel in the quiet of my dormitory room and I prayed, "Lord, as a Catholic, I believe I've already received your Spirit in baptism and in confirmation, but if it's possible for your Spirit to do more in my life than he has happened until now, I want it!" My friends, I really meant what I was praying but nothing seemed to have happened in that moment.

Just a few short days later, while on retreat, I knelt again in the presence of Jesus in the Blessed Sacrament. I knew I needed to surrender my life to God unconditionally. I prayed these words, "Father, I give my life to you. Whatever you ask of me, I accept it. If it means suffering, I accept that too. Just teach me to follow your Son, Jesus, and to love the way Jesus loves."

The next moment, I found myself prostrate, flat on my face before Jesus in the Blessed Sacrament. I was overwhelmed by the presence of God. In that moment, I was "baptised in the Spirit" and I encountered the "love of God poured out in my heart through the Holy Spirit who has been given to us" (see Romans 5:5). It was a "personal Pentecost".

St Augustine prayed, "You have made us for yourself, O God, and our hearts are restless until they rest in you." The psalmist wrote, "Taste and see that the Lord is good" (Psalm 34:8). I experienced this for myself!

Brothers and sisters, that experience of being "baptised in the Holy Spirit" has revolutionised my life and the lives of over one hundred and twenty million Catholics all over the world in the past fifty years. Just like the apostles after the first Pentecost, I began to speak to everyone I knew about the living Lord Jesus. "We cannot keep from speaking about what we have seen and heard" (Acts 4:20).

Nothing interested me as much as evangelising… proclaiming the good news! Immediately, after being baptised in the Spirit, I devoured the word of God, sometimes staying up all night, poring over the scriptures. In the margins of my Bible I would write, "This is true! This is for me!" It was as if a light were turned on in a dark room. What I was trying so hard to understand before was now bathed in light. The Holy Spirit who is the teacher, began to teach me about the power of God's word.

And not only that! The Holy Spirit increased my desire to pray from my heart and to be at daily Mass. After receiving Jesus in the Eucharist, I would say to myself, "This has to change me!"

St Thérèse said of her First Holy Communion, "It was the kiss of Jesus." Encountering Jesus in the Eucharist is the time for intimate exchange with our beloved. Because my faith came alive after being baptised in the Spirit, I approached Jesus in the Eucharist like the woman with the flow of blood, "If I only touch his cloak, I will be made well" (Matthew 9:21). In fact, one of the prayers I love to pray when receiving Jesus in communion is, "Heal me." We're always in need of some kind of healing: emotional, physical, spiritual, in relationships.

If you are hungry and thirsty to know God and to experience God's intimate love, surrender your life unconditionally to Jesus as your Lord. Ask God to baptise you in the Holy Spirit and he will. "Asks, and it will be given you… If you then, who are evil, know how to give good gifts to your children, how much more will the heavenly Father give the Holy Spirit to those who ask him" (Luke 11:9.13). Pick up the Bible in faith and say, "Speak, Lord, for your servant is listening" (1 Samuel 3:9). Approach him in the Eucharist and you will "taste and see that the Lord is good" (Psalm 34:8). ■

Patti Gallagher Mansfield has preached the Gospel for the past fifty years on all five continents. She is author of As By A New Pentecost *(New Life Publishing, 1992) and has received the Pro Ecclesia et Pontifice medal for her work in the Catholic Charismatic Renewal movement. She lives in New Orleans, Louisiana with her husband and family.*

A painful pilgrimage

Sarah Percy shares her family's painful pilgrimage.

It's a painful pilgrimage through a seemingly trackless desert. You face the unknown. Your greatest hope is that, somehow, you can lovingly support your companions on the journey. You will need each other as never before.

Deep down in your heart, you knew it was coming. There were "senior moments" of a different kind, when someone's unrelated word slipped into a conversation and you laughed together at the mistake – because otherwise, you would cry. There were – and still are – the extra household chores which you did – and still do – secretly, to avoid highlighting the increasing need for help.

Then there are the days of your loved one's anger and frustration as life unwillingly takes unfamiliar and unplanned directions; days when family life takes on new meaning as you must reluctantly explore present and future strategies and concerns.

You make the suspected diagnosis before the doctor – and then discover that the doctor faces similar challenges to yourself – and so your telephone call for advice becomes an unexpected opportunity for sharing pain and possibilities – and you both feel stronger for your conversation.

It's an excruciatingly painful pilgrimage. Sometimes you cry alone, trying to be strong for the family, yet also knowing that you're crying – and laughing – together, taking one day at a time, each uniquely helping to provide a growing kaleidoscope of support.

Yet none of you truly witnesses the inner agony and tears of the one who so lovingly still strives to protect you from pain although you are increasingly the enfolder, defender and shelter. Your ever-growing intimacy and hands-on involvement somehow tacitly acknowledges that you are also saying goodbye to the life you shared.

In their eagerness to be "there" for you, others gradually reveal their own painful pilgrimages. You are not alone – yet there is also the utter loneliness of knowing that something you had never wanted, had always dreaded, is happening within your own family. You are drawn closer together than ever before, aware that these unrepeatable days and moments will be cherished forever.

You know that this is a pilgrimage you can make only with God's help. In the midst of your unrelenting anxiety, God is holding your hand and giving you strength. As never before, you "walk humbly with your God" and are grateful for the companionship.

Your own life becomes an unending prayer for someone else's. You accidentally discover that praying the rosary together becomes an amazing way of helping a loved one to calm down and find peace. Prayer works.

It is very hard when, unexpectedly and within the space of a couple of weeks, every day holds fresh challenges and opportunities for love, compassion and understanding. You try to live "normally", although your heart and your thoughts are elsewhere, with someone very special and dearly loved, who is closer than you are to their new home in heaven.

If, like me, you are also making this pilgrimage, then be comforted. You are not alone. Cherish every moment together. Just give love, love and yet more love even if, at times, you are exasperated beyond measure and, at other moments, looking for a hankie to mop up your tears.

You can only say goodbye because you have had a chance to say hello. Your pain is because you love and are loved. Allow God to accompany you on your unwanted pilgrimage – and don't be afraid to cry in God's arms. ■

Sarah Percy, a freelance Catholic writer, claims a special status: she was born and spent her early years in Anfield whilst she attended school in Everton.

Martyrs of love amidst horror

Sîan Owen-Owen describes how the horror and poverty of nineteenth-century Liverpool led to heroic generosity and self-giving.

Take a step back in time to nineteenth-century Liverpool. Since the building of the Old Dock in 1757 and the growth of international shipping, Liverpool's burgeoning importance as a port was also increasingly cosmopolitan. Even Liverpool's hallmark cuisine, "scouse", a staple food on board ship and in poorer homes, is derived from the Norwegian *lapskaus*. It was tasty, filling and inexpensive, requiring only small quantities of the cheapest foods available.

The early nineteenth century witnessed a steady growth of two languages and nationalities as desperately poor and hungry Welsh and Irish families landed in Liverpool by the boat-load.

Liverpool and North Wales have shared close ties for more than five hundred years. With the Industrial Revolution's growing demand for coal, Welsh mining communities anticipated a secure future in spite of unrelenting and appalling hardship. When pit owners maintained shareholder dividends by reducing wages, many impoverished and starving families migrated towards Liverpool in their search for employment in shipping, railways and construction. By so doing, the estimated eight thousand Welsh people living in Liverpool in 1801 (of a total population of 77,653), experienced a six-fold increase as the city's population rose to 704,134 by 1901.

At the same time, the collapse of traditional cottage industries, successive poor harvests, increased mechanisation and horrifying conditions within textile mills and factories increasingly forced many rural English families to move towards Liverpool and Manchester.

As if this were not enough, increasing economic hardship in Ireland caused many to look towards England for food and work. A contemporary source wrote that "One vessel carried a cargo of eight hundred such passengers. They tramped through Lancashire and Yorkshire, and as far south as Nottingham and Leicester, but owing to their numbers and the state of the crops, the majority failed to find any employment. Their condition was

"The Last Court"/ Streetsofliverpool.co.uk

desperate; they tramped the long journey back to Liverpool, sick at heart and weary of the awful disappointment, which meant starvation to themselves and most likely eviction of their families, as their earnings abroad paid the rent at home." 1

The Irish potato famine between 1845 and 1852 created its own tragedies. In 1847 alone, 116,000 Irish famine refugees arrived in Liverpool's Clarence Steamship Dock. As one doctor commented, "Deck passages from Dublin cost as small a sum as sixpence, which probably tempted thousands to try their fortune in our midst."

Inevitably, many new arrivals coming into Liverpool were illiterate and spoke only Welsh or Irish, factors which created enclaves of poverty. Enormous pressures on available accommodation often forced more than one family to share a single room. Contemporary records describe situations in which more affluent householders might rent their unfurnished cellar to one or more families, who existed in penury whilst, above their heads, ship-owners, merchants and traders enjoyed a more comfortable lifestyle. In 1847, an estimated thirty thousand Irish lived in cellars in the "Irish districts" of Scotland, Vauxhall, Exchange and St Paul's.

The "Welsh districts" of Vauxhall, Anfield, Everton, Dingle and Wavertree hosted more Welsh speakers than in any Welsh city, and more than seventy Welsh Methodist chapels. Even today, a number of Liverpool streets bear Welsh names.

Throughout inner city Liverpool, largely clustered around the docks and St John's Market, where so many depended on casual labour for their survival, totally inadequate water supplies and an acute lack of even the most basic sanitation created increasingly serious problems. (A block of forty houses might have six toilets to serve more than three hundred people!) Liverpool faced cholera epidemics in 1832, 1849, 1854 and 1866. In 1832, cholera killed more than one thousand five hundred people and, in 1849, over five thousand. A typhus epidemic in 1847 caused Liverpool to be described as "a city of the Plague".

During 1847, sixty thousand people across the city were treated for typhus and another forty thousand for dysentery and diarrhoea. Eight thousand five hundred died. That year, of the 7,219 paupers buried, 5,237 were Catholics – eighty-one per cent of all pauper burials and forty-three per cent of all deaths in Liverpool. In one street alone, four hundred and seventy-two people died, most, if not all, Catholics. More than six thousand were admitted to the workhouse, where overwork, sickness, poverty and hunger drove whole families to an early grave.

Typhus and cholera travel together with horror. In the nineteenth century, with no antibiotics or intravenous fluids, no understanding of the cause and spread of the diseases, within the overcrowded squalor in which people lived, cholera and typhus epidemics were truly horrendous.

So where was the Church in all this? First of all, it must be recognised that the Welsh and Irish influx to Liverpool were largely separated, not only by language, but also by religion. The Welsh tended to be Methodists and the Irish, Catholic. According to a contemporary source, "The net result was a large permanent addition to the Catholic population, which threw further burdens on the ecclesiastical authorities. While settling down amidst their kindly kinsfolk in the crowded streets, alleys, and courts, they helped unconsciously, and certainly unwillingly, to create a set of conditions which even now, close on seventy years later, are a reproach to local administration." 2

Inevitably, Catholic priests focused on their needy Catholic parishioners.

The legacy of Fr James Nugent (1822-1905) continues today in the form of Nugent Care, Liverpool's Catholic social care agency named after the pioneer in child welfare, poverty relief and social reform. Fr Nugent's pastoral outreach extended far beyond his settled parishioners. In 1847, supported by the Sisters of Notre Dame, he set up a night shelter and refuge where homeless boys found food and lodging. By 1867, forty-eight thousand boys had received supper and, three thousand, a night's lodging. Still more was needed and so, in 1869, he opened a residential school where the boys could learn teaching, shoe-making, tailoring, joinery and printing. Fr Nugent also established a mother and baby home in Dingle and a refuge for women released from Walton Prison.

Other heroic priests also ministered in nineteenth-century Liverpool. Known as the city's "martyr priests", they literally laid down their lives in service of the poor.

In 1840 "Fever broke out, and while tending his poor flock Father Glover, O.S.B., caught the disease and died a martyr of charity". [3] At a subsequent public meeting, a Mr John Kosson declared that "Fathers Edward Glover, Fairclough, Pennington, Tarleton, Spencer, Watkinson, Pratt, and White, all of these in my recollection had rendered up their lives as sacrifices to the holy cause of imparting spiritual consolation to the dying Christian in places which had become pestilential by the dreadful visitation of cholera and typhus." He quoted a recent pastoral letter of Bishop Briggs, "which enumerated no less than twenty-five of his priests 'from youth to middle-age ' who had passed away in eighteen months owing to diseases contracted in the performance of their sacred duties." [4]

It was into these conditions that the "martyr priests" willingly carried the Eucharist, gave absolution and the sacrament of the sick, prepared dead bodies for mass burial – and themselves became ill and died.

"In January, 1847, the Rector of Liverpool informed the Government that dysentery had assumed alarming proportions, due to the cabbages and turnips which formed the only food of the first immigrants. February saw eight hundred cases of typhoid; the reading of the death-roll each Sunday morning in the churches sending a cold shiver through the immense congregations. Hurriedly the parish authorities set up fever sheds... and fitted up a hospital ship in the Mersey, to cope with the new terror. Then came the awful visitation of typhus... The handful of Catholic priests, undaunted, went from room to room in crowded houses; from cellar to garret, ministering to the sick. They were never absent from hourly attendance in the hospital wards. Here at least there was some privacy, but in the crowded rooms and cellars it was next to impossible to hear the last confession, unless the priest lay down beside the sick man to receive the seeds of disease from poisoned breaths in return for spiritual consolations." [5]

The same author continued, "The deaths of these priests made a profound impression on a town which had witnessed fifteen thousand deaths from famine and fever... The strain on the surviving clergy, most of whom suffered severely, was intense. They lay at night on chairs and sofas in their clothes, awaiting the sick calls which never failed to come, fearful lest the time spent in dressing might mean the loss of the sacraments to some poor wretch lying in his dismal hovel." [6]

On 6 July 1847, the *Liverpool Mercury* reported, "The districts of St Patrick's and St Joseph's are now in the worst condition as regards fever. The number of calls made... daily... average about forty. Some idea of the wretched places into which the Roman Catholic clergy venture in their ministerial capacity may be formed when it is known that in one house alone in the district of St Patrick's there were, besides two dead bodies, twenty-eight cases of fever." [7]

A few days previously, on 19 June, the same newspaper described Fr Richard Grayston, "the much respected senior pastor of St Patrick's", who had officiated at Fr Gilbert's funeral at St Mary's "and the following day, though he continued to visit the sick, complained of being unwell and took to his bed in the evening. He was first attacked by bilious fever, which in a few days changed to typhus. He continued to grow weaker... until Wednesday morning last, when death terminated his mortal career." [8]

Ten days later, on 29 June, the *Mercury* informed its readers that, "The Rev William Dale of St Mary's... is the eighth victim amongst the Roman Catholic clergy of Liverpool to the pestilence... He caught the fever whilst ministering to the religious wants of the poor people who now throng the unhealthy cellars... Although he felt poorly, and had done so for six or seven days, he officiated at Mass on Sunday morning... He was, however, very unwell... On Monday, he took to his bed and so rapid was the progress of the disease afterwards, that he died on Saturday evening. He was one of the worst cases..." [9]

At the Last Supper, Jesus declared, "No one can have greater love than to lay down his life for his friends" (John 15:13).

Rightly, Liverpool celebrates its "martyr priests", who risked their lives to carry the Eucharist, to administer the sacraments to people in desperate need, so many of them sick and dying. Interestingly, history has overlooked the religious and laity who cared for people's non-sacramental needs and who became ill and died – perhaps to be buried in paupers' graves alongside them. Whoever they were, known and unknown, these heroic souls, when presented with the Body of Christ in the Eucharist, responded "Amen" – and laid down their own lives in the service of others. ■

Sîan Owen-Owen is a freelance Catholic writer. During the hungry days of the nineteenth century, her family left the Welsh mining town of Pontypridd for the "Welsh district" of Liverpool.

[1] Thomas Burke, *Catholic History of Liverpool* (Liverpool:Tidling,1910) p. 63; [2] Ibid p. 63; [3] Ibid p. 63; [4] Ibid p. 63; [5] Ibid p. 87; [6] Ibid p. 87; [7] *The Great Hunger Commemoration Service* (Archdiocese of Liverpool, 1997) p. 23; [8] Ibid p. 21; [9] Ibid p.22.

Fr James Nugent. Racklever / Wikipedia

The Jesuit connection

It is no coincidence that the Jesuits, including Fr Denis Blackledge SJ, are at the centre of the life of the Church in Liverpool.

Jesuits love to be in the thick of things. After all, they're meant to find God in all things. So it's no wonder that they often started a mission in the centre of a city. And Liverpool is no exception. For well over three hundred years Jesuits have been rooting around on Merseyside, bringing Jesus to the folk of this busy, gloriously messy, historic city of trade and slaves.

At the heart of Jesuit mission is Jesus Christ. The definition of a Jesuit is a sinner called to be a friend and follower of Jesus, who strives, alongside other like-minded individuals, to make Jesus come alive in all those whose lives he is privileged to be alongside and touch with the presence of Jesus.

Throughout penal times until the present, the Mass or Eucharist has been the key focus, the ultimate touchstone of mission and ministry, the core sacrament and sacrifice which stops us all in our tracks and centres us in all we are and can become. The Eucharist is the heart of Catholic Christian identity.

Everything worthwhile begins small: the mustard seed syndrome works. Jesus started with a strange mixed bag of a dozen folk and celebrated a new Passover with them, which they failed to understand and appreciate and value until they had all faced the shame of desertion.

That mustard seed of the Eucharist, the very gift of his own self under the form of bread and wine, developed over the centuries into the source and centre of any true Christian's daily living. That sacred sacrament of the real presence of Jesus in the Eucharist has been the taproot of all mission and evangelisation throughout the past two thousand years.

But it has to become real presence in the daily living out of what is celebrated on that altar of total sacrifice. Otherwise Eucharist becomes a real pretence, not, as it is meant to be, a real living and daily lived-out presence of Jesus in each individual and community who celebrates that awesome priceless gift.

Our loving and compassionate God is the giver of all we are and can become. Each is uniquely gifted, special, with a worth only our prodigal God can give. This beauty and dignity begins with baptism, when an individual becomes another Christ, another Anointed One, another Messiah. Why do we not believe the grandeur of that wondrous prayer when, immediately after the water has flowed over the head in the name of the Trinity, the chrism is poured and another Christ is born?

What makes Jesuit presence in the heart of the city of Liverpool special is the growing desire over the decades to establish a church dedicated to the great original Jesuit missionary, Saint Francis Xavier. By the middle of the nineteenth century that desire took flesh, and a stunning edifice appeared in the thronged streets of back-to-back housing. By the late nineteenth century an extra chapel was built on, the Sodality Chapel, because of the growing number of parishioners.

With school and college added on next door, straddling both sides of the church and its tower, heart, mind and spirit were fed not just by the Eucharist, but also by a flourishing Jesuit education, from primary level to entrance to university. With A.M.D.G. (Ad Maiorem Dei Gloriam) – for the greater glory of God – atop every page of a student's written work, and L.D.S. (Laus Deo Semper) – praise God always – at the bottom, Jesuit education was all about bringing the best out of each individual, not just for their own fulfilment, but for the love and service of their sisters and brothers.

The poignant war memorial tucked in at the back of the church speaks silent volumes of lives given for God and country in the two world wars. The memory of those named individuals who gave their all is daily lit up with votive lights, and has a Eucharistic echo in "we shall remember them".

"Do this in memory of me", as spoken by Jesus at the Last Supper, has been uttered day by day in the sanctuary by

Images © LA Production Used with permission

priests too many to mention, as they fulfilled their privileged role as ordained ministers. After one hundred and seventy years of daily Masses in SFX church, it is impossible to count the number of times that these hallowed words have been pronounced over the bread and wine at the consecration, bringing the Bread of Life and the Chalice of Salvation, the Real Presence, on to the altar.

Just as Jesus took, blessed, broke and gave his living self, as word became flesh in the living Eucharist, so for one hundred and seventy years priest after priest has dared to utter those same words, with the same outcome. But there is a cost, for that taking, that blessing, that breaking and that giving are all of a piece, and there is no giving without the taking, blessing and breaking.

Devotion to the Blessed Sacrament, and to the Sacred Heart of Jesus, has been central to the life of SFX over the decades.

Maybe the old-style glamour and glitz of Quarant'Ore, the forty hours of Exposition of the Blessed Sacrament, has gone but that has not lessened worship of Jesus in the Eucharist. The living flicker of the sanctuary light is a constant daily reminder of the ever-presence of Jesus. And the number of votive lights for Sacred Heart and Our Blessed Lady attest that devotion daily and weekly.

On the Liverpool skyline from the tops of Everton Park there is a trio of churches highly visible. Two of them are cathedrals, towering at either end of Hope Street, holding out the possibility of fulfilling the prayer of Jesus for unity at that first Eucharist. Perched dead centre between them is the spire of SFX, a beacon which is now flanked by Hope University on the old site of the college, and Whitechapel Homeless Centre on the site of the old primary school. The Real Presence is the beating heart of worship which becomes a daily lived real presence of loving service, feeding minds, hearts and bodies in the relentless rhythm of daily living.

It might be worthwhile noting as a footnote that footfall at our beloved church is quietly growing, not least because SFX was privileged to be chosen as the parish for Sean Bean, as he portrayed Fr Michael Kerrigan in Jimmy McGovern's acclaimed BBC1 series *Broken*, aired in 2017, which gave an authentic picture of life for a parish priest in a northern urban scene. As writer Jimmy McGovern said himself: "It's all about the Eucharist!" ■

Fr Denis Blackledge SJ is parish priest of St Francis Xavier, Liverpool. He was Religious Adviser to Sean Bean for the BBC1 series Broken.

Archbishop Oscar Romero – a Eucharistic martyr (1917-1980)

On 24 March 1980, Archbishop Oscar Romero of San Salvador was assassinated whilst offering Mass. Are you one of many thousands who can remember where they were and what they were doing as the news broke? Julian Filochowski tells us more.

Oscar Romero was born to a family of modest means in the small town of Ciudad Barrios in El Salvador. He went to the seminary at thirteen, studied for the priesthood in Rome, and was ordained in 1942. At work in San Miguel he was a zealous pastor with a simple lifestyle, shy and bookish. In 1970 he was made a bishop; and in 1977, he was appointed Archbishop of San Salvador. There followed three tumultuous years of ministry before his assassination.

In the 1970s, El Salvador was deeply divided between a tiny land-owning elite and the mass of landless poor. There was economic exploitation, social deprivation and malnutrition in the countryside, on the coffee estates and sugar plantations. Killings, torture, disappearances, and political imprisonment were the routines of the military regime. The Church put itself alongside poor people in their struggle for basic rights and human dignity – and suffered persecution too.

Archbishop Romero had a deep and prayerful spiritual life and he loved those who are poor. His sermons were legendary. He sought to make the Word of God come alive in the lives of the poor. He preached a message of social justice and non-violent change. He became known as the voice of the voiceless. From the pulpit Romero confronted the human rights abuses, the political violence, the corrupt system of justice, the iniquitous land tenure system, and the suffering people of El Salvador. He was attacked and insulted for his prophetic words and witness. Death threats followed.

As civil war loomed, Romero spoke freely about his death and those around him tried to persuade him to wear a bullet-proof vest or have a bodyguard. In response he asked why the shepherd should have protection when his sheep were still prey to wolves. The threats intensified and, on 24 March 1980, Archbishop Romero was shot dead as he celebrated Mass in the hospital chapel where he lived.

The killing was carried out by a death squad linked to the country's armed forces. It was planned and financed by wealthy and powerful members of the Catholic and Evangelical Christian oligarchy and their military.

Archbishop Romero had known he was going to die. On the afternoon before his death he had unexpectedly visited his confessor, Fr Azcue, saying "I want to feel clean before God."

He expressed his awful fears both to his confessor and in the notes of his last retreat:

"It's hard for me to accept the violent death which, in these circumstances, seems very possible… My disposition should be to give my life for God, however it should end… He aided the martyrs and, if it should be necessary that I die as they did, I will feel him very close to me at the moment of breathing my last breath…"

The martyr of our own times overcame his deep-seated fears. He accepted it with great equanimity. He prepared himself and he went like a lamb to the slaughter. It was a given-life, a free gift with consequences, not a taken-life, with fearfulness of victimhood. Jesus is the Eucharistic martyr

Homily for the beatification of Archbishop Oscar Arnulfo Romero by Cardinal Angelo Amato, Prefect of the Congregation for the Causes of Saints, San Salvador, 23 May 2015

par excellence. Oscar Romero, his faithful follower, died "Eucharistically" in the middle of the celebration of the Eucharist – an unfinished Eucharist.

Ignacio Martin-Baró, himself martyred in 1989, said eloquently "Monseñor died as he had lived: in a priestly fashion, that is to say, offering his life as a prolongation of the sacrifice of Jesus."

Oscar Romero was a martyr who had made an option for the poor. His ministry exemplified a faith that does justice, courageously and consistently. He evokes affection and admiration across the globe, within and beyond the Church. An ecumenical icon, Oscar Romero is an inspiration to lay Christians, bishops and clergy alike, who embrace the cause of poor people as their own – and through prayer and action, join in the quest for peace and justice today.

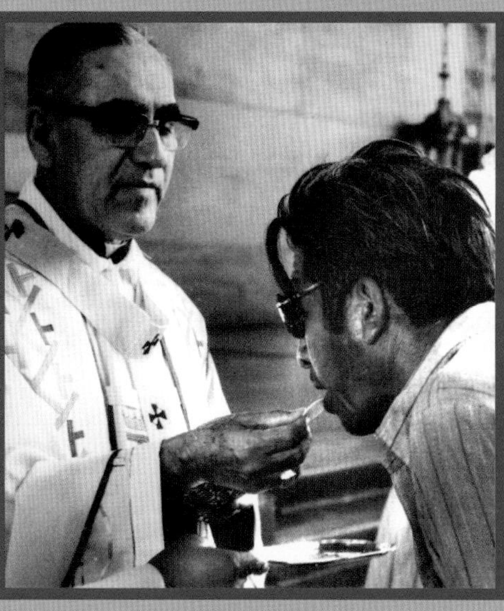

Images © www.romerotrust.org.uk /Julian Filochowski

> "The holy Mass, now, this Eucharist, is just such an act of faith. To Christian faith at this moment the voice of criticism and condemnation appears changed for the body of the Lord, who offered himself for the redemption of the world, and in this chalice the wine is transformed into the blood that was the price of salvation. May this body immolated and this blood sacrificed for humans nourish us also, so that we may give our body and our blood to suffering and to pain... like Christ, not for self, but to bring about justice and peace for our people.
>
> *Final homily of Archbishop Romero*

He was killed only seconds after this declaration of his Eucharistic faith.

In1983, Saint John Paul II stood before Romero's tomb and exclaimed, "'Romero is ours'. It is true. Romero belongs to the Church, but he also enriches humanity, which he dreamt of with a good heart, with thoughts of respect and harmony, with actions of welcome and mutual assistance. Romero is ours, but he also belongs to all because, for everyone, he is the prophet of the love of God and love of neighbour and the custodian of the right consciousness of every person. Blessed Oscar Romero, pray for us!"

On a date which will shortly be announced, he will become San Romero of America. Pope Francis will formally recognise Romero as a saint and martyr. ■

Julian Filochowski chairs the Archbishop Romero Trust, www.romerotrust.org.uk

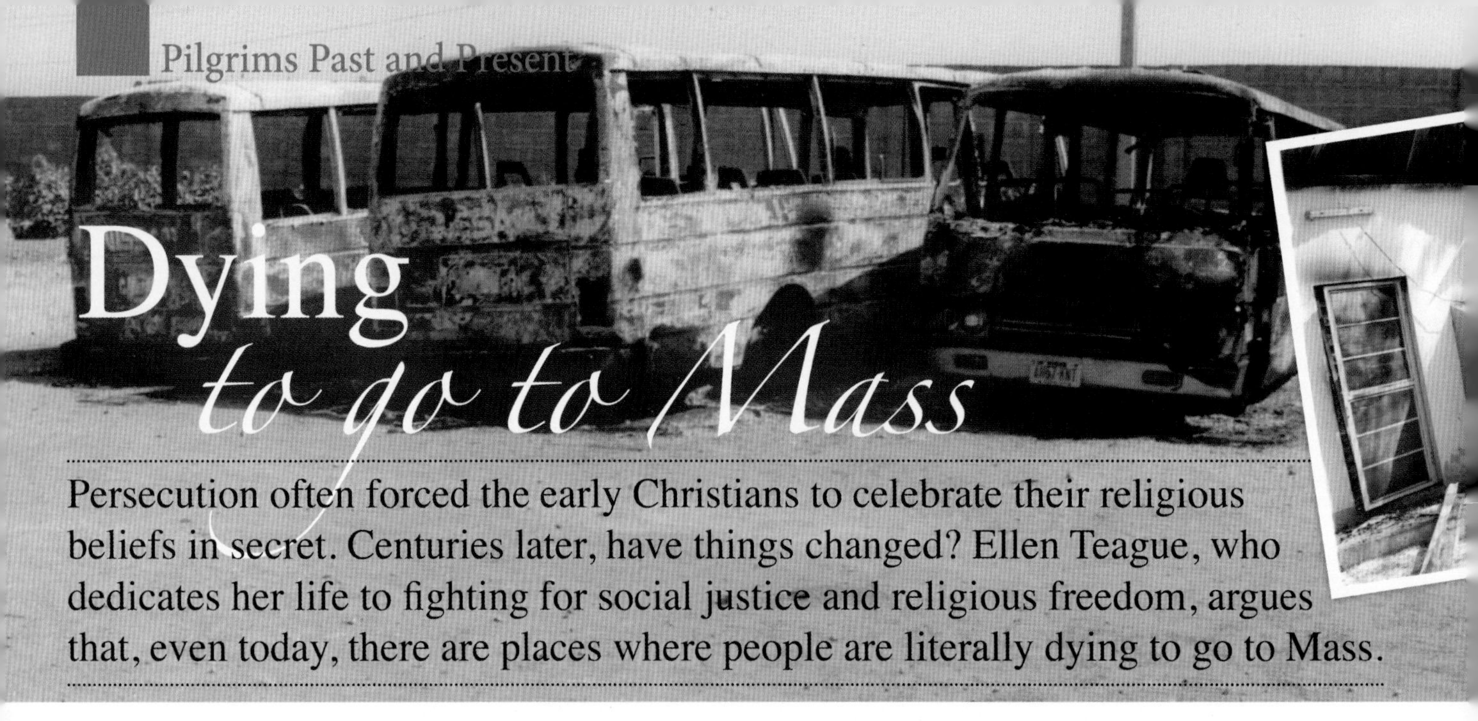

Dying *to go to Mass*

Persecution often forced the early Christians to celebrate their religious beliefs in secret. Centuries later, have things changed? Ellen Teague, who dedicates her life to fighting for social justice and religious freedom, argues that, even today, there are places where people are literally dying to go to Mass.

Did you know that for a century and a half after the Reformation, Mass could only be celebrated in Liverpool in secret? When Liverpool Jesuits built a chapel in 1736, it was demolished by an anti-Catholic mob two years later, but rebuilt in 1739 disguised as a warehouse.

Where today do people risk everything to attend Mass?

Killings and imprisonment in Africa

In Somalia, the militant Islamist group al-Shabaab wants "Somalia free of Christians". At least twelve Christians were killed in 2016. The only Catholic Church in Somaliland, which reopened after a three-decade closure in July 2017, was closed again a week later. Somaliland's government had permitted the reopening of St Anthony of Padua Church in Hargeisa for its small congregation, but complaints from Muslims persuaded them to overturn the ruling.

More than three hundred Christians are believed to be languishing in Eritrean jails and at least one hundred and thirty thousand have fled to neighbouring Ethiopia. One refugee there reported that, "in Eritrea almost every Christian faces imprisonment". In jail, he was forced to sleep with his hands and feet tied behind his back. Some prisoners were hung from trees, known as the "Jesus Christ".

Egypt's Coptic Church, as a minority religious group, is often called the Church of Martyrs. The Coptic Orthodox Church and Coptic Catholic Church have seen more than forty terror attacks since 2013. A 2011 New Year's Eve bombing of the Two Saints Church in Alexandria killed twenty-one people. In December 2016, at least twenty-five died in a bomb blast during a service at St Mark's Orthodox Cathedral in Cairo as the congregation received Communion.

In the Diocese of Maiduguri in northern Nigeria, militant Islamists Boko Haram have destroyed more than two hundred churches and Mass stations.

Persecution in Asia

Vietnamese Catholics are very proud of their martyrs, canonised in 1988, and Cardinal Nguyễn Văn Thuận, who was imprisoned by the Communist regime from 1975-1988.

Intimidation continues today. In June 2017, youths on motorbikes terrorised a Catholic community in northeast Vietnam, seriously injuring two people. "The police are ignoring what is going on," said eleven priests in a petition to the Vietnamese government, accusing it of "aiding and abetting those who cause hatred and divide Catholics from others." That same month, clergy at a monastery in a central province were viciously beaten by plain clothes police over a land dispute. Dozens of attackers pulled down a cross and a statue of Jesus.

Cardinal Nguyễn Văn Thuận © UCANews

In Pakistan, abuses of the country's blasphemy laws by militant Muslim groups are some of the starkest examples of persecution of Christians. Vigilantes and mobs have killed nearly seventy people over alleged blasphemy since 1990. In 2011 Pakistan's Catholic minister, Shahbaz Bhatti, was assassinated after pushing for reform, saying his faith gave him strength to challenge the laws. In March 2015 two bombs killed at least fourteen people near two churches in a Christian neighbourhood of Lahore.

North Korea has incarcerated tens of thousands of Christians in harsh labour camps, while others must pray secretly.

Sometimes people literally risk their lives to celebrate the Eucharist – which we can so easily take for granted. ■

Support organisations for persecuted Christians include Aid to the Church in Need (www.acnuk.org) and Open Doors (www.opendoorsuk.org).

Ellen Teague is a London-based freelance Catholic journalist who writes and campaigns on justice, peace and ecology issues.

Nigerian mission house and church destroyed by Boko Haram/Photos © Society of African Missions (SMA)

I will live the present moment to the fullest.

I will discern between God and God's works.

I will hold firmly to one secret: prayer.

I will see in the Holy Eucharist my only power.

I will have only one wisdom: the science of the cross.

I will remain faithful to my mission in the Church and for the Church as a witness of Jesus Christ.

I will seek the peace the world cannot give.

I will carry out a revolution by renewal in the Holy Spirit.

I will speak one language and wear one uniform: charity.

I will have one very special love: the Blessed Virgin Mary.

Cardinal Nguyễn Văn Thuận

To give and not to count the cost

Military training and experience teaches leadership and commitment in a way that helps people to give and to keep on giving to the local church. Dame Mary Richardson suggests that this service continues after discharge.

In the opening to his beautiful poem "The Soldier", Fr Gerard Manley Hopkins poses a question:

> Why do we all, seeing of a soldier, bless him? Bless
> Our redcoats, our tars? Both these being the greater part
> But frail clay.

Gerard Manley Hopkins was a priest serving in the parish of St Francis Xavier, Liverpool, from 1889-1891 and is commemorated by a plaque. The great-grandfather of Jimmy McGovern, author of the much acclaimed BBC series *Broken*, received Holy Communion from Fr Hopkins. McGovern, who attended St Francis Xavier School, poses a similar dilemma in *Broken,* which is filmed in that church. The church website tells us that Jimmy McGovern, explaining the title, says, "It's about broken humanity, the idea that you're at your strongest when you're at your weakest."

He has a strong Eucharistic interpretation of what that means, referring to the "solidarity and strength" which binds a community of broken people together when they take Holy Communion. "It's all about the Eucharist."

We bless and admire those who are but frail clay, says Fr Hopkins. We are at our strongest when we are at our weakest, says Jimmy McGovern. How can we reconcile these seeming and profound contradictions?

As the centenary remembrances for those tragedies of World War I come and pass, we pause for all too short a time to honour shockingly young men who gave their all. Around us at such memorial services are other young uniformed men and women with more medals than it seems possible to have earned in such young lives, marks of courage, willingness, eagerness to serve, and signs of experiences which they share but which we cannot imagine. Where did and does such moral fortitude, such spontaneous and generous giving, without stopping to count the cost, come from?

Fr Gerard Manley Hopkins says that they are nought but frail clay - or worse, foul clay - like the rest of us, open to temptation, full of the flaws which mark us as human. This is not an insult to those soldiers and sailors he saw and we see: he is honouring them beyond mere compliment. They were and are ordinary, frail and despite that set standards of ultimate heroism, never to be forgotten, but to be continually followed by new generations of servicemen and -women. That's what makes them special and makes us bless them whenever we see them, this body of men, the Pals Brigade, the regiment with fathers and sons together: this extraordinary kindred of ordinary men and women.

In the same way, Jimmy McGovern also sees the people of his imaginary parish as broken people surviving, triumphing because they too are bound by a community, by a communion of people, by the body of the Church, the Body of Christ.

Much is made today of alienation, exclusion, mental health problems and a lack of social mobility. Some young people have lost hope in their own future. Often isolated, they turn to virtual and dangerous communities for companionship and support.

Research shows that a child needs a community of values with a significant adult in order to become fully human and fully alive. This is true of a loving family, a living church, a good Catholic school or the lives of servicemen and -women. Or a gang or worse.

When I decided to join the regular army my friend decided about the same time to become a nun. She laughed when I said that the two ways of life had much in common.

It is their values which distinguish strong communities and these values seep into the young person's psyche, whole personality, by some silent and unstoppable osmosis. Those values are probably there for ever and guide attitude and patterns of behaviour.

The community and values of service life, a life of service to others, bring formation leading to integrity, moral courage, loyalty and a nobility of selflessness. Leaders are there to serve those in their care. There can be no place for excessive individualism; and the common good, the good of your friends, platoon, regiment and your military family is equally your own good.

In a gang one also has community, belonging, the wrong values and the wrong significant adult, all of which form bonds difficult to break.

I am a Liverpool woman. I was there through the Blitz and was evacuated. I went to Liverpool University and lived in the beautiful Notre Dame houses for women students in Aigburth. My cousins are in Liverpool. My father is commemorated on the Liverpool Naval Memorial on the Pier Head. My roots are deep.

But it is through Liverpool's own regiment, The King's, that I claim my Scouser pedigree.

My earliest memories are of my grandfather's stories. He, like his brothers and their father and grandfather, had joined, and some died, with The King's Liverpool. When I went up to university there was no doubt about what I wanted to do and I told my grandfather that I wanted to be an officer in The King's. He looked at me dubiously, considering my air-brain approach to life. "You have to be a bit special to be an officer", he said very doubtfully.

And he wept with pride when I went home at twenty years old, with my single pip on my shoulder. It was the most wonderful moment of my life. Nothing has ever approached that since.

Looking back on my life, I see that I have moved unconsciously from one form of service to another. So many ex-regulars I meet are leading and serving, often working with young people, perhaps cadets, teaching values, showing them how to learn from failure rather than to fear it, encouraging, developing, opening doors of opportunity to better lives. Serving the next generation. Journeying with them, in quiet communion. Living shared values.

At the end of "The Soldier", Fr Gerard Manley Hopkins has one, amazing thing to say about our redcoats and/or tars which are "but frail clay" or worse:

"'Were I come o'er again' cries Christ 'it would be this.'" ■

The King's Liverpool Regiment, 1891. Image/ Wikimedia commons.

Images / Left page: C Company of the 6th (Rifle) Battalion, The King's Regiment (Liverpool) at Kinmel Park, near Rhyl, Wales. Dated July 1931.

Right page: Bomb damage caused by the Liverpool Blitz, circa 1942. Imperial War Museums / wikimediacommons

Dame Mary Richardson is the President of SOS Children's Villages UK, https://www.soschildrensvillages.org.uk

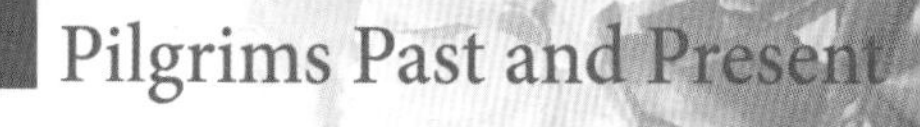

A witness in the workplace

People are bigger than their jobs. Jane Middleton describes the unforgettable witness of her aunt and uncle.

Once upon a time – because all good stories are meant to start that way – except that I think I was aged nine or ten at the time, I accompanied my mother on her weekly shopping expedition. As usual, I probably chose the most impractical and inconvenient moment to tell her that I needed to go to the toilet. This particular day was different, however, because when we eventually found its discreetly inconvenient location, to our surprise, the attendant was my beloved Auntie Betsy. She was equally astonished to see us.

From my earliest days I had worshipped the ground on which Auntie Betsy walked. I could never tire of her all-embracing bear hugs and the heart which was bigger than her (somewhat overweight) self. I didn't care where I found her: I just loved her and knew it was mutual.

It was only many years later that it occurred to me that both she and my mother might have felt a bit awkward when we found her guarding the entrance to the public toilets. "Don't forget to put your money in the slot", she called out to a woman who was attempting to gain free admission. "Do you want me to lose my job?" I feel sad that those are the last words I remember hearing Auntie Betsy say.

Let me tell you a bit about her. She was the eldest daughter in a family of eleven children, living in a tiny inner city "two-up-two-down-back-to-back". Three children died at birth or shortly afterwards during the pre-NHS, pre-antibiotic days when child mortality was still quite high. (Even when I was a child, there was a local polio epidemic in which the brother of one of my classmates was the first child to die.)

As if life were not hard enough for Auntie Betsy and the rest of the family, her younger brother joined the RAF and was killed during the war. Her father, my grandfather, had a heart attack and died on hearing the news of his son's death… but that's moving ahead too fast.

Auntie Betsy was highly intelligent, but those were the days when the eldest daughter in a big family had few options in life. She left school in her early teens so that she could help my grandmother to look after the house and her younger brothers and sisters. As a result, hers was the responsibility to hold things together during the ups and downs of family life between WWI and WWII.

I don't know at what stage Auntie Betsy found a job and started to bring in some money. Was it when she married Uncle Peter? Now if Auntie Betsy was one of my earliest pin-ups, she and Uncle Peter were nothing short of perfection. True, I don't think he went to church between the weddings, christenings and funerals, but God would be hard-pushed to find a couple who were more generous, gentle, loving and welcoming. (The word "gentle" didn't entirely fit Uncle Peter when he

listened to a football match on the wireless and his team was playing.)

Uncle Peter only had to look at a seed for it to start growing. He converted their tiny backyard into a garden by creating a wooden trough and filling it with rose bushes. How big was the yard? Would I be exaggerating to suggest that it might have been about twenty-four square metres? The yard also included an outside toilet because many inner city houses did not have the luxury of an indoor bathroom, yet, for a small child, the overriding experience was of roses, roses and more roses.

Uncle Peter worked in the construction industry. I think he was a "brickie", but I never thought to ask about his job. Any time together was too precious: he was a born listener and storyteller. What more could a child want – apart from his glorious smile, which I can still remember today, decades after his death.

Auntie Betsy took a job in a nearby factory: life had not equipped her for any dizzying heights of achievement. Rain or shine, she smiled. However boring her job, she did it. Every Sunday, there she was at Mass, gradually becoming large enough to take up more than one seat. Every Sunday, she would briefly visit us on her way home to cook the dinner. She was no theologian, but she was a dyed-in-the-wool Catholic whose spontaneous words of wisdom had lovingly encouraged far more people than she would ever know.

I didn't see her for a while, until that Saturday afternoon when my mother and I met her as the guardian angel of the public loos. Funnily enough, I've never said anything to my immediate or my extended family about the occasion. Why have I kept quiet? Perhaps because Auntie Betsy was such a wonderful person that I want everyone to remember her as the laughing, loving woman who emerged from the church on a Sunday morning, her hands and pockets full of sweets for her growing number of nephews and nieces.

So what have Auntie Betsy and Uncle Peter got to do with the Eucharistic Congress? She would have loved it and he would have found every possible excuse for avoiding anything to do with it – except, perhaps, to enjoy a visit to the Echo Arena...

I have a feeling that, if Jesus were to be on duty at the Echo Arena, he would have been the first to welcome Auntie Betsy and Uncle Peter as VIPs ahead of anybody else. You see, the Congress is about the Eucharist and about love.

Wherever they worked, whatever they did, Auntie Betsy and Uncle Peter spread love and loveliness. They didn't do anything spectacular – but they loved spectacularly.

Everybody should have an Auntie Betsy and Uncle Peter. Pope Francis would have been crazy about them. If nothing else, they showed that a person should not only be seen in relation to their employment (or lack of). People are bigger than their jobs.

The poet and philosopher Rabindranath Tagore, wrote that "work is love made visible". There's a huge amount of work involved in the Eucharistic Congress. All kinds of "everyone" will have contributed in big and not so big ways. The Congress is about making love visible – just as Auntie Betsy and Uncle Peter did all those years ago. ■

Jane Middleton is a freelance Catholic writer and former midwife.

Meeting Jesus *through drama*

Never underestimate the power of live drama to spread the Good News. Martin O'Brien describes how Ten Ten Theatre's performances of *The Runcorn Passion* were a genuinely powerful community experience.

Jesus placed storytelling at the heart of his ministry as he told parables to speak to the hearts and minds of those who followed him. In a similar way, Ten Ten uses drama, story, theatre and film to speak to hearts and minds and inspire people to "live life to the full". This was no more in evidence than the time we ran a special community project in 2013 in a town just outside of Liverpool…

The Runcorn Passion was a community Passion play performed by the people of Runcorn and Frodsham in the northwest of England, with the final performance taking place in the town's main shopping centre on Holy Saturday. An astonishing two hundred and fifty people from the local community signed up to take part. There were parishioners from the various local Catholic churches, children from primary schools, students from secondary schools, and many from other Christian denominations and communities taking part; the youngest was four, the eldest over eighty.

Runcorn is my hometown, so this project was very personal to me and my family, who run Ten Ten with me. It is a town which has suffered from the sharp bite of recession and austerity over the years. Moreover, the structures which support the Catholic faith have been slowly eroded due to a severe shortage of priests and the closing down and amalgamation of parishes. So *The Runcorn Passion* presented a unique opportunity for the Church community to come together, find strength in numbers and proclaim what they believe to the wider community.

The basis of our passion play was "Born For This", the beautiful reflection on the stations of the cross in words, music and action written by Jo Boyce from CJM Music. Rehearsals took place over a six-week period. Each gathering would begin with a time of prayer and reflection on the Passion of Our Lord, followed by an intense but fun session of rehearsals led by professional actors and musicians from Ten Ten. For this, the participants signed up to various groups: choir, the band, soloists, actors, dancers, readers, prayer leaders, stage managers, marketers, set builders and stewards to name but a few. There was a job for everyone, irrespective of experience, interests or skills, and many took on more than one role.

It was a true community project in every sense of the word. At weekends, participants trawled the streets to display posters in shop windows and hand-deliver flyers about the event to letterboxes throughout Runcorn and Frodsham; the first print run of ten thousand were dispatched within four days and so a further ten thousand were ordered and quickly delivered. Children in primary schools worked hard learning songs and sign language as part of their contribution. The community manipulated every press opportunity available to them, and as a result the event was featured in many local newspapers as well as given a prime spot on the local BBC radio station. One well-known disc jockey, who lives in Runcorn, was assailed with dozens of emails and calls from local people asking if he could help!

It became evident quite early on that many of the people taking part were deeply touched by reflecting on Christ's Passion in this way. Each week, we invited participants to write responses to various prompt questions, which proved humble reading;

Ten:Ten

Life to the full

Photos/Rosie Allt
The Runcorn Passion
www.tententheatre.co.uk

Ten:Ten

Life to the full

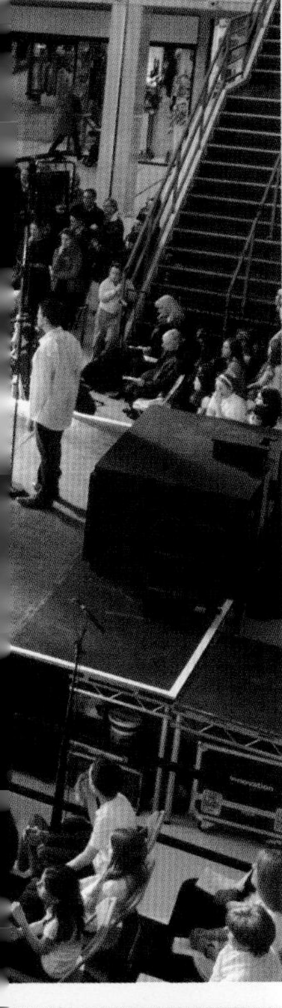

the overwhelming response to the question of "what does faith means to you?" was simply "everything".

As the final performance at Halton Lea Shopping Centre approached, so did a growing conviction amongst the participants that they wanted to proclaim their faith to their neighbours, their colleagues, their friends. There was also, naturally, a reticence. In particular, there was a concern that the shopping centre would attract those who would vocalise their opposition, or teenagers hanging out at the centre who could disrupt and undermine the event. However, people prayed. They prayed for their own courage, and they prayed that their witness to Christ would touch the hardest-to-reach people.

A week before the event itself, the project was thrown into jeopardy. As the entire company of two hundred and fifty were about to come together for the one-and-only chance to put all of the elements of the production together, starting with a Mass celebrated by Bishop Mark Davies, the town of Runcorn was buried underneath a rush of snow. Many roads were shut. The school where rehearsals were due to take place had closed down. The pathway to the hall was lethally icy. We thought that was the end of it. Without a dress rehearsal, the performance would simply not be ready.

Then, shortly before 9am on that cold, snowy, dazzlingly white Saturday morning, the first of the participants turned up at the rehearsal venue with a shovel. Then the next one arrived. Then the next. By 9.30am there were dozens of us clearing the snow from the car park. By 10am, half of the participants had turned up and were able to get into the rehearsal venue. By 10.30am, all but a handful had been able to make it, with some trekking miles across town through the snow to get there. The faithful, Spirit-led determination of the community was remarkable.

On Good Friday evening, men from the local community erected a huge stage and PA system in the centre of the shopping centre. Many of these men had not wanted to take part in the performance itself but were willing and eager to help in other practical ways. As they worked, they shared. I was privy to one particular conversation between two family men about their kids and the challenges of bringing them up within the Church, a conversation which would not have happened if they had not been working together on a project of this nature.

Over one thousand people turned up to watch *The Runcorn Passion* on Holy Saturday across two performances. Many more shoppers stopped and watched, some for a short time, some for the entire hour-long presentation. I remember very clearly the face of one woman – a shopper not connected to anyone in the cast – who looked slightly bedraggled and world-weary and yet was utterly transfixed by what she was watching with tears welling up in her eyes. A teenage girl watching the performance was heard to say, "I'm crying but I don't I don't know why."

There were one or two moments of disruption when, for example, a drunken man made disparaging comments, and a group of teenagers shouted from a distance, but these were drowned out by moments of utter silence and stillness, creating an extraordinary feeling of reverence and prayer on a busy weekend for shoppers. It was a true witness of faith in a very public sphere.

One participant wrote to us afterwards to say that she prayed to the Holy Spirit that her husband would turn up to watch *The Runcorn Passion* because he never steps foot in a church. He did, and was deeply moved.

Another woman, not usually one for religious expression, told us that a couple of days after the event, she found herself praying publicly and openly for a stranger who was in need of healing. We heard story after story of how people were affected by the experience, and how faith was shared and grew in so many ways.

We made a twenty-minute documentary which was filmed during the making of *The Runcorn Passion*. On film, the people reflected on what they had told us about what their faith means to them and it was very powerful. One participant said: "I've been touched by the faith of others. I really admire this in people and it helps me as a questioning, sometimes wavering and often cynical Catholic to be more grounded in what is at the core of our faith."

In *Evangelii Gaudium*, Pope Francis talks about pastoral ministry at a local level. He says, "I invite everyone to be bold and creative in this task of rethinking the goals, structures, style and methods of evangelisation in their respective communities." The people of Runcorn and Frodsham achieved precisely this.

For *The Runcorn Passion* proved that, despite the hardship, faith is still strong within these communities. Through faith, the ordinary become extraordinary, the spiritual meets the practical, the lost are found and the person of Jesus Christ becomes tangible, real and very much alive. ■

Martin O'Brien is the Artistic Director of Ten Ten Theatre.

Reconciliation

Never *more needed* than today

Dr Bridie Stringer points out that the outcast woman, forgiven her sins, saw what the authorities missed: that they were in the presence of God.

There is an old Irish joke in which a tourist asks for directions to Dublin, only to be told: "Well sir, if I were you, I wouldn't start from here." So where is the best place to start a reflection on the sacrament of reconciliation? Some might suggest the *Catechism of the Catholic Church*, where it is described as a "sacrament of penance and reconciliation". However, the emphasis on "straying into sin" and the necessity for disclosure or confession to a priest as an essential element of the sacrament might result in the penitential "tourist" heading for the hills rather than Dublin's fair city. So I will not start from there.

A small minority might start the journey in the pages of the Code of Canon Law and the rules about who should avail of the sacrament and when they must do so. But again, this might be perceived as legalistic and rather like a transaction – "If I do this, God will do that."

Others might start with the creation story of Genesis 3 and the fall from grace which bequeathed a sad legacy to us all because Eve encountered a very scheming reptile.

While each of these has its own merits, I choose as my starting point the dust of first-century Jerusalem.

According to the Gospel of John 8:1-11, a group of self-righteous religious officials decide to kill two birds with one stone, or more accurately, several stones. They want to execute an adulterous woman and, at the same time, publicly disgrace an iterant backwoods preacher who is beginning to gain popularity with ordinary people and possibly threaten the Temple status quo.

Jesus, of course, simply writes on the ground before delivering his killer one-liner: "Let anyone among you who is without sin be the first to throw a stone at her." He resumes writing in the dust and then asks the woman: "Woman, where are they? Has no one condemned you?" She says: "No one, sir" and Jesus responds with one of the most beautiful and merciful sentences of the Gospels: "Go your way, and from now on do not sin again."

We do not know what he wrote on the ground. Some suggest that he was listing the faults of those who had set out to entrap him and that this disclosure had caused them to slowly slink away. There is also some dispute over this story and some manuscripts of the Gospel of John do not include it, but, as one eminent contemporary scripture scholar puts it: "The story sounds like Jesus, has his unmistakable accents... and culminates in the beautiful dialogue in which the woman is no longer treated as bait, but as a human being, invited to speak for herself and regarded by Jesus as a responsible adult."[1]

Interestingly, in some translations, the scribes and Pharisees call Jesus "teacher" or "master" while the woman calls him "Lord". The outcast from the margins has recognised what those in authority have missed.

This account of course is very critical of the religious authorities and it is not my intention to draw comparisons with our Church leaders. I think, though, that it is helpful to examine the role of the priest as the official reconciler within the Church.

The priest does not himself forgive sin but rather pronounces forgiveness in the name of Jesus and welcomes the person who sits or kneels before him back into the community from which they feel excluded. This does not mean they have been ostracised by others but that they, themselves, feel in their hearts that they are not fully alive within the Church community.

The sacrament of reconciliation, undertaken either as one-to-one confession with the priest, or as one-to-one confession within a communal reconciliation service is a ritual which speaks to that part of us which responds to sign, symbol and metaphor.

To give some other examples, a graduation is an event which confirms, in a joyful solemn ceremony, the achievement of the new graduates. They already know they have passed their exams but the ceremony is a public, symbolic act which testifies to their achievement, the sacrifices they have made, and is also an opportunity for their friends and relatives to show they are proud of them.

A Military Salute for the Farewell Parade.
Martin Gillman / shutterstock.com

A military passing out parade does a similar thing. It is a formal, structured, publicly recognised acknowledgement that an important milestone has been reached.

In a way, we are hard-wired for ritual. Through ritual we have affirmation and confirmation by authorised third parties, such as the university vice chancellor and the military commanding officer, that an important event has occurred.

So how does this relate to the sacrament of reconciliation? I would suggest that the moment we acknowledge to the Lord that we are sorry and wish to be reconciled, we are forgiven. Our visit to the confessional or the reconciliation service is the public recognition of this and the words of absolution spoken by the priest (the authorised third party), in the place of Jesus, affirm this on behalf of the local community and the universal Church. It is not an exercise in humiliation, but confirmation to us that we are truly loved and forgiven.

Pope Francis assures us that no one is excluded from the joy brought by the Lord[2] and he reminds priests that the confessional must not be a torture chamber, but instead an encounter with the Lord's mercy which spurs us on to do our best.[3] He has called the Church a field hospital, echoing the response of Jesus in Luke 5:32 to those who criticised his followers for eating and drinking with outcasts: "The healthy have no need of a doctor – no, it's those who are ill."

A further Gospel reminder of wholeness and being sacramentally reconciled to the Church community comes from Luke's Gospel and the curing of the man with leprosy in 5:12-16. In this story, he asks for healing and does the unthinkable – he stretches out his hand to Jesus and touches him saying: "Lord, if you choose, you can make me clean." Jesus heals him and commands him to tell nobody but to go and show himself to the priest, as prescribed by the Law of Moses.

This visit to the priest would have been the equivalent of going to the public health inspector to be reassured that there was no longer any risk of infection and that the cured man could resume his life with his family and community. He was already cured when he arrived with the priest.

So, for those of us who feel fear or anxiety about presenting ourselves before the priest in the confessional, perhaps we should remember that, unlike the tourist asking for directions, our journey to the Lord starts from where we are. God is with us as we travel and it is not where we begin that matters, but where we end.

In bringing this reflection to a close and to keep with the journey metaphor a little longer, the modern traveller, on arrival at the airport, checks in the baggage and feels relieved when this has been achieved. If they are anything like me, at this point they normally heave a sigh of relief and think of having something good to eat as they anticipate the next phase of their trip.

As a faith community, we do exactly the same. Having checked in the luggage – the things which have hitherto been weighing us down – we know that, for this particular journey, we do not have to collect this baggage again. It has been totally taken care of – gone for good. We now feel that we can joyfully proceed to the Lord's table to partake of the food God offers us. We do not have to be perfect to approach the table: we just have to be there.

As Pope Francis reminds us: "The Eucharist, although it is the fullness of sacramental life, is not a prize for the perfect but a powerful medicine and nourishment for the weak".[4]

We remember too, from Mark's Gospel 6: 31 that Jesus invited his closest followers to go with him into a quiet place to rest awhile because they did not even have time to eat. After they had done so, the crowd still showed up and Jesus fed them all.

Perhaps Liverpool's Adoremus will offer the opportunity to do likewise – to check in the baggage of our sorrows and our failings, to go into a quiet place to rest and reflect and, finally, to joyfully consume the Lord's gift of himself in the Eucharist, so that we can continue the most important journey of life in its fullness to the Father's house. ■

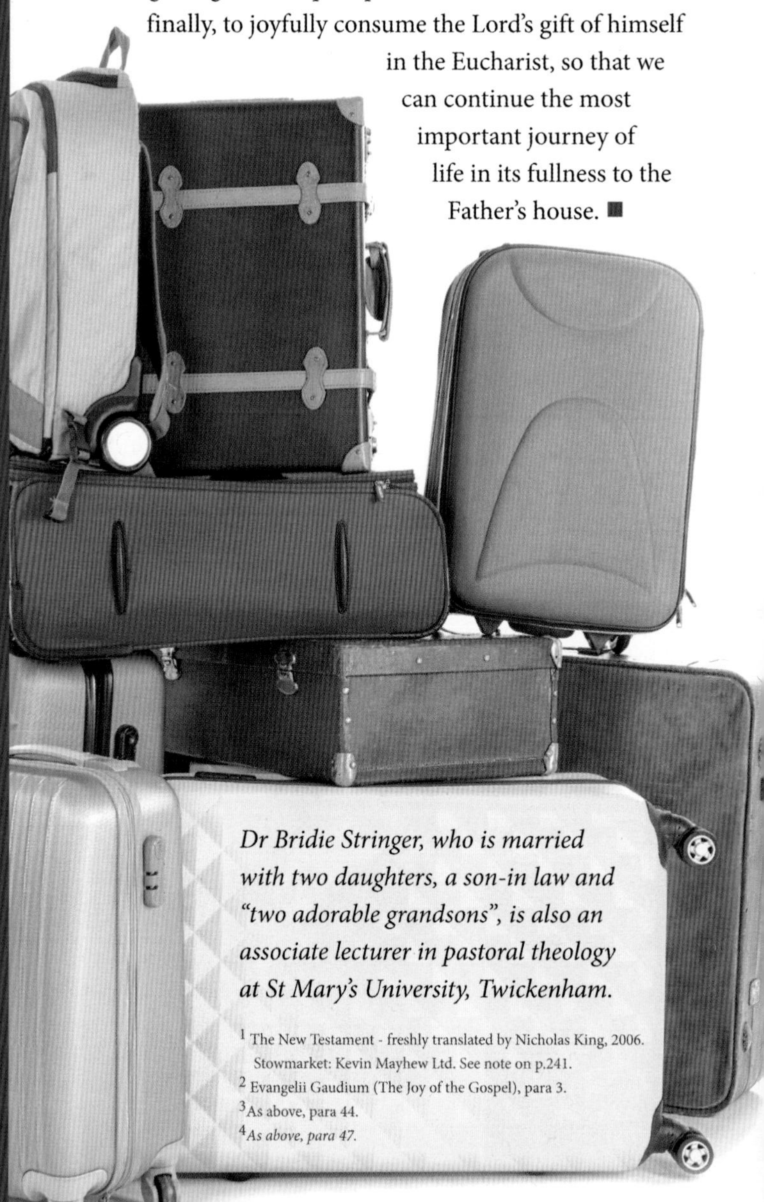

Dr Bridie Stringer, who is married with two daughters, a son-in law and "two adorable grandsons", is also an associate lecturer in pastoral theology at St Mary's University, Twickenham.

[1] The New Testament - freshly translated by Nicholas King, 2006. Stowmarket: Kevin Mayhew Ltd. See note on p.241.
[2] Evangelii Gaudium (The Joy of the Gospel), para 3.
[3] As above, para 44.
[4] *As above, para 47.*

A text message prompts an *act of faith*

If you thought you had only half an hour to live, how would you spend that time? Would the sacraments be YOUR top priority? Some people in Hawaii unexpectedly found themselves with that choice.

We've all done it: push the wrong button and something that should not happen happens. Most times, it doesn't make for disastrous consequences: we accidentally switch off the fridge instead of heating the kettle. However, at 8.07am on 13 January 2018, as Hawaii's Governor David Ige later explained, "It was a mistake made during a standard procedure at the changeover of a shift and an employee pushed the wrong button."

Whatever the cause, an emergency alert went to Hawaii's residents, warning them of an incoming ballistic missile. "Everyone knows you have about fifteen minutes until detonation", a Hawaii resident subsequently explained.

"Ballistic missile threat inbound to Hawaii. Seek immediate shelter. This is not a drill."

How would you have responded if you had unexpectedly received such a text message on your mobile phone? In all probability, you would have urgently sought shelter, every other plan for a Saturday morning shelved indefinitely in your anxiety to save your own life and your loved ones.

Not so in the St Stephen Diocesan Centre in Kaneohe, an island district of Honolulu. Fr Mark Gantley was distributing Holy Communion to about forty-five people in a deacon formation programme.

When Deacon John Coughlin, the programme director, interrupted to show him a text message, people realised that something unusually urgent must have happened. "The first thought that came to me was that I am going to finish Mass," Fr Gantley explained later. "I am not going to interrupt it."

To everybody's surprise, Bishop Larry Silva strode into the church, still dressed in his t-shirt, and announced that he was going to give everybody a general absolution, abandoning any liturgical formalities. As the *Hawaii Catholic Herald* later declared, "It was the first time he had ever performed the rite – the absolution of sins given to a group of people at one time allowed only in grave circumstances, such as situations of great danger or imminent death, or for soldiers going into battle, when private confessions are logistically impossible."

"I just thought, 'Let's get this thing done.' If there ever was an occasion that was it," he said. "It was scary." Bishop Silva gave a very brief explanation of his actions, asked everyone to pray and then gave absolution.

Although local sources described people in the congregation as "visibly upset", the sacrament of reconciliation had an "amazing" calming effect. Eva Andrade, one of the deacon formation staff, called the absolution "the most powerful reconciliation ever. It was deeper, richer... In that moment when you really don't know [if you are going to die], your heart reaches out for that forgiveness." She added, "In that moment everything changed and was made right. You could feel the presence of God in that room."

Thirty-eight minutes after the false alarm, the Hawaii Emergency Management Agency issued a second message, declaring that the first had been sent in error.

Yet someone's mistake also prompts an important question: if you thought you had only half an hour to live, how would you spend that time? Would the sacraments be YOUR top priority? ■

Forgiveness in spite of everything

To renowned screenwriter Frank Cottrell-Boyce, "Forgiveness is always a surprise ending."

Anton Chekhov famously said that if the audience sees a pistol hanging from the wall in Act One, it has to be fired in Act Three. It's one of the first and most important lessons you learn as a writer. Stories need endings just as chords need to be resolved. The murder is avenged. The mystery is solved. Love is requited, or tragically unrequited.

In 1969 in Glasgow, James Nelson murdered his own mother. What's the proper ending for that story? A life spent in jail haunted by her ghost? In fact Nelson served his time, studied theology and applied to be a minister in the Church of Scotland. He was not a spectacular penitent. He didn't give inspirational talks about his conversion or describe himself as the greatest of sinners. He simply challenged his Church to demonstrate its belief in the possibility of redemption.

The Church rose to the challenge. He found a parish. When, ten years later, the press tried to rake up and sensationalise the story, his parishioners wrote letters of support to the papers.

Of course a Church recognising that a sinner can repent and believe in the Gospel is not the same as a victim – or the parent of a victim – forgiving someone who has sinned against them personally.

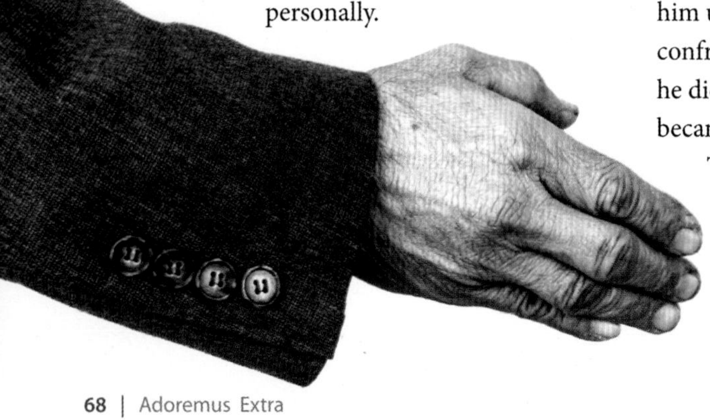

This Eucharistic Congress is taking place in Liverpool – a city that is still haunted by the murder of one child – Jamie Bulger – by two others. The continuing pain of that story disturbs our senses and seems to have no ending.

And just as the unresolved chord jars your brain, so the lack of a satisfactory ending produces rage. If you look at social media, you get the sense that, for many people, the only real ending would be a death sentence for the killers. Certainly the opposite ending – forgiveness – seems too much to ask of the boy's parents. The title of his mother's autobiography – *I Let Him Go* – seems to suggest that she has not yet forgiven even herself for her own tiny part in his loss.

There are people who have forgiven in similar circumstances. In this same city, Anthony Walker's mother publicly forgave the boys who murdered her son in a racist attack not far from here, in Warrington.

There are tales of spiritual and moral heroism but more often forgiveness takes us by surprise.

I spent many years putting together a film about "the Railwayman" – Eric Lomax – who was tortured while a prisoner on the infamous Burma railway. That feeling that the story was not over left him unable to function emotionally until he had confronted his torturer – Takashi Nagase. When he did so, all his rage fell away and he and Nagase became friends.

That's the story as I told it.

Once the film came out, however, I became friends with Eric's daughter, Charmaine, and discovered that to her, the sentence I'd so blandly said so often in pitch meetings and auditions. "He was unable to function

The comeback of Prodigal son scene by Josef Kastner in Erloserkirche church, Vienna, Austria. Renata Sedmakova / Shutterstock.com

emotionally," – meant years of living with a chaotic, untrustworthy father who had, in turn, undermined her ability to form relationships.

Eric Lomax also needed to be forgiven.

The rule of Chekov's pistol really comes down to the fact that, morally and emotionally, actions have consequences. One thing leads to another. Thus the torturer reaches through his victim to torture the next generation.

We are bound by the chain of events – unless the chain can be broken. And by and large, it is broken not through moral effort, but through grace.

One of the other victims to whom I spoke while working on the film of *The Railway Man* was a Dutch prisoner who had successfully hunted down his torturer. When he finally confronted him, the torturer had a heart attack.

You might think that this was the perfect ending, but in fact his victim rushed to give him CPR and phone an ambulance. When the torturer's family turned up, the man was – much to his own surprise – sitting at their father's bedside, a hero – and he was trapped in this heroic scenario from then on.

I love this story. I love the way his own instinct to save kicked in and changed the ending. And where did that instinct come from?

In Newtonian physics, actions lead to reactions. But thanks to Einstein we know that though this appears to be the case in daily life on earth, it is not the whole story.

A well-turned story is one in which the pistol we saw in Act One is fired in Act Three – hopefully in a way that is both satisfying and surprising.

But there's another kind of story – far harder to tell – in which the gun does not go off.

Just as there's another view of the universe in which things are weightless and time is not a relentless tick-tock countdown to the grave.

At the end of "Gawain and the Green Knight", for instance, the Green Knight refuses to take his revenge on Gawain. And most extraordinary of all, at the end of the Prodigal Son, the father does not punish his son but – in a sentence that Ernest Hemingway said was the most beautiful ever written – runs to meet him.

It's worth remembering how unexpected that ending is.

The son was not looking for, or hoping for, forgiveness, but only for a job. The fatted calf, the cloak, the ring… now that's what you a twist in the tale.

Forgiveness is always a surprise ending – at least for the prodigal and for his better-behaved brother.

The father, though, was waiting, standing where he could see the figure approaching on the road. The father always knew that the story was not over, that a different kind of ending was coming, one in which the chains of consequence, time and gravity would be severed and he would run towards us. ■

Frank Cottrell-Boyce is a renowned screenwriter who counts God on Trial, The Railway Man *and* Goodbye Christopher Robin *amongst his screen successes.*

Eucharist and Mission

Eucharistic mission

Liverpool's city centre Blessed Sacrament Shrine is a precious space for many Liverpudlians, as Simon Hart explains.

"It is clear to everyone what a welcoming and attractive place has been created here for the worship of God, for meeting Christ in the sacraments and for experiencing friendship and rest."

These were the words of the Most Reverend Derek Worlock, the Archbishop of Liverpool, at the dedication of the Shrine of the Blessed Sacrament in Liverpool in November 1985. More than three decades later, the Shrine on Dawson Street continues to offer Catholics in the busy city centre a precious space for prayer and devotion amid the daily to and fro of their busy lives.

Run by the Blessed Sacrament congregation, the former furniture warehouse is a place where Catholics have access to three daily Masses, confession, and the Exposition of the

Blessed Sacrament, which takes place between Masses and up to 5.30pm each day.

In the basement below is St Joseph's Hall, which welcomes visitors for tea and coffee during the day and acts as a venue for meetings. Down the years the Shrine has hosted a wide range of events, from all-night vigils and scripture talks to a recent "Life in the Eucharist" programme. One evening a week, it welcomes the Cenacolo support group – set up for the families of children struggling with drug and alcohol addictions – for prayer in the chapel and a meeting.

The idea for a Blessed Sacrament foundation in Liverpool originated with an Australian priest, Father Thomas McNevin, who had seen the positive impact of a city centre church for shoppers and office workers back in Melbourne. The long search for a suitable location in Liverpool led eventually to an unlikely site: the Jacey sex cinema on Clayton Square. "Sex cinema to be chapel" declared the front page of the *Catholic Pictorial* when the news broke in June 1972. Five months later, on 21 November that year, it had its blessing and inauguration.

Brother Timothy McLoughlin was there in the early days at Clayton Square and remembers: "The shrine was a great success – on holy days there were lines outside waiting for Mass rather than queues for the cinema! On those days we used to open the circle, which still had the cinema seats, and send people up there." One of the notable features of a cinema, of course, is its sloping floor and it was not unusual to see newly purchased tomatoes and apples rolling out of shopping bags and down the aisle during Mass – and even the odd pram.

After the move to Dawson Street, the congregation celebrated twenty-five years of a city-centre presence in November 1997 with the then superior, Father Jim Duffy, saying, "It would be impossible to calculate how many people have been strengthened by the Shrine's presence in the city centre."

Today regular Mass-goers remain highly supportive, though the wish for Brother Timothy is that this year's Congress will provide a spur to "rediscover some of the energy and zeal" of those early days when the numbers for adoration were so much higher. ■

Simon Hart is the Editor of The Catholic Pic*, the Liverpool archdiocesan magazine.*

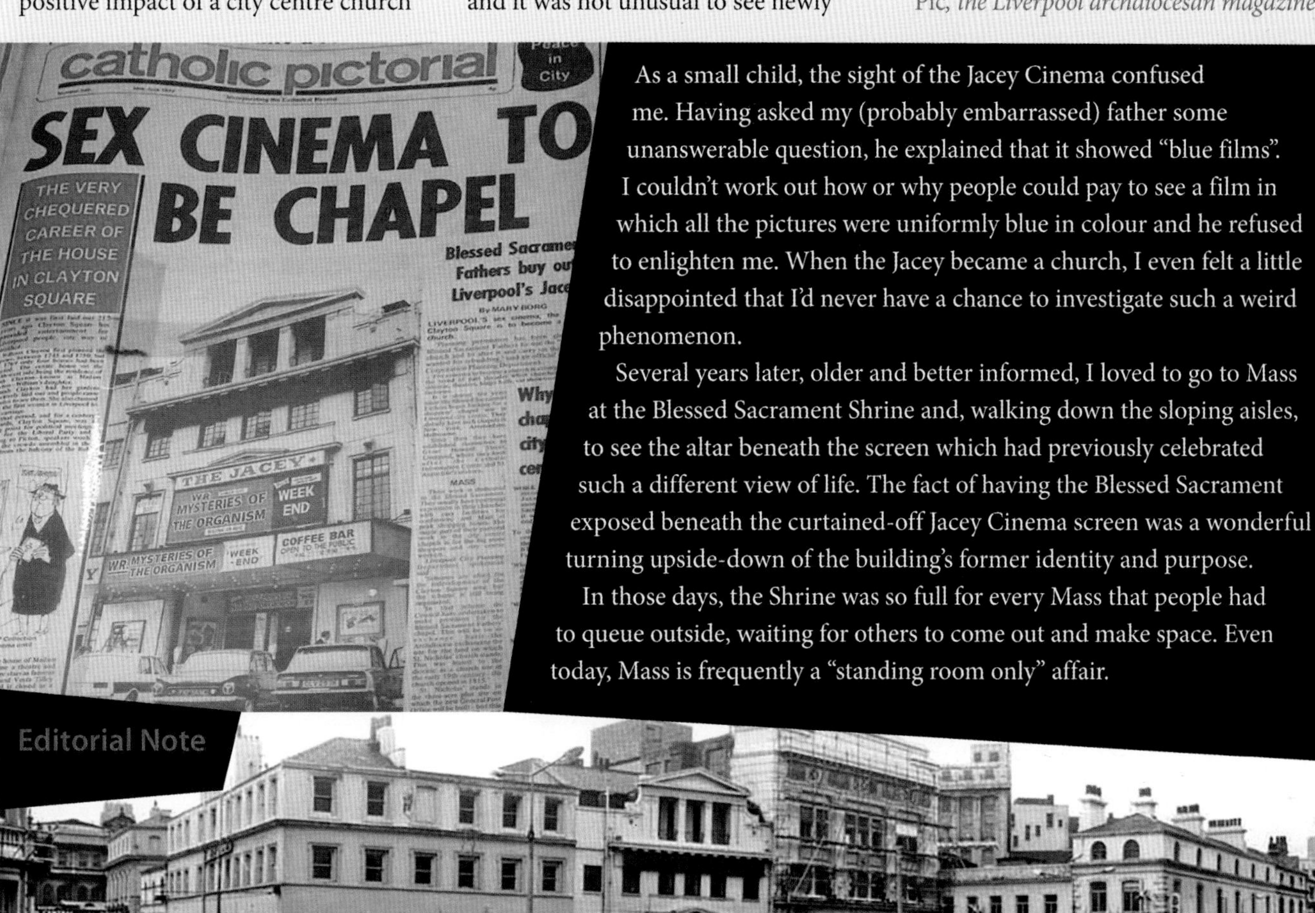

As a small child, the sight of the Jacey Cinema confused me. Having asked my (probably embarrassed) father some unanswerable question, he explained that it showed "blue films". I couldn't work out how or why people could pay to see a film in which all the pictures were uniformly blue in colour and he refused to enlighten me. When the Jacey became a church, I even felt a little disappointed that I'd never have a chance to investigate such a weird phenomenon.

Several years later, older and better informed, I loved to go to Mass at the Blessed Sacrament Shrine and, walking down the sloping aisles, to see the altar beneath the screen which had previously celebrated such a different view of life. The fact of having the Blessed Sacrament exposed beneath the curtained-off Jacey Cinema screen was a wonderful turning upside-down of the building's former identity and purpose.

In those days, the Shrine was so full for every Mass that people had to queue outside, waiting for others to come out and make space. Even today, Mass is frequently a "standing room only" affair.

Editorial Note

Image / Left page: www.blessedsacramentuki.org, Right: photo © Simon Hart, Right bottom: "Clayton Square"/www.streetsofliverpool.co.uk

Eucharist is mission

Fr Paul Mooney MHM spent many years working as a missionary in the Philippines. He recalls one very special occasion…

Photo © Fr Paul Mooney

Images © UCANews, 51st Internatinal Eucharistic Congress, Cebu, January 2016.

It was my privilege in January 2016 to participate in the fifty-first International Eucharistic Congress in Cebu City, Philippines. For one week, fifteen thousand participants from some seventy-three countries around the world gathered to focus their prayer and attention on God's greatest gift, the gift of himself to us in the Holy Eucharist, and to explore the implications of our participating in the Eucharist for our lives.

Cebu, the "birthplace" of Christianity in the Philippines, was the perfect setting for this festival of faith. Cebu is a city already familiar to me, since I had worked as a Mill Hill Missionary in the neighbouring city of Iloilo for many years. The whole city and its people rose to welcome us and work with us to make the Eucharistic Congress a beneficial experience and a blessing for all.

Each day, in the purpose-built conference centre, we prayed together, listened to faith testimonies and catechetical speeches from laymen and -women and senior members of the hierarchy of the Church. We laughed; we cried and shared our faith, as we grew in our appreciation of this wonderful gift of God, the Eucharist.

From the start it became apparent that the Eucharistic Congress was going to be a practical appreciation of how the celebration of the Eucharist and our participating in Holy Communion affects our daily lives. In other words, how this table-fellowship with God, receiving him into our lives, sets before us the mission to go and bear fruit, to take him to all whom we encounter each day in all circumstances, to evangelise the small part of the world we inhabit, to bring about the transformation of the earth for which Our Lord prayed.

As a priest, I have celebrated the Eucharist in many magnificent churches, in small self-constructed chapels, on the lakeside in Galilee, on hillsides, in fields and on seashores with the faithful.

The Last Supper continues to be celebrated continuously, and the entreaty remains the same as Our Lord shared with the apostles in that Upper Room before his passion; "Go!". We cannot restrict the Eucharist to a building or a tabernacle. The Eucharist, by its very nature, is given to be shared, to be offered practically.

The world pines for this Bread of Life, this altruistic gift of God. What a beautiful responsibility God has given us to share, to bear fruit that will last, and to transform the world! The task before us is to enter into dialogue with the world: our family, relatives, friends and neighbours and strangers; to offer, to listen, to respect, to learn, these are all essential aspects of the mission set before us; to resist the temptation to restrict God's grace only to ourselves or those who share our faith, and, instead, to reach out in his name with the assistance of the Holy Spirit to all. We are called to extend our care especially to the poor, the marginalised, the persecuted, the exploited, those who are denied justice, those denied the peace they deserve and that God wants for them, the stranger who feels beyond forgiveness and without hope, and those who promote secularism and a culture of death.

The Eucharist is our bread for life. The Eucharist will give us the spiritual sustenance we need to journey through life in accord with God's will and give expression to the faith we profess as we step forward to receive Our Lord in Holy Communion.

My responsibility is to make sure that the Eucharist I celebrate and the presence of the Lord whom I receive penetrates and positively transforms all aspects of my life; my attitudes, my behaviour, my words and deeds. My life must demonstrate what I believe and what I have received.

"Mission", in this regard, means that I must find effective and affective ways of sharing what I have received. It may be the helpful gesture I extend to someone in need, the smile I share, the kind word I express, the friendship I offer to friend and stranger alike, the humility to seek forgiveness and reconciliation from the one I have wronged, to practise less judgement and more tolerance; the possibilities are boundless! This is truly the "efficacy" of the Eucharist finding expression through me.

By virtue of my baptism, confirmation and the receiving of Our Blessed Lord in Holy Communion, I am, like the first disciples, compelled to "Give them something to eat." What a positive sign of contradiction such self-giving could become in our selfish society today! Such selfless love, empowered by the Holy Spirit, holds the potential of really changing the face of the earth.

Love alone will foster greater care and compassion and increased inter-dependence, satisfy the common thirst for the eternal and encourage collaboration in addressing the needs of the world; all beginning with myself responding to the cry of the poor. Here, I must avoid the temptation to focus on my unworthiness, my limitations, my faults, my failures and sin. Rather, Jesus urges me to rely on the affective grace that flows from him in the Eucharist.

If I am to be "salt to the earth and light to the world", then I must quell the anger that so prevails in the world today and replace it with respect, as I approach, reach out, assist, care for and dialogue with the world and its peoples. This is what Our Lord did before me. This is what he asks of me today. Only in the Eucharist will I find true meaning and lasting satisfaction. Even the tranquillity and peace I experience after receiving Holy Communion will fan the fire of faith into a flame, burning in my heart, excited, as the first disciples were, to share the good news that brings hope, love, peace, truth, justice, purpose, direction and life. Truly, in the Eucharist I become a new creation, fit for mission and ready to glorify God through my life. ■

Fr Paul Mooney describes himself as "A Gospel Traveller with the Mill Hill Missionaries, who has worked in Kenya, Pakistan and the Philippine Islands."

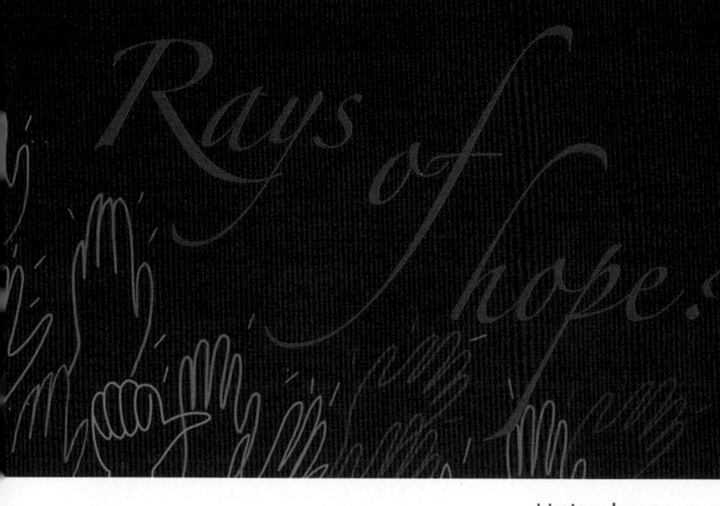

Receiving the Eucharist is not always straightforward, but there is hope, as Dr Helen Costigane, a theologian and Canon lawyer, points out as she reflects on some of these complex circumstances.

In the aftermath of the Second World War, many children, rescued from concentration camps, were traumatised by starvation and deprivation. Though finding themselves in new settings which were secure, offered healing, and where food was more readily available than they had previously experienced, their carers noticed the inability of these children to sleep at night. Realising that the children were anxious about whether they still might have food when they awoke the next day, the adults gave each of them a piece of bread to sleep with. This gave the children reassurance that, when they awoke, they could be sure of something to eat. It also became a pledge, a symbol, that they were safe and no longer alone.

On Holy Thursday, Jesus gave a similar assurance to us that he would not leave us bereft, gave us a tangible sign of his care and love, a sign that we would never be hungry, and that we would not be alone. He instituted the Eucharist as the memorial of his death and resurrection and commanded his apostles to celebrate it until his return. As the *Catechism of the Catholic Church* says, he did this "'In order to leave them a pledge of this love, in order never to depart from his own and to make them sharers in his Passover" (paragraph 1337).

There are, however, some commonly perceived difficulties with receiving the Eucharist, and this short article discusses two of these, while trying to see where there are "rays of hope" that can be detected.

United yet separated

The first of these difficulties arises, in terms of reception of the Eucharist, where a Christian marriage exists but one spouse is a Catholic and the other is a member of another Christian Church which is not in full communion with the Catholic Church.

Since the Church came into being there have been many divisions, the first major one being with the Orthodox Churches in 1054, and then followed by Protestant Churches (sometimes referred to as "Reformed") beginning in 1517. While all Christians share many beliefs – in Jesus Christ, baptism, the Bible as the word of God – major differences in beliefs still do exist, including the primacy of the Pope, the sacrificial priesthood and the nature of sacraments, including what the Eucharist is.

Protestant theology differs from Catholic theology in regard to the Eucharist over the real presence of Christ and transubstantiation. While much progress has been made since the Second Vatican Council, to discuss these differences with various Christian groups, such differences are held by the Catholic Church still to "break the common participation in the table of the Lord" (*Catechism of the Catholic Church*, paragraph 1398).

Notwithstanding this, there are some rays of hope. The 1983 Code of Canon Law makes provision (and an exception) for emergency cases. In terms of members of the Orthodox Churches, who primarily disagree with Catholics over the authority of the Pope, the Second Vatican Council's *Decree on Ecumenism* (1964) noted that, although they are separated from the Catholic Church, they "possess true sacraments, above all – by apostolic succession – the priesthood and the Eucharist" (paragraph 15).

This being the case, the 1983 *Code of Canon Law* stipulates that the sacraments of reconciliation, Eucharist, and anointing of the sick may be administered to members of the Orthodox Churches if they ask on their own for these sacraments and are properly disposed (Canon 844, No. 3).

Furthermore, the same canon notes that, in danger of death or other grave necessity and following a judgement made by the diocesan bishop or the Bishops' Conference, Catholic ministers may licitly administer the sacraments of reconciliation, Eucharist and anointing of the sick to other Christians "who cannot approach a minister of their own community and on their own ask for it, provided they manifest the Catholic faith in these sacraments and are properly disposed".

Much dialogue has taken place between Christian Churches over a number of years, and a further ray of hope may be detected in a joint declaration signed by Pope Francis and Lutheran bishop, Munib Younan, President of the Lutheran World Federation, on 31 October 2016. This acknowledged that:

Many members of our communities yearn to receive the Eucharist at one table, as the concrete expression of full unity. We experience the pain of those who share their whole lives, but cannot share God's redeeming presence at the Eucharistic table. We acknowledge our joint pastoral responsibility to respond to the spiritual thirst and hunger of our people to be one in Christ. We long for this wound in the Body of Christ to be healed. This is the goal of our ecumenical endeavours, which we wish to advance, also by renewing our commitment to theological dialogue.

Following this and in discussing this document, Cardinal Kurt Koch noted an important distinction. While the term "Eucharistic communion" refers to a more regular situation of the reception of Communion by people recognised as belonging to the same family and is problematic for the reasons already discussed, "Eucharistic hospitality", on the other hand, is used to refer to welcoming guests to the Eucharist on special occasions or under special circumstances as long as they recognise the real presence of Christ. This is clearly a ray of hope, and one which could generate more light as the dialogue continues.

Community but not Communion

Although entered into with the best of intentions and hope for the future, it is a reality that some marriages fail and a divorce is sought. Often a divorced spouse may decide to remain single or to seek a declaration of nullity of the first marriage (sometimes referred to as an "annulment") so as to get married again in church.

Sometimes, though, it is the case that, for various reasons, such a declaration is not obtained and one (or both) of the spouses wishes to marry again. Since they are still bound by the bonds of the previous marriage (even though divorced in the eyes of the state), they may enter a second, non-canonical, marriage. There is no difficulty with someone who is either separated or divorced from approaching the Eucharist, although they may wish to reflect on to what degree they may have contributed to the marriage breakdown.

However, a problem arises with the status of the Catholic in a second civil marriage who wishes to approach the Eucharist.

The language used in Canon Law to describe people in such a situation has been significantly tempered from the Code that was promulgated in 1917, which referred to "bigamists" and threatened "excommunication" on those who did not resolve their "unlawful" situation. Such people were excluded from the Eucharist until they had shown signs of repentance, amendment of life, and had publicly repaired the scandal caused by their actions.

The revised Code of 1983 no longer uses such language, and the divorced-remarried are not specifically identified, although Canon 915 states that those who "obstinately persevere in manifest grave sin" are not to be admitted to the Eucharist.

The sin is made explicit in the *Catechism of the Catholic Church*, paragraph 2384: contracting a new union, even if it is recognised by civil law, puts the remarried spouse in a situation of "public and permanent adultery". This then excludes those who have entered into a second non-canonical marriage.

That said, various synods of bishops have raised this question of exclusion from the Eucharist as a most pressing pastoral problem, one which has recently been discussed in various papal documents.

Pope John Paul II, in *Familiaris Consortio* (1981), noted a distinction between those who tried to save their first marriage but were unjustly abandoned and those who destroyed a canonically valid marriage. There are also those who entered into a second union for the sake of their children and those who are subjectively certain in conscience that their previous and irreparably destroyed marriage had never been valid. While reiterating that the divorced-remarried are unable to be admitted to the Eucharist, there is a call to pastors to make a careful discernment of different situations.

Pope Francis takes up these ideas in his Apostolic Exhortation, *Amoris Laetitia*, in which he speaks of the need to integrate people living in "irregular" situations. He continues:

Such persons need to feel, not as excommunicated members of the Church, but, instead, as living members, able to live and grow in the Church and experience her as a mother who welcomes them always, who takes care of them with affection and encourages them along the path of life and the Gospel (paragraph 299).

The Pope's call for mercy, to be attentive to people's distress in difficult and complex situations, and the need to avoid judgements which fail to take account of these can be considered yet another ray of hope to those who, for whatever reason, are excluded from the Eucharist. ■

Dr Helen Costigane is a member of the Society of the Holy Child Jesus and is Programme Director for the MA in Theology at St Mary's University, Twickenham.

Pastoral Engagement

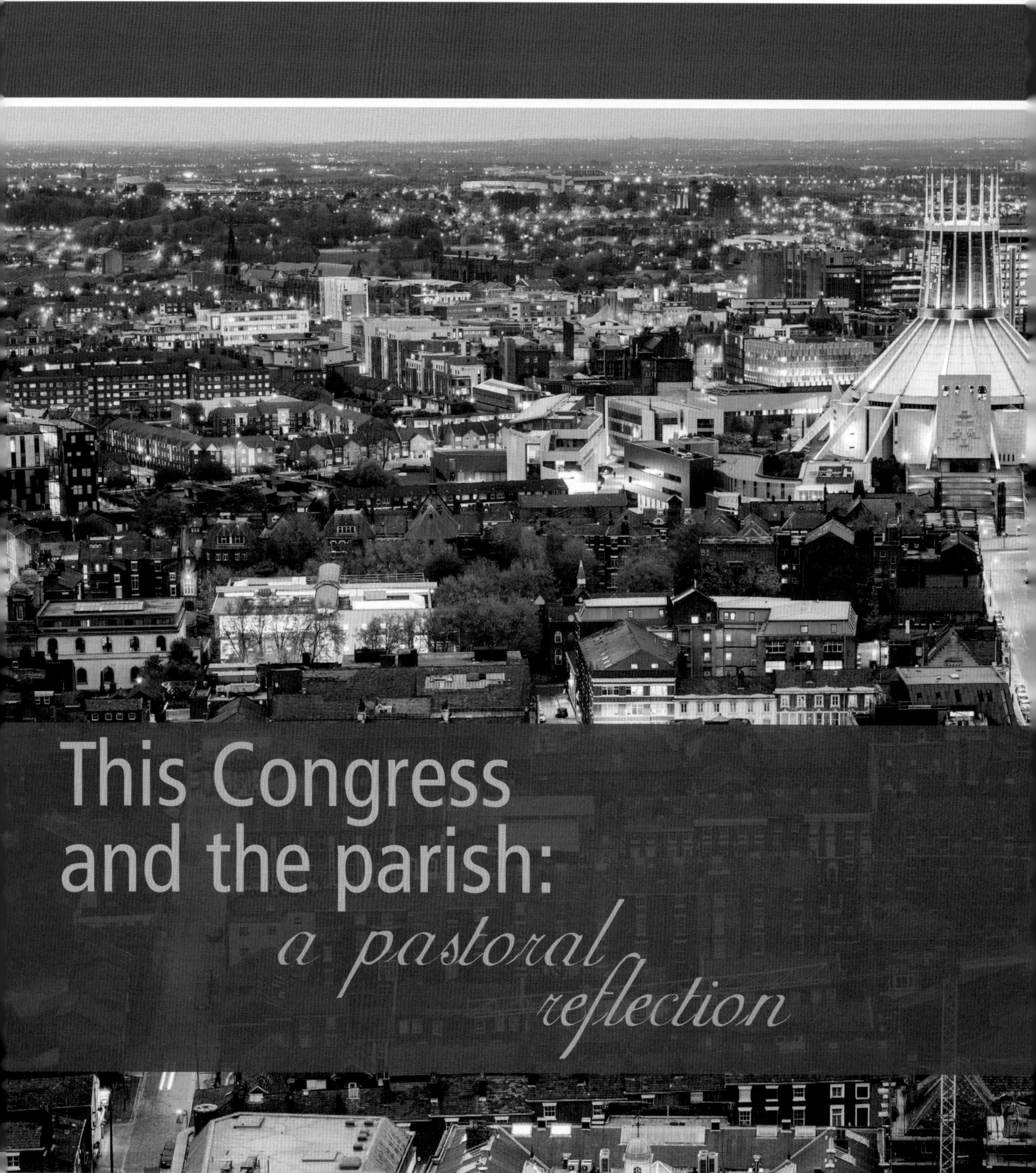

This Congress and the parish: *a pastoral reflection*

The Eucharistic Congress and Pilgrimage taking place in Liverpool from 7-9 September 2018 is described as "a national event supporting the local Church."[1] Some ten thousand people are expected to attend and participate from every diocese in England and Wales.

This particular Congress however, is much bigger than the three days or actual location assigned to it. This is a sound pastoral initiative which presents many cascading opportunities for engagement, reflection and the challenge of pastoral priorities. It could well become a highly significant moment for the life of the local Church, primarily experienced in the context of the parish community.

The focus of the entire event is the centrality of the Eucharist, "the source and summit of the Christian life."[2] The Eucharist impacts on every parish in the land so this gathering of the Church in prayer is a three-day celebration of God's greatest gift. It opens doors to the sacred, calls the people of God together, asking us to explore and articulate the primary cornerstone of our faith. John Paul II took the view that "the Eucharist is the most precious possession which the Church has in her journey through history."[3] So for three sharply focused days we are all invited to encounter the person of Christ and actively participate in something greater than ourselves.

Aerial view of Liverpool city and the Metropolitan Cathedral. Shahid Khan / Shutterstock.com

Fr John Mulligan

The success of this Congress depends on prayerful preparation, invitational leadership, empowerment, stewardship, on-going formation and legacy consideration. The event itself will be a crossroads moment of pause, prayer, discernment and wonder. While its purpose is to inspire reflection and contemplation, it cannot be just a one-off national event in Liverpool. If this is to be an investment for the future of the church in England and Wales, we have to broaden the pastoral scope of the moment, see the bigger picture emerging and hear the challenging conversations of life unfolding.

Bringing the Gospel into respectful dialogue with the culture of our time is a formidable challenge for every Christian today. Pope Francis maintains that "the Lord does not disappoint those who take this risk."[4]

Some of the essential implications of this Congress may be hidden way below the surface. The Pastoral Constitution of the Church draws our attention to the internal dilemma of conscience[5] for every person and the moral necessity of correctly informing our decision process on the complex voyage of life. The issues we bring to the Lord in prayer undoubtedly dominate our minds. They are the things that really matter as we journey on the road. The internal baggage carried to Liverpool could well define some life-changing moments. Perhaps this Congress will provide a prophetic moment of awareness when we begin to hear and understand those who are broken and wounded on the frontiers of parish life and Eucharist.

Pope Francis, as leader of the Catholic Church, reminds us that "the Eucharist is not a prize for the perfect but a powerful nourishment and medicine for the weak."[6]

This Congress is a moment to be mindful of those to whom the Eucharist, or indeed the Church, is no longer particularly relevant. Their families and friends are present in every parish congregation. It may well trigger some uncomfortable but vital questions that will reach out to those who are searching for a word of welcome, accompaniment, healing, reconciliation and re-engagement. Perhaps we need to check again that we have the correct address on all the Congress invitations. There is no limit to the distance an invitation, or indeed a question, can travel. This is the pedagogy of God.

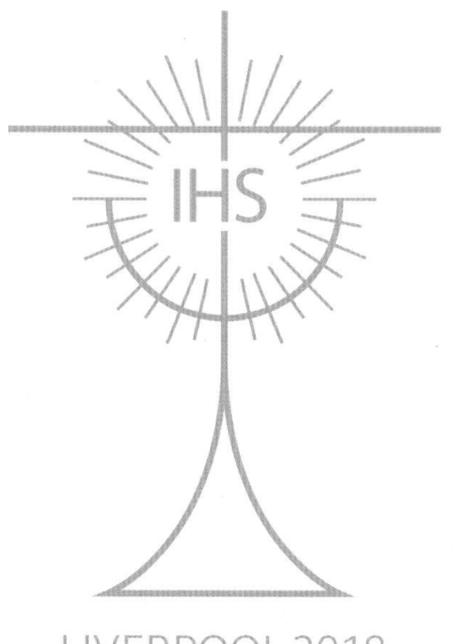

The Congress challenge to the parish

The local parish community remains an extraordinary place of encounter. It is here that this Congress needs to be realised. The parish is the Church in miniature, where we first meet the person of Jesus. The parish is the sacred space where "people gather, welcome each other, listen to the Word, celebrate the sacraments, learn about faith, minister to one another and witness to the world."[7] With all its perceived faults and failings, it is a rich tapestry of humanity and an anchor of life for many who are searching for God. Richard Gaillardetz makes the point that "the whole purpose of the Church is to illuminate the person of Christ and the whole purpose of your parish is to facilitate that illumination."[8]

The parish is also a challenging jigsaw where the committed, the casual and the disengaged are frequently thrown together because they often stem from the same household. This Congress introduces a unique pastoral opportunity for every parish to stop, look back, look around, look within, and look out at the broader landscape of life where people struggle to find God in the "bits and pieces"[9] of every day.

Over time, parishes can grow stale and stagnant from rite, ritual and relentless routine. This Congress provides a strategic opportunity for every parish to reflect on its life, mission, purpose and trajectory. It also provides the challenging moment to ask "what is missing", or "who is missing" from our parish community? Perhaps a more fundamental question is "why are they missing"? This Congress provides the people of God with an amazing chance to discern and see beyond the predictable, parochial timetable.

Every parish community is invited to send delegates to Liverpool. The Congress specifically invites parish representatives, catechists, extraordinary ministers, RE leaders, clergy, religious orders, seminarians, hospital and prison chaplains, who are all on the front line of evangelisation. Chosen, volunteered, elected or cajoled, the chosen delegates are experienced practitioners and ambassadors for us all.

Images © Mazur/ catholicnews.org.uk

Surrounded by prayer, they are commissioned and sent out on a journey to engage again with the ancient tables of the word, the Eucharist and life itself. These delegates must go, absorb, return and empower. Undoubtedly, they will be reaffirmed both in ministry and in mission, but they also face some tough ecclesiological challenges in the parish communities from which they come.

While all these ministries share the sharp challenge of evangelisation in their various communities, they are strongly supported by multiple layers of other, unseen ministries, all connected to Eucharist. Welcomers, flower arrangers, church cleaners, ushers, collectors, gift aid organisers, sacristans, servers, singers, musicians, artists, parish pastoral councils, parish secretaries, youth leaders, counters, auditors, IT ministers and numerous community organisations… These collectively form an intrinsic and vital infrastructure for every parish. Perhaps these indispensable ministries, so fundamental to the life of the parish, have pride of place on the real guest list for this Congress. They may not all get to the Congress but maybe its message needs to find its way to them for a "mutual exchange of gifts."[10]

With such a rich reservoir of talent, the parish itself is infinitely more than what we initially encounter or perceive. There is a vast network of life and energy at work behind the scenes. There is a great spiritual wisdom here because it is linked to, and centred on, the Eucharist. The parish community is the site of an exciting local theology that shapes a profound reflection at the interface of faith and life.

Sadly, for some people in today's Church, their ministry has become clericalised, tired and predictable. For others there is a nostalgic hankering for a model of Church that was safe and secure, cautious and lifeless.

Today we are often trapped in a world of gadgets and technology where the virtual community takes precedence over the real one. But if we are to read the signs of the times, we need to take on the "bold and creative" mantle encouraged by Pope Francis in *Evangelii Gaudium,*[11] the curriculum of parish life.

This Congress is a welcome pastoral opportunity to evaluate our parish journey and re-imagine our parish ministry in the service of God's kingdom. The competition for time and connectivity is high. People will only commit to what is relevant to their lives. Yet the weekly Sunday gathering presents a unique opportunity to connect and excel in every aspect of ministry. This Congress is a pastoral and practical signpost and signposts always point to something greater than themselves.

We may never arrive at the perfect model of parish but sometimes the journey is more important than the arrival. ■

Fr John Mulligan, a Southwark parish priest, is also the Southwark archiocesan lead for Adoremus.

[1] Bishops' Conference of England & Wales, London, June 2017.
[2] Documents of Vatican II, *Lumen Gentium* #11, 1965.
[3] John Paul II, Rome 2003, *Ecclesia de Eucharistia*, #9.
[4] Pope Francis, *Evangelii Gaudium* #3, 2013.
[5] *Gaudium et Spes*, #16.
[6] *Evangelii Gaudium*, # 47.
[7] Mulligan, J. "Parish Ministry – Servant of Mission", DThMin thesis, 2014.
[8] Gaillardetz, R. National Conference on Ecclesiology, Communion and Co-Responsibility, Ireland, Sept 2012.
[9] Patrick Kavanagh, *The Great Hunger*, 1942.
[10] *Gaudium et Spes* #40.
[11] Pope Francis, *Evangelii Gaudium*, #33.

Building blocks for the pastoral life of the Church

What are the building blocks in your life? What would you add to any these? How might your parish construct something really beautiful for God?

Five building blocks creating a firm foundation for the pastoral life of the Church are:

- **Scripture** – in which we come to meet, know, understand, love and follow God
- An **understanding of the Church** – so that we can more effectively "be Church"
- **Mission** – so that we can carry the Good News to the world around us
- **Formation** – so that we deepen and cherish our understanding of our faith, helping others to follow our example
- **Music** – helps us to get in touch with and express what is deepest in our hearts, binding us together in celebration and prayer

Yet there are also other blocks which are vital if we want a strong parish community gathered around our keystone: Christ. You can probably add to the list of loveliness. ■

Scripture

In order that the family walk well, with trust and hope, it must be nourished with the Word of God.

Pope Francis

The Church

The Church is called to draw near to every person, beginning with the poorest and those who suffer.

Pope Francis

Mission

Who are the first to whom the Gospel message must be proclaimed? The answer, found so often throughout the Gospel, is clear: it is the poor, the little ones and the sick, those who are often looked down upon or forgotten: those who cannot repay us.

Pope Francis

Formation

The Spirit guides us towards the entire truth, until he leads us fully into the mystery of Christ and enables us to see all things as he does.

Pope Francis

Music

The voices of the faithful are multiplied when joined in prayerful celebration with musical accompaniment.

Pope Francis

Music nurtures a Eucharistic dimension

Canon Alan McLean is known throughout the Southwark archdiocese for the amazing diocesan choir which he helps to inspire and animate. He and the choir, through their music, can be guaranteed to bring extra layers of meaning to a liturgical celebration.

A Eucharistic Pilgrimage and Congress should always deepen our love and spiritual understanding of the power of the Eucharist in our lives. If it doesn't, as the Catholic family, it will have failed. No one would want this 2018 moment to be anything but a success. In the Archdiocese of Southwark, we have grappled with the many themes and priorities that have been presented. Many words have been used to explain what could become part of this journey – Adoration, Formation, Mission, Ecclesiology, Eucharist and, guess what, Music.

It does not surprise me that in our diocese, music is seen as a key word, as very often the use of music has helped us express our living faith. "See us Lord about your altar, though so many we are one." This is such a great hymn that helps our community express who we really are. It continues: "Wheat and grape contain the meaning; food and drink he is to all."

For us to truly understand the power of this amazing mystery every element of who we are needs to have expression: head, heart, body and spirit. Is it any wonder that when we feel things strongly the sung voice is always there? Whether we are at our lowest, or experiencing great happiness, we sing as "many souls by love united in the heart of Christ your Son."

As we prepare for the Congress, music will help us express in a public way our deepest thoughts of our love for God and God's overwhelming love for us,
as thanksgiving.

"The Servant Song" by Richard Gillard expresses for me what God wants us to be. Through word and sacrament we must be Christ to others.

Eucharistic music must always lead us to the altar or from the altar into our everyday life: "In bread we bring you Lord, our body's labour." This hymn is probably sung in most churches, often too fast. It takes us from word to sacrament and then to action.
It is my hope that this Eucharistic Pilgrimage and Congress will deepen our understanding of why we come to Mass, why word and sacrament are central to our life.

I offer some suggestions of hymns that I have found work and help us deepen our understanding of the Eucharist and its consequences:

Alleluia, sing to Jesus
At this great feast of love
Love is his word
Of the glorious body telling
O praise our great and gracious Lord
Praise now your God
Seed, scattered and sown
The heavenly word, proceeding
The night before our Saviour died
The time was early evening
Those who were in the dark
We celebrate this festive day
Welcome, all ye noble saints
In bread we bring you
Jesus, you're the one I love
Let all mortal flesh
Upon thy table, Lord
We bring you this bread and wine
An upper room
Bread of life, truth eternal (CJM)
Draw nigh and take
Bread for the world (Walker)
Bread of life, hope of the world (Farrell)
Behold the Lamb of God (CJM)
Broken for me
Father, we give you thanks
Gifts of bread and wine
Holy gifts
I received the living God
Lord, your love has drawn us near
My God, and is thy table
Now in this banquet
O thou who at thy Eucharist
One bread one body
One bread we break
See us Lord, about thine altar
Take this and eat it
This is my body
We come to your feast
We have gathered
When the time came
Within the reign of God (Haugen)
All the gifts of God (Lee/Adams)
And when you eat this bread
At the supper, Christ the Lord (Mowbray)
Author of life divine (Wesley)
Be known to us in breaking bread (Montgomery)
Blessed Jesus, living bread
Bread of life from heaven (Haugen)
Bread is blessed and broken (Bell)
Come, Christ's beloved (Quinn)
Come, risen Lord (Briggs)
Cup of blessing (Soper)
For the bread which you have broken
Glory, love and praise and honour (Wesley)
Holy manna from above (Warner)
Jesus, God among us (Dufner)
Jesus, you are the bread (Farrell)
Life-giving bread (Chepponis)
One in body, heart and mind (Walker)
Strengthen for service, Lord
Take and eat (Joncas)
The bread that we break (Dean)
There is something holy here (Walker)
This is the body of Christ (Bell)
We hail thy presence glorious
We who live by sound and symbol (Bell)
We will take what you offer (Bell)
You are the bread of life (Leckebusch)
You are our living bread (Joncas)
Psalm 116 (Dean)
Our blessing cup (Joncas)
Psalm 34 Taste and See
Soul of my Saviour
We come to share our story (Haas)
Thanks be to God (Dean)

Through song our celebration of the Eucharist should create a deeper desire to spend more time in prayer, contemplation and adoration that leads to action.

"The Mass is ended. Go in peace" Our lives are often so busy, that stopping time and contemplation do not exist. I remember those moments, when I, as a child, went shopping with my mum. We would never go past a church without a visit. It was a short moment when I wanted to go to the statues that I liked and light a candle while mum knelt in the bench before the Blessed Sacrament. She always had a smile as we left the church.

Benediction was part of our life at school once a week and then, once I became a server, we had Benediction on a Sunday as well as going to Mass. We also had the Forty Hours (Quarant'Ore) of exposition that looked magnificent and seemed equally special.

Did I understand what was going on? No. Did I really understand what was happening? Did the music help? I liked the tunes, but "No". Yet, as an adult and now almost forty years ordained, much of that music is very real, even if some of the hymns are a little sentimental.

Some of these older hymns have touched our lives and rise in our memories. I offer a list that may help these moments of prayerfully reflective nostalgia:

O bread of heaven
Adoro te devote
Santo, santo, santo
(Bread of life from heaven)
Sweet sacrament divine
Music from Taizé
Chants from Margaret Rizza

It strikes me that our Eucharistic life is very much a time of spiritual encounter. It is not a one-way track. Some of the music of the past made us look only in one direction. We were the unworthy people, gazing at our God in adoration of Jesus Christ. Some of the music we use today enfolds us in God's love for us and encourages us to action as well as giving praise and thanksgiving.

I return to the hymn I first quoted: "See us Lord about your altar; though so many we are one; many souls by love united in the heart of Christ your Son."

I hope that some of these suggestions and thoughts may help in our Eucharistic preparation for the Congress and deepen our love for the Eucharist and sustain our life that flows from it. ■

Canon Alan McLean is the parish priest at the London parish of The Most Holy Trinity, Dockhead.

Hidden homage

Ssanctuary of San Damiano, Assisi, Italy

A Poor Clare Colettine from Ty Mam Duw in North Wales describes the "miracle of miracles" that is the Blessed Sacrament.

In September 2018 the city of Liverpool will become the herald of the Great King. She will proclaim her faith in her Eucharistic Lord, who took on flesh for our sake and united himself to our humanity, promising to be with us even to the end of time. Isn't this a great promise? Yet how often do we really think deeply about this and take it on board and come before him with full confidence in the Blessed Sacrament?

We come to worship and adore our Eucharistic Lord who is present before us in the tiny white host. Here, heaven and earth meet. Here we encounter Jesus, the one who was laid in a manger; who walked this earth healing and teaching; who was crucified; the one who rose from the tomb on the third day and ascended into heaven. Here, in the Eucharist, we have the victorious one who fulfils his promises. Here, Jesus is revealed on the altar. We are taken to heaven to meet the Father who loved each of us so much that he gave us his only beloved Son Jesus, so that we may come to that knowledge and experience his love.

Something unbelievable happens when we come before the Lord exposed in the Blessed Sacrament. Our eyes behold God and he beholds us. The miracle of miracles that we search for takes place. All that is in us and all in our world is exposed to that great loving heart of God. The pain and anguish, the sorrow and fear that we feel and that our world experiences, all the sin and the falsehood, we can place before the great healer and lover to touch.

In the Eucharist, we come to see this great God of ours, united to us as the best friend that we could ever have or imagine, the one we can trust completely.

Saint Clare trusted her Eucharistic Lord so much that, one day, when soldiers were scaling the walls of San Damiano to attack the Sisters, she took the monstrance and went out into their midst. As she did so, she said to the Lord, "I am no longer able to protect your handmaids. Only you can do this." Immediately the soldiers ran away and St Clare heard the consoling words, "I will always protect you."

In times of trial let us follow Clare's example, placing our trust in the power of Jesus the King of Kings present in the Blessed Sacrament. Let us run to him, full of confidence in his strength to protect us from all harm.

We Poor Clare Colettines will be with you all the way as you make your pilgrimage to encounter Jesus in the Eucharist and proclaim your faith in Jesus the Bread of Life.

In this great Eucharistic celebration let us behold him present in the Eucharist, hold him before our eyes and enfold him into our daily life. Jesus, this mighty God of ours, is always present with us. ■

The Poor Clare Colettines of Ty Mam Duw in Hawarden, North Wales, are a contemplative Franciscan community whose life of prayer is part of the wider world's powerhouse.

A Sacred corner for adults

Denise Cottrell-Boyce explains some words and ideas which some readers might otherwise find unfamiliar.

Benediction

Benediction is a service of simple adoration. We take time to wonder at Jesus' divinity. The hymns, the monstrance, incense and ornate vestments all help us to feel God's otherness and how blessed we are to be invited to share it with him. They help us appreciate what Christ gave up in order to share our humanity.

Monstrance

On special occasions, the Blessed Sacrament is put into a beautifully decorated display case on a stand. This is called the monstrance. The word comes from the Latin verb meaning "to show". Jesus Christ is shown in the sacred host so that we might feel the pleasure of his company.

Tabernacle

When the priest has consecrated the hosts they become the sacred body of Christ. They are kept in a place of honour in the sanctuary of the church, often behind the altar, in what is called a tabernacle. It is a sacred space inside a sacred space. We keep a light shining there to show that Jesus is here with us.

Adoration

When we pray, we are usually asking for God's help. But sometimes it's important just to be with God and be aware of God's wonder, to allow the mystery of his being to touch us. When we do this we find ourselves adoring him.

Pilgrimage

There are times when we feel a great need to "go to God" in a way that our local church cannot fulfil. The physical act of moving towards a holy place with thousands of others symbolises the reality of our life's journey towards God, accompanied and supported by our fellow pilgrims.

Visits to the Blessed Sacrament

Jesus is always with us but we are not always with him. Because we are physical creatures, it is comforting to us to visit the physical presence of Christ in the tabernacle. When we visit the Blessed Sacrament, we take our anxieties, our sufferings and our joys and share them with him.

Colour these images as you reflect...

Reconciliation
Sin puts distance between us and Jesus. Hurting ourselves and others means we are moving away from looking at his world through his eyes. The sacrament of reconciliation gives us the chance to close that gap, to get back on the right path and to love as God loves.

Evangelisation
Evangelisation is the great desire to share the joy and comfort of our faith with those around us. Everything we do and say can be an expression of what we believe. Words are not always necessary. The most important evangelists are parents.

Congress
The Church is a living, growing body blessed with a huge diversity of strengths and talents. Sometimes we need to join together at a national and international level so we can share our faith, knowledge and experience. We celebrate the faith we have inherited while thinking about how to pass it on to our children.

Chalice
During Mass we use the chalice to offer wine for the consecration. It's a beautiful goblet, usually made of a precious metal, which helps us to show honour to Jesus' presence in his precious blood. Some priests prefer to use a simpler cup to commemorate the Last Supper more authentically.

Activities

1. **Ask the priest to let you examine and hold the monstrance and the chalice.**

2. **What is the difference between the wine sold in the shops and altar wine?**

   No difference at all provided the wine is made only from grapes.

3. **Can you name ten Catholic pilgrimage places? Which is nearest to where you live?**

   Lourdes, Walsingham, Rome, the Holy Land, Knock, Iona, Put, Banneux, Fatima, Vailankanni, Guadalupe, Compostella, Lisieux, Avila...

4. **At Benediction, we pray the Divine Praises. Look them up and pray them from time to time. Which one is your favourite? Why?**

5. **What is a "Recusant chalice"? Why is it sometimes unscrewable or the size of your index finger?**

   A recusant chalice sometimes had an unscrewable base because it could be more easily hidden.

Denise Cottrell-Boyce is the mother of seven children and a parish catechist.

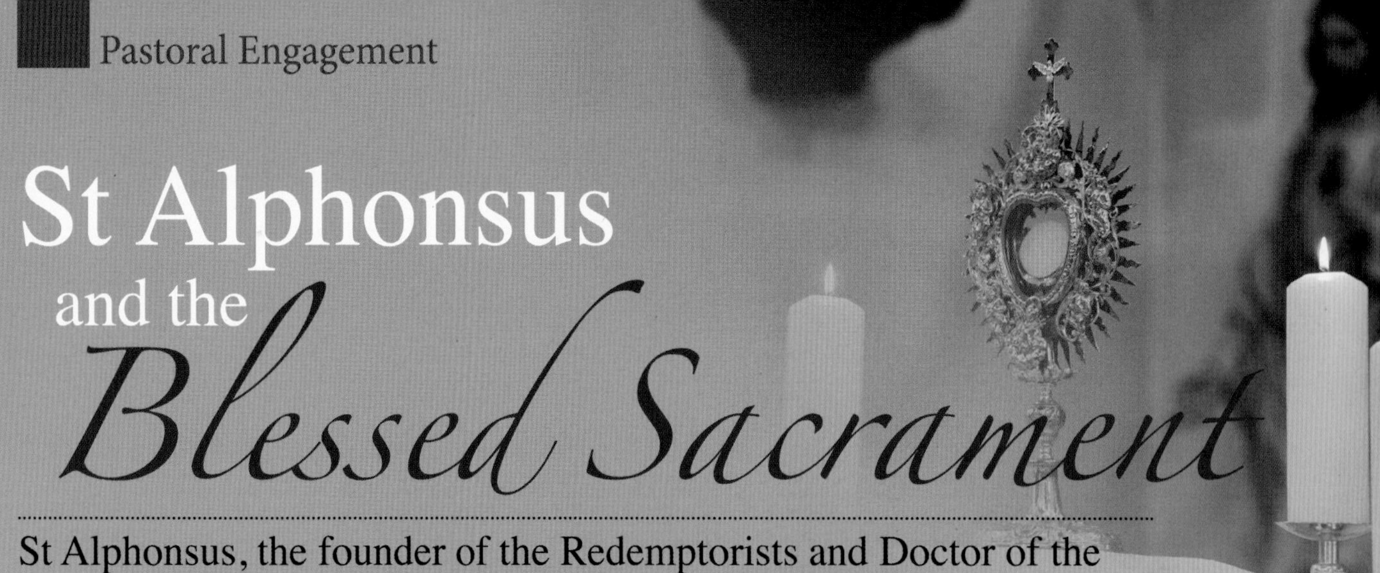

St Alphonsus and the *Blessed Sacrament*

St Alphonsus, the founder of the Redemptorists and Doctor of the Church, worked to inspire people with an ever deeper love of Jesus, present in the Blessed Sacrament, as Fr Ronald McAinsh C.Ss.R. explains.

"Come to me all you who labour and are overburdened, and I will give you rest".

In every age we experience an upsurge in devotion to the Blessed Sacrament in new and fresh ways, in response to the needs of the age and of society. That is why the Adoremus initiative of the Bishops' Conference of England and Wales is so important.

Through Adoremus, the National Eucharistic Pilgrimage and Congress, every parish community can celebrate the Eucharist in a revitalised way, perhaps including the Forty Hours' Devotion in their programme. Every parish in the country will also be represented at the final Eucharistic Congress.

Eucharistic devotion seems to be on the increase in many parts of the world. In numerous parishes in this country and even more so in the United States, there is Eucharistic devotion twenty-four hours a day, seven days a week. This allows a parish to create, night and day, a grace-filled place and an uninterrupted atmosphere of love, praise, petition and thanksgiving to God.

But why have Eucharistic adoration when we have the Holy Mass?

The sacrament of the Eucharist was instituted to nourish us and draw us into communion with one another.

In the early days of the Church there was no tradition of Eucharistic devotion, although the Blessed Sacrament was always reserved with special care and honour for dying people who needed Viaticum ("food for the journey").

Christ is present in many different ways in our world and our lives: through his presence in the Blessed Sacrament, the scriptures – the living word of God – and in the heart of every baptised person.

In the history of the Church, Eucharistic adoration has peaked and waned from time to time.

When Saint Alphonsus wrote *Visits to the Blessed Sacrament*, initially for Redemptorist students, it was in the aftermath of the Reformation and the Council of Trent. The Reformation had, in effect, banned the public celebration of Mass and therefore any devotion to the Blessed Sacrament. The Council of Trent wished this celebration to be reaffirmed very strongly at the heart of our Catholic faith.

"Jesus never wearies of listening to our cares when we visit him in the Blessed Sacrament", wrote Saint Alphonsus in the preface to *Visits to the Blessed Sacrament* in 1743. Overwhelmed by the thought that Jesus gave himself entirely for us in the Eucharist, Saint Alphonsus' entire focus was on amazement, gratitude and praise.

Since then, this little booklet has inspired people from every walk of life and social status – including popes. Intended to assist those who spend time before the Blessed Sacrament in prayer, it has been through countless translations and editions. Now, for the celebration of Adoremus, we shall print a new version, equally faithful to the author whose principal desire was to enkindle love, devotion, zeal and boundless confidence in the living Jesus, present in this sacrament.

Great saints like Blessed Charles de Foucauld and Saint Teresa of Calcutta found great consolation at the feet of Jesus in the Blessed Sacrament.

Someone once asked Mother Teresa what was essential in the life of her Sisters. She replied, "a deep and personal love of the Eucharist and finding Jesus in the Blessed Sacrament," adding, "When they have done this they can go out and find Jesus in their neighbour and serve him in the poor".

May the experience of Adoremus be, for each one of us, a rekindling of our love for, and confidence in, Jesus, present in the Blessed Sacrament.

> Acquire the habit of speaking to God as if you were alone with him, familiarly and with confidence and love, as to the dearest and most loving of friends.
>
> *St Alphonsus*

Fr Ronald McAinsh is the Provincial of the London Province of the Redemptorists.

A creative revolution: *one bread, one body*

Cristina Gangemi tells us that, for children with learning disabilities and for their families, sharing in the Eucharist makes sense.

Over the past twenty years a revolution has begun to occur in the lives and education of people who have been disabled. The development of personalised language systems, symbol-supported texts and the development of technology have meant that exciting new ways to communicate have been developed. This has offered us, the Church, a creative and accessible way to ensure that we all contribute to the building up of the Body of Christ (Code of Canon Law, 208).

In my role as a disability adviser, I have witnessed these changes. I have watched as the use of signs and symbols has transformed people because they have enabled many to share and celebrate their story within their journey to the sacraments.

In the past, it was presumed that people, especially those who are intellectually disabled, were just not able to engage in the catechetical programmes that exist and therefore not permitted to receive the sacraments. However, with the growth of creative journeys towards the sacraments of reconciliation and Eucharist, such as *I Belong Special* [1], many amazing stories are being expressed.

Many parishes have begun to celebrate diversity as, Pope Francis declared in 2016, a "way to improve and to be more beautiful and richer". "They have become Bread of life for all".

One issue that has been important in my own journey has been to understand what is meant by the word "disabled". I have only ever shared faith with people of many abilities, amazing people with amazing stories.

The only time I have met a ***dis***abled person was when I have witnessed how physical and intellectual barriers have prevented people from living their life and their faith to the full.

If a building does not have access, people who use wheelchairs, or have heightened physical needs, cannot get in. If a sacramental programme is made up only of words, without signs and symbols to help people understand, they remain "intellectually disabled" by this lack of access.

The joy of the past twenty years has been to witness how new and creative approaches have begun to remove these barriers and as such enable people with learning disabilities to flourish within the Body of Christ.

This has been a wonderful journey and, even though we still have a way to go, we are a generation of the Church that minsters at the birth of this awesome revolution.

We must authentically proclaim that "Every human being is created in the image of God" [2] (Long 2016) which is, in Christianity, the very essence of the *gift of life*.

As we reflect on the words, "I am the Bread of Life", we have to recognise that, if we are each made in God's image then Every-Body's [3] (Gangemi 2010) story is also a form of nourishment. We each have the capacity to share that Bread of Life with one another, no matter what our ability might be.

Diversity is our richness. It is what helps the bread to rise. Let me tell you one such, nourishing, story.

Once sharing with one of our bishops, about the "revolution" that was occurring, he told me of an event that had transformed him, in Liverpool Cathedral.

He was asked to give First Communion to a child on the spectrum of autism. Knowing that the child had been prepared, through a carefully planned programme of signs and symbols, he was happy to give her the Bread of Life at the Sunday Mass.

As he watched a family approach, their child in her wheelchair, he was overjoyed to share Christ with her. He was rewarded by an open hand and a total sense of peace as she looked at him and smiled. No word was spoken but her body said "Amen."

Following this, however, another young girl, also on the spectrum of autism, came forward for the Eucharist. He looked carefully at the parents, who proudly smiled and the child, also held out her hand. "This is the Body of Christ." He offered the Eucharist and she answered, peacefully "Amen."

Following the Mass, thoughtful about the two girls, the bishop went into the sacristy, followed by a very worried mother. "Your Grace, please… I am sorry, my daughter received the Eucharist today, but she has had no preparation."

Things began to turn over in his head: he must have given the Eucharist to both children, one who had received a formal formation and one who would now need some immediate formation.

Before he could give the mother an answer, her sister came running in to the sacristy… "You must all come", she said, "please follow me." It turned out that, as the aunt was beginning to feed the little girl, the other child, who had received formation, came to where they were feeding. Without words, she moved the child's aunt out of the way, taking the spoon from her hand, and began to feed the little one.

The bishop, seeing this, said that her formation had begun, for here she was "fed by the child who had been catechised: this is my body… given for you… take it and eat it, this is the Bread of Life".

For anyone who knows anything about children with autism, eye contact, surprise, change of routine and strangers always present a problem or initiate fear. However, here the revolution had been lived out! Each child had, with ease, put out her hand to receive Christ and, as each shared in this loving act, she shared rich signs and symbols and both were catechised. The bishop looked and told the families "Well, her catechetical journey has begun."

So that our parishes can be enriched by the hundreds of lives and stories, such as that of these two young girls, sacramental programmes must reflect a place of belonging and mirror the grace for which they prepare.

Preparation for reconciliation and the Eucharist should be rich in the use of signs and symbols, Makaton sign language and any other form of communication that remove barriers that disable.

Sacramental programmes must always be adapted to meet the individual's way of being and creative way of learning: only then can we truly make up the Body of Christ in the world. Programmes must therefore include:

- Motivational stimuli
- A multi-sensory and tactile approach
- Music and drama
- Signing, symbols and visual material to support the understanding
- Selecting different ways to bring stories and messages to life (e.g. animation, representational objects, puppets, songs, role play, etc.)
- Non-verbal communication (i.e. body language, use of voice accompanied by gesture, movement, facial expressiveness, slower pace, simple language, routine and timing.

It is important that a person is creatively enabled to distinguish the Body of Christ from ordinary food, even if the recognition is evidenced through manner, expression in their eyes, gesture or reverential silence rather than verbally.

Using these varied approaches ensures that there is sensitivity towards different ways of communication so that people can truly enjoy their place of belonging within God's promise "I will take you as my people, and I will be your God" (Exodus 6:7).

A true relationship understands beyond words or sounds, communicates beyond definitions, freeing people to be at their best and who they were born to be. Opportunities must be created to develop faith-filled relationships, where "the full and active participation" (*Sacrosanctum Concilium* 2) of all people can celebrate stories and enable faith to be expressed, so that each and everyBody can enter into a deep and meaningful union with Christ and with each other, for, together, we are one bread, one body. ■

[1] *I Belong Special*, Redemptorist Publications, 1995.
[2] Long, quoted in the journal *Living Fully* vol XXIV 2016 n.3, *Cultura e Fede special* edition.
[3] *EveryBody Has a Story*, Cristina Gangemi, University of Aberdeen, 2010.

Cristina Gangemi has been privileged to share in the lives and stories of many people. Her ministry as a disability adviser is enriched and nourished by their generous witness. She was recently able to give a copy of *I Belong Special* to Pope Francis.

Cristina Gangemi is a disability adviser, and consultant and the Director of The Kairos Forum.

I Belong Special is available from Redemptorist Publications, www.rpbooks.co.uk

The Daughter of Jairus by James Tissot (1836–1902) Brooklyn Museum/ wikimedia commons

Into the *homes*

Cecilia Skudder, a Eucharistic Minister, finds joy in taking Jesus to the homes of her fellow parishioners.

"Who knows how they're feeling, who understands their needs?
Who wants them to be joyful, so, when they're floundering who intercedes? "

Often after a lifetime of serving in their church, sickness or frailty may confine loyal parishioners to their home. Receiving the Blessed Sacrament not only gives them great grace, but also keeps them feeling they are part of the community of the Church.

Home visiting was not new to me. I had been a district nurse and then a Macmillan nurse before I retired. I have also carried out home visiting for over thirty-eight years as a volunteer on behalf of a charity.

I was privileged to become an Extraordinary Minister of the Eucharist in January 2016. What an honour and a joy it is to take the Blessed Sacrament to the sick and housebound at home and in hospital!

Before embarking on my first home visit I was given a list of prayers and Gospel readings from which I prepared a short service, printed two copies and laminated them. I bought a pyx to hold the Blessed Sacrament, which my parish priest blessed, a free-standing crucifix and a battery-operated candle. (I also visit nursing homes where naked flames are inadvisable.) A small white cloth serves as an altar cloth. There are twenty-one people in my parish who receive Holy Communion at home each week – not all from me, I hasten to add.

The very first person I visited at home was a single, elderly lady who had previously thought that only a priest should give out the Blessed Sacrament. Our parish priest told her that none of us, including priests, is worthy to carry the Blessed Sacrament, but the Church has sanctioned chosen laity to be Extraordinary Ministers of the Eucharist to carry out this ministry. The lady accepted this answer.

Often it is not a question of just taking the Blessed Sacrament to the home. People, including their families, may be in pain, distressed or have other problems that may need addressing and a friendly listening ear will prove invaluable. If the person needs professional help or faces a situation which is beyond my capability I can refer them to an appropriate organisation.

Each person is at a different stage in their spirituality, so my visits and prayers are adapted to where they are in their journey of faith. Each needs to realise that God loves them as an individual, having formed them in their mother's womb and known their name before they were born. It is important for him or her to know God's love and readiness to accept all their worries and concerns and then to give him- or herself to them in the Eucharist.

When I started visiting people in their homes, I quickly

realised that they often appreciated a spontaneous prayer for their personal needs, perhaps laying my hand on their shoulder or holding their hand whilst we prayed together.

I learn more about the person at each visit and in my prayers I feel my own faith is deepening. Several of those I go to see have dementia, yet they know when prayers are being said for them and that they are receiving the Blessed Sacrament, giving the responses at the right time.

One lady of ninety-two, with a broad Irish accent, always thanks me for bringing the "Lorrrd" to her. In her awareness, each time that she receives the Eucharist in her own home is the first such occasion! Her joy is so visible and tears fill her eyes. She is often confused, yet her faith is evident. We were saying the Our Father one day and when I reached the words "lead us not into temptation", she touched my arm and said, "I always say let us not into temptation." How profound!

When I think of those who have dementia, their childlike state, their innocence, I do see total trust in their faith shining through any confusion.

As well as doing home visits I joined the Chaplaincy Volunteer Service at the local hospital and visit on a rota basis. The hospital requires its volunteers to attend induction days and training, but all are truly valued and considered part of the health trust. I have met people in hospital who may have been admitted either through accident or illness, who have been in tears and shown such relief and joy to receive the Eucharist in their time of need. That indeed was a joy for me.

Yes Jesus is truly with the suffering and to see this is a great grace for me to witness.

There have been times when a wife or a husband has been a non-believer and I have tried to find opportunities to talk about faith matters with them.

One man I visited regularly was being cared for in a nursing home as his wife was too frail to look after him at home. I would phone her from his bedside so they could talk to each other, and occasionally she would accompany me in my car when I went to see him. She was not a Catholic and when he became too ill to receive Holy Communion she suggested I need no longer go to see her husband. I said, however, that I wished to continue so that I could pray with him. The wife had commented that her husband no longer recognised her, so, at my next opportunity, I prayed that he would be more lucid one more time so she could speak with him. That prayer was answered on her very next visit. He died soon afterwards.

How blessed I am to witness the joy of those I am serving… ■

Cecilia Skudder, a retired nurse and Macmillan nurse, is also an Extraordinary Minister of the Eucharist in her home parish.

Ideas for the parish

The priests and people of the Southwark archdiocese recently came together to talk about parish life…

Delegates and others representing the Southwark archdiocese at the Eucharistic Congress came together for a workshop at the Kairos Centre, Roehampton.

They discussed possible parish ideas and initiatives which could maximise the opportunities which the Congress offers for nurturing and celebrating the Eucharist in our lives.

What follows is based on suggestions made at the workshop. These are questions and ideas which might help parishes in their preparations.

Traffic lights

This is partly a brainstorming session so all ideas are welcome. Suggestions are grouped according to their usefulness and ease of implementation.

Red: not possible in our parish at this time

Amber: worth thinking about – further thinking needed

Green: let's go for it!

And here are some of the results from Southwark's brainstorming…

Red

- Some of these will be unique to each parish depending on its circumstances. So, for example, setting up a soup kitchen to feed homeless people might be very reasonable in a town or city but not in a small village where everybody knows everybody else and homelessness is not a problem.

Amber

- Can everybody in our parish take an active part in the Mass regardless of their physical, mental limitations and vulnerability?

- Can we increase the opportunities for Adoration within our parish and deanery?

- How can we build upon what is already happening in our parish?

Is the final blessing the ending of the Mass, or the sending forth in mission to share Jesus with others?

- Brainstorm ideas for extending the role of Eucharistic Ministers.

How can we help them to enrich their personal and parish appreciation of their important role?

Are they visiting sick and housebound parishioners?

- How might we meet people where they are, not where we want them to be?

- How might parish communication, future planning and strategies become more effective and all-embracing?

- Are parishioners able to use their talents to enrich parish life? What more could be done?

- How will this parish unite itself with the Eucharistic Congress during the weekend of the Congress?

- Would a parish survey help parishioners to identify how they would like to move towards the future?

Consider starting a *Lectio Divina* group within the parish.

- How can we encourage membership and outreach of such groups as the St Vincent de Paul (SVP), Union of Catholic Mothers (UCM) and others?

- What resources might help parishioners to increase their understanding and appreciation of the Eucharist?

- Could we, individually and collectively, study St John's Gospel and the Letter to the Romans as a preparation for the Congress?

- How might the parish use the media (including social media) more effectively as a means of communication and evangelisation?

- What can this parish do so that the Congress can make the Eucharist a real and lasting personal experience of Jesus?

- Can we make a parish pilgrimage during the year as a preparation for the Congress?

- How could our children and young people use their enthusiasm and talents to highlight the Congress message for the whole parish?

Loving God, help us to be open to the freshness of your Spirit. Fill us with enthusiasm for the Good News. Invite us into a deeper relationship with your Son, Jesus Christ, truly present in the Eucharist. Make us more aware of where there is need for new life. Help us to reach out to those who feel lost or abandoned, those who are searching and questioning, those who have walked away from you and those who are eager to know your love. We ask this through Christ, Our Lord, Amen.

Eucharistic Pilgrimage and Congress, 2018

Green

- Let's communicate, celebrate, listen and share our faith and our identity as a Eucharistic community!
- Is there a way of encouraging adults and children to visit Jesus in the Blessed Sacrament?
- Let's pray for each other! Could we put a book in the church where people could write their prayer intentions?
- Let's try to make Jesus so real in our own lives that others will also want to be friends with him.
- Identify people, especially parishioners, with whom we do/do not communicate. Why? How could we communicate more effectively?
- Let's recognise our own richness, potential and giftedness. We are the best resources the parish can offer each other and the world!
- Let's pray for our diocese that it will help people to more deeply appreciate the Eucharist.
- Pray the Congress Prayer at each Mass (as part of the intercessory prayers).
- Increase our welcome towards and engagement with newcomers to the parish.

O Sacrament most holy,
O Sacrament divine,
All praise and all thanksgiving
Be every moment thine.

Ideas for your parish

A church cleaner goes to Holy Hour

Jessica Turnbull offers a different take on Exposition.

Hi, Lord, it's me again, Jessica, no stranger around your sanctuary as you well know. I'm popping in for a bit to say hello. As you know, I'm usually in my apron, sweeping and hoovering and dusting, to make sure your house is spick and span. I'm not OCD about it, thank God, like those strange warriors you see on the TV who clean their kitchen floor twelve times a day and then go out to help people who inhabit an absolute mess. You see them in white overalls and masks, looking nauseated, as though they are part of a forensic team at a gruesome murder. Not me.

Dear Lord, I reckon that coming from Nazareth you would be no stranger to a bit of dust or a cobweb here and there – no offence to your dear mother, of course. Or dear Joseph, who must have made a pretty mess with all the wood shavings and stuff. I mean who cleaned all that up?

Forgive me for fighting with the flower ladies this morning. They believe they have a unique talent as they place agapanthus and yellow tulips and greenery into a collection of vases, eternally standing back to admire their "delicious arrangement" as they call it. Dear God, you are in the background with this crowd and the "arrangement" takes full focus. This is the Holy Hour of flowers with the Host at the back.

They mean well, I know, but they have an easy talent for annoying us cleaners, as if we belong to a different species with no artistic talent for arrangement. While we only collect dust, they manage to gather beautiful flowers and acres of greenery, to construct architectural floral displays that are meant to leave people breathless in wonder at their creativity. If they ever came to the Holy Hour, I doubt, dear Lord, you would get much of a look in.

Sorry, that is unfair. Just me again, though I do believe some of our precious flower ladies are a bit undernourished when it comes to people skills.

Anyway, I have ditched the apron and am now wearing, as you can see, my new two-piece costume in silk lavender – although nobody calls it a costume these days – and am here to visit you, all shining and proper. The parish priest didn't recognise me when I came in early, asking me if I was rehearsing for a wedding on Lake Como. (He is Italian, God bless him, from somewhere called Menaggio.) But the cheek of Don Paulo, really! The silk lavender is for you, dear Lord. I used to dress up for my husband, but he gradually failed to notice any difference about me. I think if love is anything, it is basically about noticing, paying attention. You know your husband is falling out of love with you when he doesn't notice anything any more. Derek, the husband, has now gone off because he noticed someone else – devoted to her, apparently.

I am here to notice you, dear Lord, up there in our new monstrance. Hope you like it. The old one was stolen two months ago. When the policeman came to make a report, he asked Don Paulo what a monstrance was and he replied it was a receptacle for holding Jesus. The policeman looked at me desperately for help, God bless him, and I drew a picture on the back of our *Sunday Plus* newsletter to explain what our monstrance looked like. He went away none the wiser, it has to be said, though he said he would check out eBay.

Sorry, Lord, I am supposed to be praying, not updating you with my silly talk. Let me pray my favourite psalm:

O Lord, you search me and you know me,
you know my resting and my rising,
you discern my purpose from afar.
You mark when I walk or lie down,
all my ways lie open to you... ■

Sunday Plus *is available from Redemptorist Publications, www.rpbooks.co.uk*

Fr Denis McBride C.Ss.R. visited the V&A and found himself captivated by the intricacies of a beautiful monstrance.

The monstrance had a late start in the life of the Church – after 1264, following Pope Urban IV who instituted the Solemnity of Corpus Christi on the Thursday after Pentecost as a universal feast for the whole Latin Church.

Although it took some fifty years for the feast to become popular as widespread practice, it eventually became an important event in celebrating the real presence of Christ in the community, dramatised in the Corpus Christi procession. A carrier was needed for the sacred Host – hence monstrances were made by creative craftsmen, mostly silversmiths or goldsmiths, for this purpose.

The word monstrance is from the Latin *monstrare*, to show – hence the purpose of the monstrance is to display the sacred host.

My favourite monstrance is in the Sacred Silver section of the Victoria and Albert Museum. It was made by Johann Zeckel, a leading goldsmith, in Augsburg, Germany, in 1705. As well as being a beautiful work of craftsmanship, it contains beautiful teaching.

This monstrance is elaborately decorated with imagery. The imperial crown at the top represents God the Father. The cornucopias, the horns on either side, hold ears of corn and grape vines. These symbolise the wine and bread of the Eucharist that become the body and blood of Christ.

Below the window that holds the Host, there is a silver relief depicting the Last Supper, the meal where Jesus broke bread for his disciples and said, "This is my body, given for you." While you see the apostles seated around the table, you notice that Christ himself is absent. You can see only a tiny gilt chalice. All look at it, except one – the figure of Judas who turns away, clasping a money bag.

You realise the absence of Christ is deliberate: he is absent until the sacred Host is placed in the window. Instead of an image of Christ, you now see Christ really present in the sacred Host. The monstrance comes alive only when the sacred Host is at the centre. When that happens, we are in the living presence of the Lord. ■

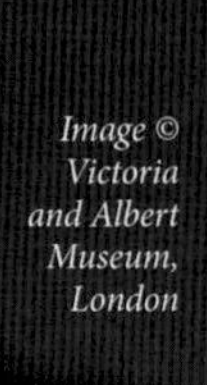

Image © Victoria and Albert Museum, London

For Children and Young People

School chaplaincy: *a family experience*

Kathleen O'Sullivan, a chaplain in a large sixth form college, believes that the school chaplain's role is also a sacred responsibility.

Christ the King Sixth Form College has a successful, long-established tradition of welcoming students of all faiths and none. It has three campuses in Lewisham, Brockley and Sidcup, with a yearly intake of around three thousand young people aged sixteen to nineteen. All three sites share the same vision and ethos:

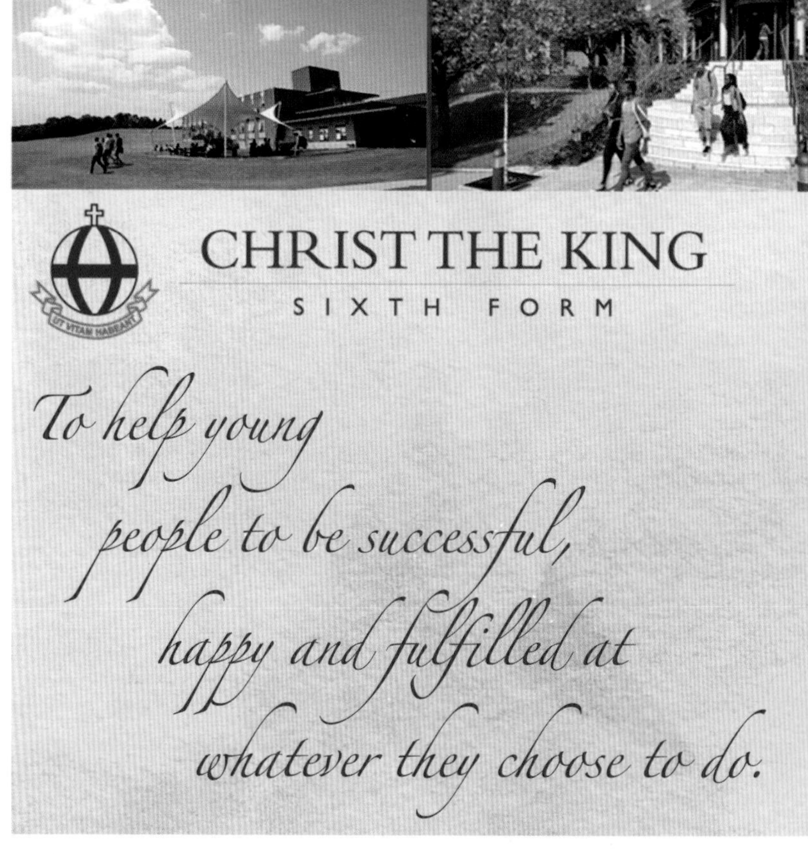

Images / www.ctksfc.ac.uk

Chaplaincy on all three sites facilitates prayer and worship within the college community. Its role is to support students and staff on their journey by listening and walking beside them. We offer many different activities ranging from a Gospel choir to fundraising for charities and retreats.

On each site the chaplaincy has a common room space and a chapel. Students are required to sign into the space, helping to instil a sense of commitment and a pause for reflection upon entering. The common rooms have easy chairs, books, musical instruments, games and resources to show films and presentations. The students use these rooms to socialise, rest and reflect. The chapels are reserved for Mass and quiet prayer.

I am the chaplain at the campus in Brockley and have been in this role for three years. One day I overheard two students in the process of signing into the space. Upon flicking through the sign-in book, one of them commented on the fact that they had been there on many occasions. To my joy, the other replied,

"Well, it's like home."

For me, that remark summarises the over-arching concept of chaplaincy: a space where we feel at home, where we can be family for each other. It is a place of sanctuary and safety, harbouring staff and students while offering the wide embrace Jesus embodied in his own ministry. His ministry always reached out and included those whose spiritual practice was weak or non-existent. The students' and staffs' use of the chaplaincy allows for the opening of dialogue. The divine moves in all sorts of ways and directions, and who are we to judge what should be included?

Our chaplaincy team mirrors the concept of chaplaincy as home. We are like a family, welcoming and very diverse, including both men and women, young and old, lay and ordained. Some have many years of chaplaincy experience and other, newer members, none at all. All are included and encouraged, guided and formed. The college has given opportunity for professional development on the team. Some have studied theology, Catholic social teaching and spiritual direction. Being part of a team gives valuable day-to-day support because we can phone or email each other for advice, a different perspective or just the chance to offload.

Each site has at least one resident chaplain, daily present and available between 10am and 3pm, engaging with the students and staff in the common space. The chaplain is a presence within the space, someone who remains aware, joining in when needed, while allowing young people to be themselves. Sometimes we will invite an opinion or pose a question and at other times we remain in the background, watching. The young people can explore and get to know one another.

As a chaplain, you learn a lot about problems and stresses from just listening at the touchlines. The young people learn to trust you from your regular, constant presence. Often, they are cautious of those outside their personal circle and it takes a long time of just being there before they trust you enough to share problems or troubles.

Students like you to be a constant, in the same place at the same time, rooted… otherwise you face questions of "Where were you, Miss?" Sometimes as come they along the corridor towards the common room you can tell talk is not needed: in fact all they need is to express themselves and you just need to listen. Sometimes they just need to sit and be.

Often it's each other's company that they seek, but they also like to be able to throw the odd question in your direction. Comforted by a presence, they will often ask if they have been missed or will be when they leave. Like all of us, they need to feel valued and remembered.

The slow work of chaplaincy is one way the Church can really support and listen to young people. It is not a job in which we can just tick a box and then wipe our hands, saying we have provided the information, job done! Chaplaincy, like family, requires patience and consistency with no expectation of obvious results. All we can do is be there.

Our chaplaincy is rooted in our Catholic tradition, confidently reaching out and walking humbly with students and staff at what are often critical points of their lives.

Every day in chaplaincy is different,

depending on what is happening in people's lives. People can have close relations or colleagues die. Students' mental health can be fragile. Sometimes staff or students have to come to terms with pregnancy. Poverty is very real and families struggle with all sorts of societal pressures. The chaplain is privileged to be able to love and hold people when they are most frail.

As with everyone, periods of change or transition cause a great deal of anxiety and stress. Sixth-form college is filled with this kaleidoscope of concerns, ranging from starting as a new student to taking exams and thinking about what to do in the future.

Often students feel pushed or crushed, needing time to step back and pause in order to stop and reflect. The retreats which chaplaincy offers can provide this kind of space, as does the silence and stillness of the chapel. Often during the exam season you will find more students seeking the peace of the chapel and asking you to pray for them. Frequently not much talking is needed: you can tell from looks how things are, how little sleep there has been and how the pressure is getting to them.

As with a family, we are there through the highs and lows. We are present to share in the joy of success with exams passed, university places confirmed or jobs offered. "Rejoice with those who rejoice, weep with those who weep" (Romans 12:15).

Chaplaincy work is not always easy and sometimes it can be met with resistance. At times, the students use the common space to be boisterous or shout over each other. Having a contemplative attitude helps the chaplain to gaze on them with love whatever the situation. We can impose behavioural rules when we think lines have been crossed, but it is important to do this without being judgemental. God shows love and mercy to us, so we can share it with each other. By remaining open, we can often see behind behaviour without being clouded by prejudice. Young people have stories that need to be heard; stories that are personal, individual to them as human beings. We should listen without images of what we believe they are telling us. Chaplaincy provides a confidential safe space for people to talk and to be heard. By keeping a regular prayer life, seeking spiritual direction and using retreat opportunities, we as chaplains are able to cope and remain open-minded to all.

Feeling welcome, being able to find a space to sit and reflect, allows people to stop, give time to ponder and move away from the idea of "self".

Modern living with its constant communication and doing does not allow for a reflective routine. The world is rapidly changing, dominated by technology and a "throw-away culture", to which we need to respond with greater listening, respect and dialogue.

Chaplaincy tries to create mindful opportunities for silence and rest by leading students in stilling prayer or silence. Images and music are also used as ways into contemplative practice. Instilling a reflective outlook can help young people to grow and make informed choices for themselves.

The young people with whom we work are able to express the divine in their lives and the effect it has on them. They ask questions and explore opinions. Sometimes they express frustration with institutional religion but also appreciate speaking with people who are unafraid of "God talk". They question and challenge the chaplains: making you explore your own faith in a new depth. This becomes a never-ending circle.

Questioning strengthens our own relationship with God, so we can, in turn, help others to listen to God for themselves.

Sometimes, it is impossible to verbalise our personal experience with God, but by listening to others, we can find a voice. The joy in life which students show is infectious and they are not at all what they appear or are portrayed as being.

As Pope Francis says "accompanying young people requires going beyond a preconceived framework, encountering young people where they are, adapting to their times and pace of life and taking them seriously." [1]

Seeing the journey through their eyes makes you realise how vulnerable we all are, how badly we need each other and how important a place of home is. ■

Kathleen O'Sullivan is a school chaplain at Christ the King Sixth Form College, London.

[1] Pope Francis to young people on the occasion of the presentation of the preparatory document of the Fifteenth Ordinary General Assembly of the Synod of Bishops.

TEENS TALKING

"Prayer gives me hope when things are dark. Faith is a *light*."

"Faith ***guides*** you with decisions."

"To me, prayer is a way of ***reflecting*** my thoughts: almost like a conversation with God."

"Prayer is a conversation: a way of communicating with God and receiving his blessings. Prayer is a way of seeing your heart's desires."

"Faith is showing your ***love*** for God."

"Prayer gives me ***strength***, not to be afraid."

"***Singing*** with the choir is my way of ***praying***."

"Faith is having a **strong purpose** and trust in God."

"I feel that prayer to me means to talk to God and to get ***closer*** to him. It also helps us to know ***what God wants*** us to do."

"Prayer ***helps*** me believe God loves me."

"Faith means ***believing*** that things will go better."

"I am able to pour out my ***deepest thoughts*** and ***confessions***. I am also able to get closer to God."

"To me prayer strengthens me when I feel weak and down. It gives the chance to connect to God as well as empowering me. Prayer is a major key to success and a way to get you through difficult times of life."

"Pouring out my problems to God **helps**."

"Faith is having a strong ***trust*** in God."

A sacred corner for children

Denise Cottrell-Boyce explains some words and ideas which some younger readers might otherwise find unfamiliar.

Benediction
In Benediction we remember that Jesus is God as well as human. So we worship him with special Latin hymns and lovely incense. The priest wears golden robes.

Monstrance
For Benediction we use a special display case to show everyone the Host. It is a beautifully decorated circle on a stand with a little window in the middle for the Host.

Tabernacle
After Mass we put any extra Hosts in a special cupboard, hidden behind beautiful curtains at the back of the altar. It is holy because Jesus is there: there for us.

Adoration
Because Jesus became human to be with us, we sometimes forget that he is God – mighty and powerful – but when we do remember and thank him, it feels great. This great feeling is called "adoration".

Pilgrimage
A pilgrimage is a journey to a place where holy people have lived. Some are places of healing. Visiting them helps us feel closer to God and to each other.

Visits to the Blessed Sacrament
No matter where we are we can talk to people – including Jesus – but it even better to be with them. We can be with Jesus when we pray near the tabernacle. We can share anything with him.

Reconciliation
In the sacrament of reconciliation, we tell the priest about how we might have hurt ourselves and others. This helps us understand how to be closer to Jesus and to the people we love.

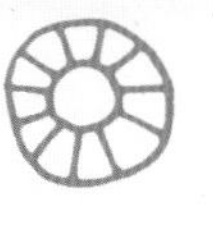

Activities

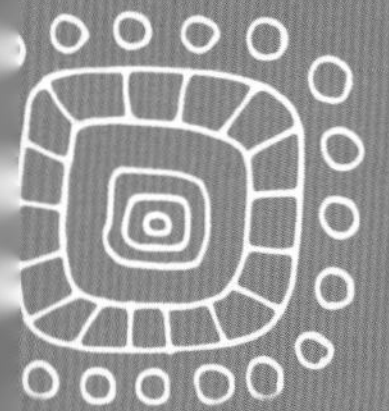

1. Draw a chalice and a monstrance.
Write the names of three people you want to pray for.

2. When you next go to church, look for the tabernacle and the sanctuary lamp.

3. Tell Jesus you love him and want to be his friend.

4. Name three places where people go on pilgrimage.

- ....
- ....
- ....

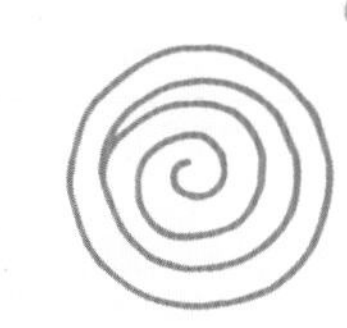

5. Why are Lourdes and Fatima famous? Name the children who saw Our Lady.

6. In the picture below, find the following:

- Priest
- Chalice
- Crucifix
- Altar

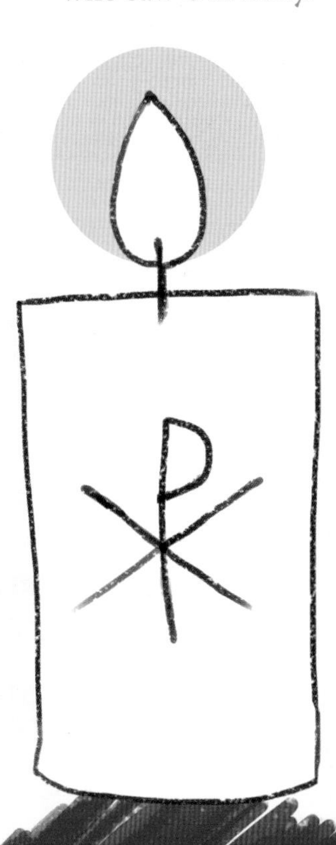

7. Colour the candle. Why do we use candles at Mass?

Evangelisation

Everything we do and everything we don't do, says something about what we believe and who we trust. We show our faith in God through our words and actions. This is evangelisation.

Congress

Sometimes the Church has a huge get-together of people, priests and bishops, from far and wide, so we can share, celebrate and learn more about the things we believe.

Chalice

A chalice is a beautiful cup in which we offer up the wine during Mass. It's special because when the priest blesses it, it will contain the sacred blood of Christ.

Denise Cottrell-Boyce is the mother of seven children and a parish catechist.

Sr Hyacinthe Defos du Rau OP writes about a new First Holy Communion programme which she has introduced into the Portsmouth diocese.

How can we make the time of preparation for first reconciliation and First Holy Communion a moment of evangelisation? How can we transform a prescribed and limited sacramental formation into an encounter with the living God, who cannot be contained in time and space? How can the culmination of our catechetical efforts – the day of First Holy Communion – become, for our children, the beginning of a lifelong journey of faith and love for Jesus in the Eucharist?

Evidently, a new programme or resource will not be able to achieve this. It is the Holy Spirit who alone can convert and lead to Jesus. Yet the aim of *I Want to Make my Home in You*, a new resource published by Redemptorist Publications, is precisely to open children's hearts to the presence and action of the Holy Spirit, through the word of God and prayer, and so enable them to encounter Jesus.

This new "journey" towards the sacraments of reconciliation and the Eucharist gives them time, in twenty-two sessions, to grow in faith, hope and love, and to freely respond to the invitation of Jesus, spoken to them in the words of scripture and in the silence of prayer.

Using a progressive, evangelising approach, the authors, members of Notre Dame de Vie Institute in France, offer a resource which focuses on the faith development of the children, through a method of dialogue on the scripture. This dialogue, in which the children come to understand the essential truths of our faith, is helped by beautiful silhouettes especially designed for the resource, which portray the spiritual attitudes which the children are invited to adopt.

The resource first offers eleven sessions to evangelise the children and prepare them for the sacrament of reconciliation. The evangelisation of the children begins with the baptism of Jesus and his invitation to them to follow him. The children then learn to pray, to love, and to obey like Jesus, before the power of Jesus over sin and death is presented to them, as available for them today in the Church.

After a session on the discovery of their conscience, the children are then led, through the parable of the Prodigal Son, to understand and follow the various steps of the sacrament of reconciliation, which they freely and joyfully embrace.

Next, the resource offers eleven sessions to discover Jesus, the Word of the Father and the Bread of Life, who gives himself to us in the scriptures and in the Eucharist.

The sessions present the Eucharistic teaching of Jesus to the children: the multiplication of loaves, the discourse of the Bread of Life, and the Last Supper.

Then the celebration of the Eucharist itself is discovered, first in the church building, dwelling place of God, and then in the Mass. Finally, the mystery of Holy Communion, of Jesus-with-us, which extends in charity to the whole world, is presented through Zacchaeus, the pilgrims of Emmaus, and the image of the vine and the branches.

The most beautiful feature of this resource, however, is the use of two intervals which allow the children to freely prolong their time of prayerful encounter with Jesus at the end of each session. These precious minutes, freely given to God in silence, are the immediate but unpredictable outcome of a resource which gives time and space for the Holy Spirit to work in the children's hearts – and the children really do use the time available for prayer. ■

Sr Hyacinthe Defos du Rau OP is a Dominican Sister of St Joseph and a member of the Portsmouth diocesan Formation for Mission team.

For more tutorials visit www.rpbooks.co.uk

First Holy Communion: reflections from a catechist

Anne Dharmpaul, a parish catechist, describes the First Holy Communion programme in her parish.

First Holy Communion takes place every year from October to May and has twelve hour-long sessions on Saturday mornings with breaks for school holidays at Christmas and Easter. First reconciliation is celebrated during Lent and children receive their First Holy Communion over the course of four celebration Masses in May. The preparation course is aimed at children in Year 3 who originate from our parish school but, increasingly, children attend from non-Catholic primary schools in the surrounding area.

A useful strategy at reconciliation is to invite in a visiting priest so that parents may themselves take the opportunity to celebrate the sacrament.

It is not unusual to have up to eighty or more children who are divided between four groups, each with four adult volunteer catechists. All are Disclosure and Barring Service (DSB) checked.

Children's sessions take place in the church and the parent sessions, which happen simultaneously, are in the community centre. The parent sessions are led by a separate team of catechists including two members of school staff. This provides an invaluable bridge between the school and the parish.

Other important team members are the tea makers, crèche leaders, admin department and the calligraphers who prepare memorable certificates for the big day. The preparation programme really does operate as a trilogy – the family, the parish and the school.

Several programmes have been tried and tested throughout the years but the most effective and enjoyable has proved to be *I Belong*, which is also a popular choice in surrounding parishes. The books come in three formats – one for the children, one to assist the parents and one for the group leaders. The children's books are colourful and interactive and have prominent stories from the Old and New Testaments. Many of them are translated into everyday life, encouraging discussions during the sessions and also with the family at home.

Families attend special Masses throughout the preparation to strengthen the bond of prayer and faith sharing among all the participants. This also serves to introduce the children and their families to the rest of the congregation.

As a catechist, introducing the children to the person of Jesus is an amazing privilege. Most are nervous and not sure what to expect if they are not regular attendees at church, or if they have not been brought up in the Catholic faith. Eight months might seem like a long time in the life of a First Holy Communion programme but it gives the children time to feel comfortable with sharing their thoughts in group discussion.

It is rewarding and very joyful to see the children grow through the programme and then celebrate reconciliation and Eucharist. It is an even greater joy to see some of them become altar servers and, in later years, taking part in the liturgy in other ways.

Every year we have an evaluation session with parents who have said that the programme has caused them to re-examine their own faith journey as they find their own group discussions insightful and enlightening. Sadly, not everybody's journey continues along the prescribed path. Some, inevitably, take other roads. But the seeds sown at First Communion may well come to life another day. ■

Anne Dharmpaul is a catechist in a London parish.

I Belong *is available from Redemptorist Publications, www.rpbooks.co.uk*

My First Holy Communion

Children from the Most Holy Trinity Parish, Dockhead

It means to receive Jesus and be part of his family. *Rhys*

Being welcomed into God's big family. *Oliver*

Receiving Jesus and being very special. *Sophia*

Now I can receive Jesus every time I go to Mass. *Roanne*

Going up to the altar on the day with my mum & dad – wow! *Rachel*

I felt so special – I did not want the day to end. *Patrick*

I feel blessed now that Jesus is with me. *Lisa*

It's so special – all my family came to see me. *Alex*

Adoremus Kids

Activities & Puzzles

COME TO THE PARTY

Everyone is invited to Jesus' special party

Gather the guests and bring them together for the feast.

Hunt the guest

Jesus told a story about a king who sent his servants to invite people to a feast.

Can you find people hiding around this page who the servants could invite?

Word search

JESUS the **BREAD** of **LIFE** makes us **STRONG**, **LOVING** and **KIND**.

Can you find the coloured words in the word search?

L	O	V	I	N	G
I	X	G	J	M	Q
F	B	R	E	A	D
E	W	L	S	B	N
P	Y	X	U	T	I
K	R	Y	S	B	K
S	T	R	O	N	G

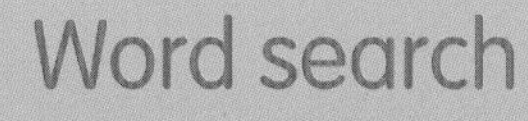

Jelly maze

Time for pudding! Can you get to the centre of the maze?

Sharing

In the slices of bread draw or write what you will share this week.

Dot Puzzle

Answer: Jesus is the Bread of Life

Colour in all the shapes with a dot in the middle to reveal something about Jesus.

Match the loaves

Draw a line between the loaves of bread which match.

Dot to dot

This is the Last Supper that Jesus had with his friends. He shared bread and wine, just as we do today at Mass.

Join the dots, then colour the picture.

Making bread

Have you ever made bread at home? Put the jobs in the right order…

A Mix yeast and sugar in warm water and let it grow.

B Add yeast and water and make a stiff dough.

C Leave the dough to rise.

D Knead, then put the dough into a tin to rise again.

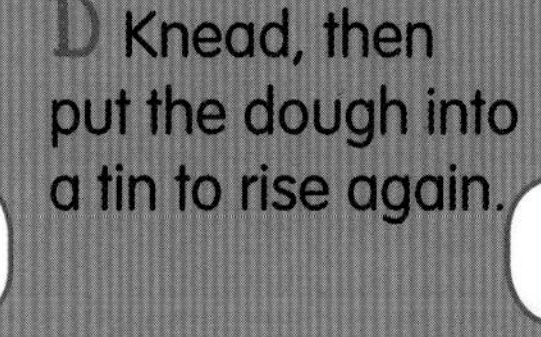

E Carefully put the dough into a hot oven.

F Mix flour and salt and oil in a bowl.

G Take the bread out and enjoy!

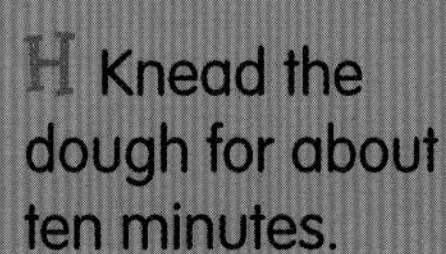

H Knead the dough for about ten minutes.

Answer: A=1 B=3 C=5 D=6 E=7 F=2 G=4 H=8

If we believe

Break the code to see what Jesus is saying.

Jesus said that if we believe in him we shall never be...

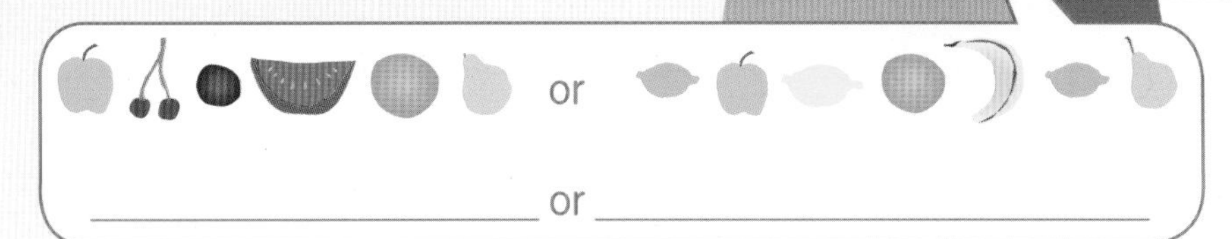

_______________ or _______________

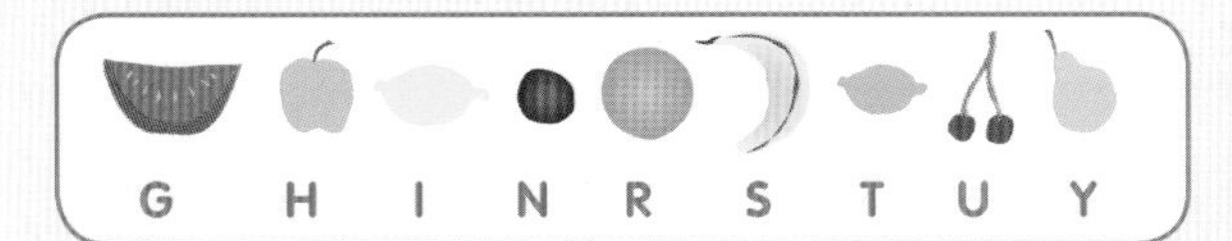

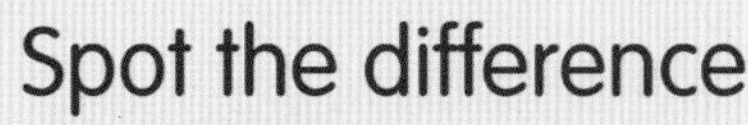

Spot the difference

These children are receiving Jesus' body in Holy Communion. Can you spot the five differences in the pictures?

Answer: shoe, chalice, robe, candle, hair

Food for life

Our food gives us energy. What is your favourite food? Draw or write it onto the plate.

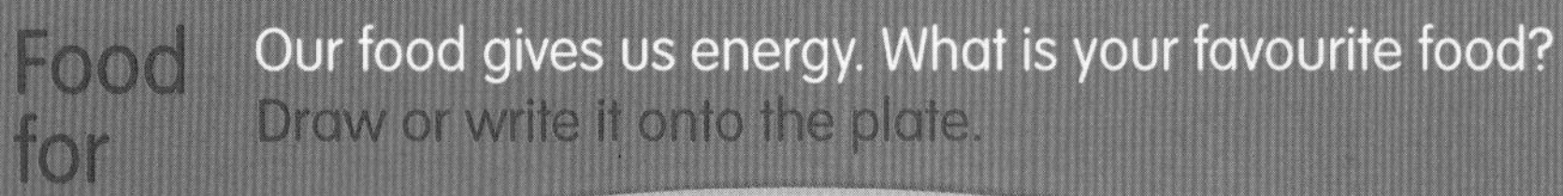

We need energy to follow Jesus and live like he did. Fit in the missing vowels to find out what will give us this energy.

H_ly C_mm_n_ _n (oouio)

Choosing to follow Jesus

Which words show we are following Jesus? Write them in these loaves of bread. Jesus says these things will make us happy.

Jesus loves us

We hear in the Bible about a Roman centurion whose servant was sick. The centurion had heard about Jesus, He knew he not deserve Jesus' help, but the centurion believed that Jesus had the power to heal his servant. Jesus was amazed by the centurion's faith and healed the servant, without even going to the centurion's house!

Put the missing vowels (a,e,i,o,u) in the right space to see the prayer we say in Mass that is inspired by the centurion.

"L_rd, I _m n_t w_rthy th_t y_ _ sh_ _ld _nt_r _nd_r my r_ _f, b_t _nly s_y th_ w_rd _nd my s_ _l sh_ll b_ h_ _l_d."

Sudoku

Can you fill the grid with the different types of bread? Each row, each column and each mini-grid should have just one of each picture.

Jesus, the Bread of Life, wants to heal us all

Sometimes we can't see when someone is ill. They are hurt inside. Jesus wants to make everyone better. Which piece will mend the heart? Colour the matching right piece of jigsaw.

Jesus can mend our hearts. If we are hurt inside Jesus can make us whole agian.

Answer: 3

JESUS IS THE BREAD OF LIFE

Jesus said that whoever comes to him will never be hungry.

Can you find the way for the children to reach the bread?

Recipe for life

What do we need for a good life? Create your own recipe. The first two ingredients are there. What will you add? Write your ideas.

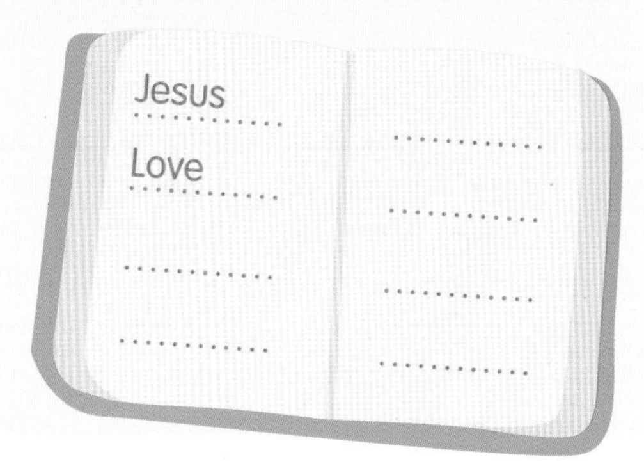

Challenge Crossword

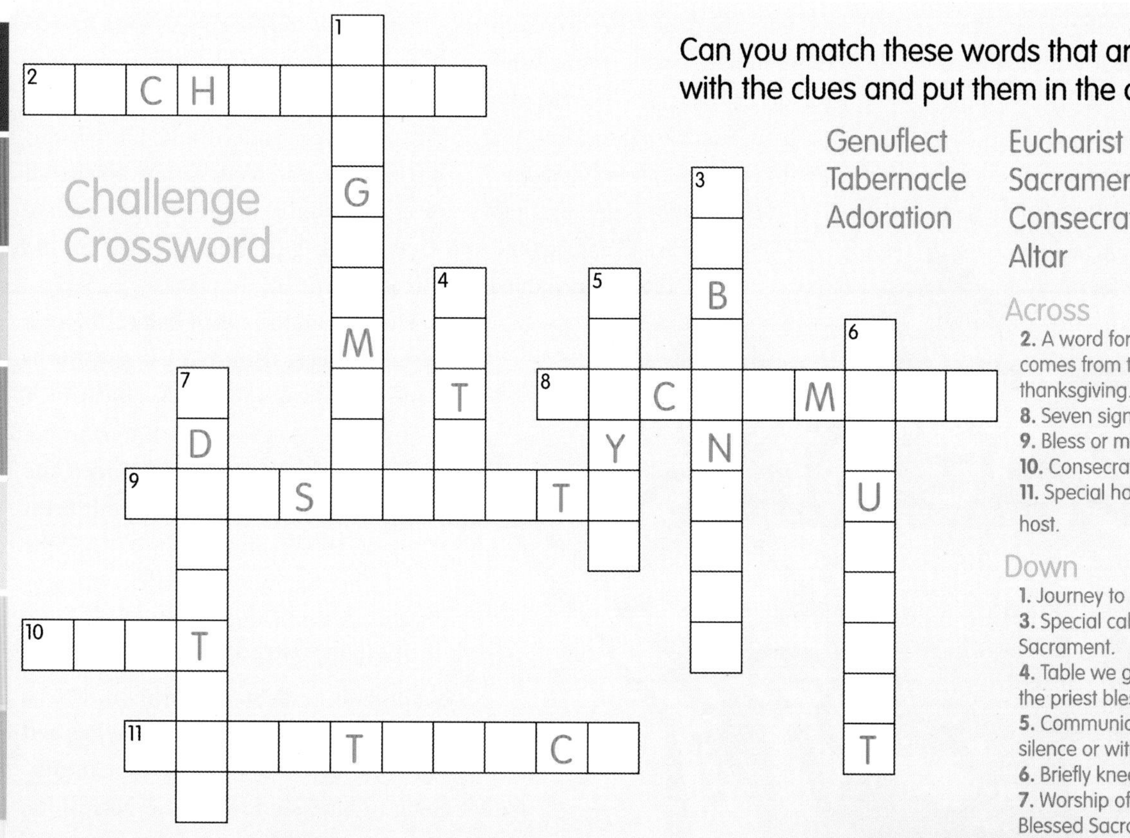

Can you match these words that are used in church with the clues and put them in the crossword?

Genuflect	Eucharist	Prayer
Tabernacle	Sacrament	Pilgrimage
Adoration	Consecrate	Host
	Altar	Monstrance

Across

2. A word for Holy Communion that comes from the Greek word for thanksgiving.
8. Seven signs that God loves us.
9. Bless or make holy.
10. Consecrated bread in the Eucharist.
11. Special holder for the consecrated host.

Down

1. Journey to a holy place.
3. Special cabinet for the Blessed Sacrament.
4. Table we gather round at Mass where the priest blesses the bread and wine.
5. Communicating with God, maybe in silence or with words, music or actions.
6. Briefly kneeling respectfully.
7. Worship of Jesus present in the Blessed Sacrament.

Freddie Freckles

AND THE HOLY HOUR

Fr Tim visited Freddie Freckles' Year 5 class and encouraged the children to become involved in a special project.

Freddie Freckles and his pals had moved up to Year 5 and were beginning to feel very grown up as they moved through their primary school. In the previous year they had all made their First Holy Communion and they had been used to Fr Tim, their parish priest, popping into class to see how they were getting on.

Their new form teacher, Mr Burns, told them that Fr Tim had something important he wanted to share with them and would be coming into class at the beginning of the following week. They began to wonder what it was all about, but presumed that he had written some new stories and wanted to try them out on the children. In fact, it wasn't that at all and when he arrived he said he had come because the bishop had written to him, asking for help to prepare for a big event which was coming up the following year. Because Freddie and his pals had all just made their First Holy Communion, Fr Tim had decided they were the ideal group to help with the project.

The event the bishop had written about was called a "Eucharistic Congress" and, before anything else, Fr Tim realised that even the title needed some explaining. Freddie loved quizzes and was pleased when he realised they were going to have a quiz on words.

Fr Tim began by asking if any of the children could think of other words for Holy Communion. Sarah immediately put her hand up and said "The Bread of Life." "Brilliant, Sarah," said Fr Tim, "that is the key phrase for next year's Congress."

Freddie put his hand up and said "The Eucharist," and again Fr Tim was delighted, but then he asked Freddie if he was good at Greek, because the word was originally a Greek word. Freddie's head dropped because, if he had been told, he couldn't remember. But, wonder of wonders, Peter Pickles, Freddie's best friend, somehow had the idea that the word meant "thanksgiving," and he was right.

Fr Tim was even more pleased when a couple of the other children came up with "the Mass", "the Lord's Supper" and "the Blessed Sacrament". But what about the word "Congress"? he asked. Immediately loads of hands went up and Caroline was able to tell him it meant a gathering of people. "Perfect!" said Fr Tim. "It is indeed and the bishops of England and Wales want people all over the country to gather and celebrate God's great gift to us of Jesus as the Bread of Life."

He went on to explain that the Mass is so called because the old Latin words to send us forth were "*Ite missa est*" which just tells us to go because the gathering is finished. And he reminded the children that the Mass is our great way of offering thanks to God the Father with Jesus, which is why it is also called the Eucharist.

Freddie's little head was beginning to spin with all these explanations, but he did understand what Fr Tim was saying, and now came the big invitation. "Boys and girls, we are going to have some special events in the

parish and in the diocese and one of them is a 'Holy Hour' for young people. I need a new team of servers because many of our older servers have grown up and gone off to university, so can you all think about this and, if you are interested, please take a form and discuss it with your parents. In a week's time I will come back and see how many of you have brought back the forms and want to train as servers."

A week later, Fr Tim was delighted that he had eight new volunteers, including Freddie and Peter, Sarah and Caroline. Over the next few weeks they came along for training and in no time they were able to serve Mass perfectly.

The people in the parish were really impressed by the way they showed such great reverence, moving slowly, genuflecting on one knee with great precision and without flopping around, knowing when to bring up the wine and water, when to ring the bell, how to carry the cross and the candles.

But there was more: there was this Holy Hour to prepare for, and so, after Christmas, Fr Tim arranged for further meetings and other boys and girls from the class, who had not wanted to be servers, agreed to help prepare and present the Holy Hour. For example, some of the best readers in the class volunteered their services and agreed to prepare special Bidding Prayers for the occasion.

Fr Tim came back into class one day to talk about devotion to the Blessed Sacrament. He explained that from the earliest days of the Church, two thousand years ago, Holy Communion had been taken to the homes of those who were too sick to go out to church. Gradually the custom of keeping Holy Communion in readiness to take to the sick or the dying at any time meant that we needed somewhere to keep the Blessed Sacrament reserved and that is why we have our tabernacles, a word which means little tents or houses.

He went on to explain that this is why, when you go into a Catholic church, you always see the little red light burning: it is a wonderful reminder of Jesus' promise that he will always be with us. Fr Tim said, "The more people thought about the wonder of Jesus' special presence in the church, the more they began to pray before the tabernacle. Then, they started taking the Blessed Sacrament out of the tabernacle, using a monstrance, which is another Latin word, meaning a show-case. When the Blessed Sacrament is in the monstrance we call this a time of Exposition. And finally, children, showing their love for Jesus, the people started having processions, sometimes even carrying the monstrance around the streets of the town or city."

Now Fr Tim asked the children why people would make Holy Hours before the Blessed Sacrament. Somehow, Freddie worked it out straight away.

He remembered that because his First Holy Communion was coming up, he had gone to Mass on Holy Thursday evening with the family and he remembered that after the Mass the Blessed Sacrament had been carried around the church and put into a special tabernacle in a side chapel, called the altar of repose. He knew that this was to remind us that after the Last Supper, Jesus had left the Upper Room with his disciples and gone to the Garden of Gethsemane, where he asked them to pray with him, but they had fallen asleep. Then Jesus had asked Peter: "Could you not keep awake one hour?" Freddie, hoping this would be the right answer, shot up his hand and offered the explanation to Fr Tim. Fr Tim was amazed and congratulated Freddie on brilliantly putting the jigsaw together. It gave Fr Tim the opportunity to reassure the children that although an hour may seem like a long time and people do sometimes fall asleep before the Blessed Sacrament, Jesus doesn't really mind: he is just happy that they have made the effort to be there and just as he was with the apostles, Jesus is always patient with us.

"Nevertheless", said Fr Tim, "we are going to make our Holy Hour so inspiring that no one is likely to fall asleep."

Then they set about the detailed preparations. The whole class was involved in working out the programme, and although it was aimed at the young people of the parish, people of all ages would be welcome.

They would begin by explaining the origin of the Holy Hour as Freddie had worked it out and Michael, who was an excellent reader, would be given the task of welcoming everyone and explaining what was going to happen and why.

Then the servers would come to the sanctuary with Fr Tim and the Blessed Sacrament would be exposed in the monstrance. The servers would have to learn to use something called a "thurible", because on these occasions incense would be burnt.

Fr Tim explained that the incense was a reminder of the gift brought by the Wise Men to the baby Jesus in Bethlehem. The incense was a precious gift, telling us that Jesus was truly God's son. Fr Tim explained that it is sending out the same message to us when we use it in church: and added that it also

reminds us that we are precious because Jesus has made us his adopted brothers and sisters and therefore also children of his Father in heaven. Throughout the hour they would be singing some wonderful hymns, including some new ones being written especially for the Eucharistic Congress. There would also be some short readings from the scriptures, especially the one about Jesus praying to his Father in the garden.

Towards the end of the Holy Hour they would have a procession, not just around the church, but around the grounds if the weather was alright.

But Fr Tim spelt out that at the heart of the Holy Hour would be a time of quiet, when they would simply sit and look at Jesus in the Blessed Sacrament. "Children," he said, "before we do this, one of you will read a simple reflection, reminding everyone that we are all children of God and that prayer does not need us to use lots of words. It is better simply to rest quietly in God's loving arms." Fr Tim used one of his favourite images, reminding the children of what he always says at the baptism of babies: "Look at this little child in the arms of his parents and remember that no matter what your age you are always a child of God; so let God gently hold you and love you and you will be praying."

Freddie couldn't wait for the Holy Hour. He knew loads of people were going to come and he was very pleased that because of his wonderful answer in class he had been chosen to carry the thurible and look after the incense. ■

Illustrations / Jane Morgan. Copyright © Redemptorist Publications.

Fr Tim Buckley C.Ss.R. is a Redemptorist priest. He was engaged in mission and retreat work across the UK and is now based in Liverpool. He retains a close friendship with Freddie Freckles.

His previous accounts of Freddie Freckles' activities are available from Redemptorist Publications, www.rpbooks.co.uk

A Holy Hour and service of

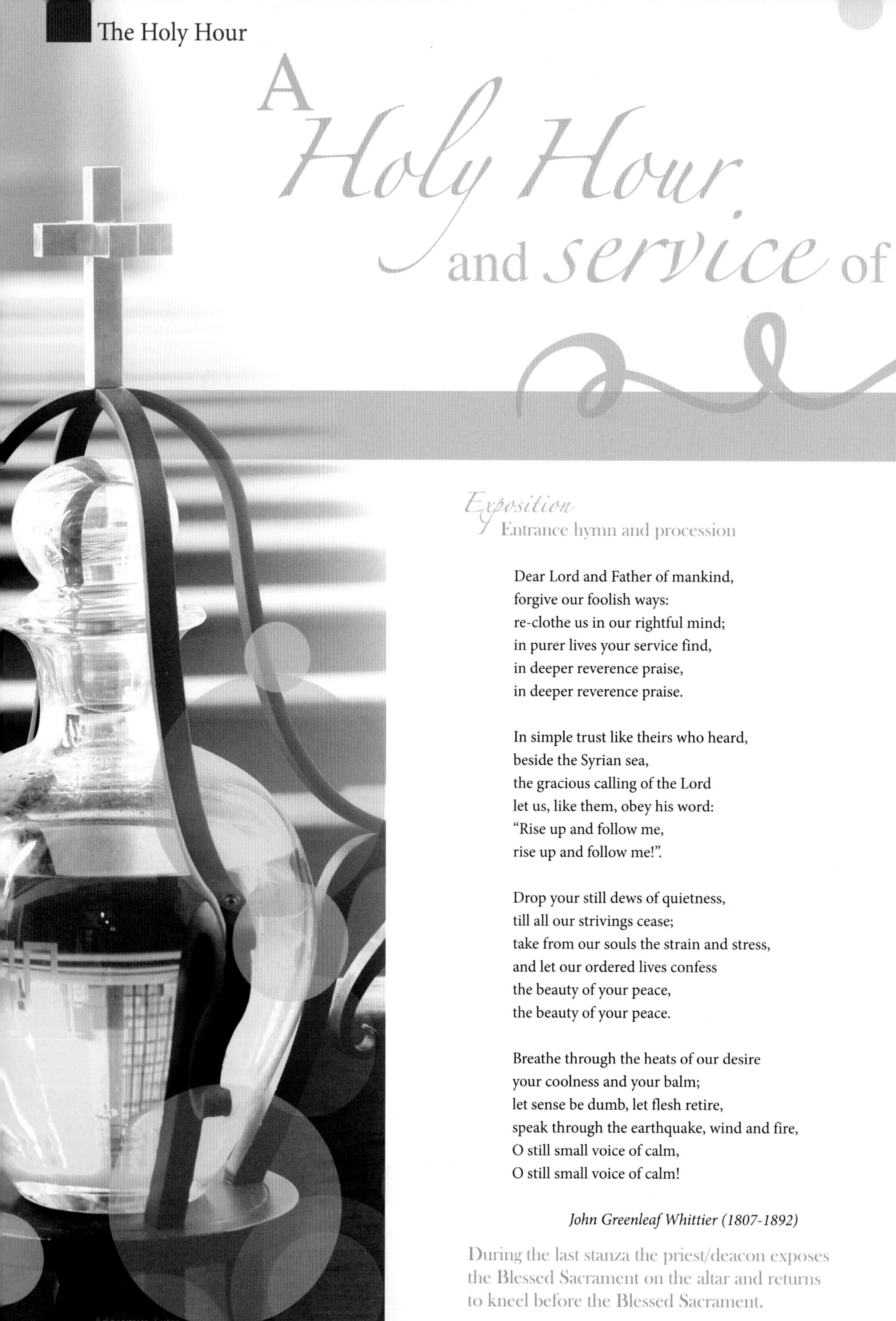

Exposition

Entrance hymn and procession

Dear Lord and Father of mankind,
forgive our foolish ways:
re-clothe us in our rightful mind;
in purer lives your service find,
in deeper reverence praise,
in deeper reverence praise.

In simple trust like theirs who heard,
beside the Syrian sea,
the gracious calling of the Lord
let us, like them, obey his word:
"Rise up and follow me,
rise up and follow me!".

Drop your still dews of quietness,
till all our strivings cease;
take from our souls the strain and stress,
and let our ordered lives confess
the beauty of your peace,
the beauty of your peace.

Breathe through the heats of our desire
your coolness and your balm;
let sense be dumb, let flesh retire,
speak through the earthquake, wind and fire,
O still small voice of calm,
O still small voice of calm!

John Greenleaf Whittier (1807-1892)

During the last stanza the priest/deacon exposes the Blessed Sacrament on the altar and returns to kneel before the Blessed Sacrament.

the *anointing* of the sick

Opening prayer

Let us pray:
Our Lord Jesus Christ, we bless you with full hearts
that you are truly present in the Blessed Sacrament on this altar.
You welcome everyone who comes to visit you,
whatever our condition, whatever our trials and troubles,
whatever our joys and small triumphs.
We come before you as we are:
you see us better than we see ourselves.
Reach out to us with your loving arms;
transform us with your healing presence.
Teach us the joy of living in your presence,
the contentment of gazing upon you,
the delight of knowing that you look on each of us with love.
We give thanks to you in your holy name, Jesus Christ our Lord.
All: Amen

The congregation now sings:

O saving Victim, opening wide The gate of heaven to us below: Our foes press on from every side; Thine aid supply; thy strength bestow.	O Salutaris Hostia Quae caeli pandis ostium: Bella premunt hostilia, Da robur, fer auxilium.
To thy great name be endless praise, Immortal Godhead, One in Three! O grant us endless length of days, In our true native land with Thee. **All: Amen.**	Uni trinoque Domino Sit sempiterna gloria, Qui vitam sine termino Nobis donet in patria. **All: Amen.**

During the singing, the priest/deacon puts incense on the charcoal and then incenses the Blessed Sacrament.

Adoration

After a period of quiet two readers approach the lectern.

Paul's Canticle of Love
(after 1 Corinthians 13:1-13)

Reader 1
If I speak in the tongues of mortals and angels
but do not have love,
I am nothing
but a noisy gong or a clashing cymbal.

Reader 2
If we have powers of prophecy,
and understand all mysteries and knowledge.
And if we have faith even to remove mountains
and have not love,
we are nothing.

Reader 1
If I give away all my possessions;
if I give my body over to be burned,
but have not love,
I gain nothing.

Reader 2
Love is patient, is kind;
love is not envious or boastful;
is never arrogant or rude;
it does not insist on its own way,
is not irritable or resentful.

Reader 1
Love does not rejoice in wrongdoing,
but rejoices in the truth.
Love bears all things, believes all things,
hopes all things, endures all things.

Reader 2
Love never ends.
Prophecies will come to an end;
tongues will cease;
knowledge will come to an end.

Reader 1
When I was a child,
I spoke like a child, I thought like a child;
when I became an adult,
I put an end to childish ways.

Reader 2
Now we see in a mirror, dimly;
then we will see face to face.

Reader 1
Now I know only in part;
then I will know fully,
even as I am fully known.

Reader 2
Faith, hope, and love abide,
these three;
and the greatest of these is love.

All now sing (sung 3 times):

O come let us adore,
O come let us adore him,
Christ the Lord.

Time of quiet for 15 minutes

Prayers of Pleading

Reader 1
**The response to the verse is, Lord,
in your mercy, hear our prayer.**

We pray for Christian people throughout the world;
for peace in the Church;
for the healing of divisions;
that in faith and unity we may be constantly renewed
for the mission and service of the Gospel.
**All: Lord, in your mercy,
Hear our prayer.**

We pray for all those who suffer;
for the victims of war and terror;
of persecution and aggression;
of disaster and accident.
**All: Lord, in your mercy,
Hear our prayer.**

We pray for the homeless and the hungry;
for all refugees and asylum seekers;
for those who have no home place
or hearth to lay their head;
for the lonely and those who are always overlooked;
that all may find strength and hope.
**All: Lord, in your mercy,
Hear our prayer.**

We pray for all those who are sick in our community,
for those in hospital or those living at home;
for those whose spirit is broken;
for those who turn to us for healing and comfort
that, together in the Lord, we may find wholeness and peace.
All: Lord, in your mercy,
Hear our prayer.

We pray for one another and for ourselves,
that we may be instruments of the Lord's peace and joy.
May we know for ourselves, and mediate to others,
the wholeness and healing of the Lord.
All: Lord, in your mercy,
Hear our prayer.

Priest/deacon

Gracious Lord, in whose presence we are gathered, listen with kindness to these our prayers as we make them in your holy name, Jesus Christ our Lord.

Time dedicated to the anointing of those who are unwell

If possible, and if space allows, the row in front of the seated congregation is kept empty so that the ministers can walk along and easily distribute the sacrament to those who wish for it. The priest/deacon first anoints the forehead and then the hands, saying:

Through this holy anointing
may the Lord in his love and mercy
help you with the grace of the Holy Spirit.
All: Amen.

May the Lord, who frees you from sin,
save you and raise you up.
All: Amen.

During the anointing quiet music is played.

After the anointing the ministers wash their hands at the credence table.

The priest/deacon now approaches the altar, genuflects before the Blessed Sacrament, kneels and invites the assembly to pray:

The Divine Praises

Blessed be God.
Blessed be his holy name.
Blessed be Jesus Christ, true God and true man.
Blessed be the name of Jesus.
Blessed be his most Sacred Heart.
Blessed be his most precious blood.
Blessed be Jesus in the most holy sacrament of the altar.
Blessed be the Holy Spirit, the Paraclete.
Blessed be the great mother of God, Mary most holy.
Blessed be her holy and immaculate conception.
Blessed be her glorious assumption.
Blessed be the name of Mary, virgin and mother.
Blessed be St Joseph, her most chaste spouse.
Blessed be God in his angels and in his saints.
All: Amen.

Benediction

The *Tantum Ergo* is now sung:

Therefore we, before him bending,
this great Sacrament revere;
types and shadows have their ending,
for the newer rite is here;
faith, our outward sense befriending,
makes the inward vision clear.

Tantum ergo Sacramentum
Veneremur cernui:
Et antiquum documentum
Novo cedat ritui:
Praestet fides supplementum
Sensuum defectui.

Glory let us give, and blessing
to the Father and the Son;
honour, might, and praise addressing,
while eternal ages run;
ever too, his love confessing,
who, from both, with both is one.
All: Amen.

Genitori, Genitoque
Laus et iubilatio,
Salus, honor, virtus quoque
Sit et benedictio:
Procedenti ab utroque
Compar sit laudatio.
All: Amen.

During the hymn the priest/deacon incenses the Blessed Sacrament and then rises to proclaim/sing the traditional responsory:

You have given them bread from heaven.
All: Having within it all sweetness.

Panem de caelo praestitisti eis.
All: Omne delectamentum in se habentem.

Let us pray:
O God, who in this wonderful sacrament have left us a memorial of your passion: grant, we beseech you, that we may so venerate the sacred mysteries of your body and blood, as always to be conscious of the fruit of your redemption. You, who live and reign forever and ever.
All: Amen.

Oremus:
Deus, qui nobis sub sacramento mirabili, passionis tuae memoriam reliquisti: tribue, quaesumus, ita nos corporis et sanguinis tui sacra mysteria venerari, ut redemptionis tuae fructum in nobis iugiter sentiamus. Qui vivis et regnas in saecula saeculorum.
All: Amen.

The blessing with the Blessed Sacrament

The priest/deacon kneels and puts on the humeral veil. He rises, genuflects, approaches the altar, holds up the monstrance and then blesses the assembly.

The priest's hands are covered by the humeral veil to show that it is Jesus, not the priest, who blesses his people.

The priest/deacon reposes the Blessed Sacrament in the tabernacle and returns to the front of the altar.

Closing responses

Priest/deacon
For all that God can do within us,
for all that God can do without us.
All: Thanks be to God

Priest/deacon
For all in whom Christ lived before us,
for all in whom Christ lived beside us.
All: Thanks be to God,

Priest/deacon
For all the Spirit wants to bring us,
for where the Spirit wants to lead us.
All: Thanks be to God.

Priest/deacon
We have worshipped the Lord
and received his healing and blessing.
Let us go in the peace of Christ.
All: Thanks be to God.

Recessional hymn:

Now thank we all our God
with heart and hands and voices,
who wondrous things has done,
in whom his world rejoices;
who from our mothers' arms
has blessed us on our way
with countless gifts of love,
and still is ours today.

O may this bounteous God
through all our life be near us,
with ever joyful hearts
and blessed peace to cheer us,
to keep us in his grace,
and guide us when perplexed,
and free us from all ills
of this world in the next.

All praise and thanks to God
the Father now be given,
the Son and Spirit blest,
who reign in highest heaven
the one eternal God,
whom heaven and earth adore;
for thus it was, is now,
and shall be evermore.

Martin Rinkhart (1586-1649), translated by Catherine Winkworth (1827-1878)